MARRYING
MR. MAN
of GD

IDENTIFYING GOD'S PLAN *for*
YOUR HAPPILY EVER AFTER

Jordan Smith

◀◀◀ BROOKSTONE
PUBLISHING GROUP

Brookstone Publishing Group
P.O. Box 211, Evington, VA 24550
BrookstoneCreativeGroup.com

Ordering Information:
Special discounts are available on quantity purchases by corporations,
associations, and others. For details, contact
Brookstone Publishing Group at the address above.

Acknowledgements

"MAY MY MEDITATION BE SWEET AND PLEASING TO HIM;
AS FOR ME, I WILL REJOICE AND BE GLAD IN THE LORD."

—PSALM 104:34 (AMP)

SWEET JESUS, THIS WHOLE BOOK IS THE MEDITATION OF MY HEART of Your loving kindness, and the dedication of my will to Yours. Above all else, Lord, I hope it pleases You.

To my parents, Keith and Robyn Wray. You helped write this story from day one, guiding me and teaching me how to live. Your relationship with each other gave me the perfect example of what a godly marriage should look like. You two have gone above and beyond the call of a parent. I'm blessed to have you both as mine.

To my best friend, Julia Hartberger. You have been with me through every up and down. You were the encouragement I needed at exactly the perfect time. God knew I needed you.

And lastly to my Pastors, Gary and Diane Hoffman. You fed my spirit, encouraged my passions, and invested in my calling. I am forever grateful for your leadership and love to and for your people.

Dedicated to my Mr. Man of God,
my husband, Seth Smith.

You are my greatest testimony and
my favorite love story.
You are living proof that God
does what He says.

I love you, and I hope these words
help you see yourself how I see you.

Contents

Introduction

Above all, love each other deeply, because love
covers a multitude of sins.
—1 PETER 4:8 (NIV)

This is a journey, not a fairytale. This is a miracle, not make believe.
This is a reality, and not a romantic novel.

This is a love story.

It won't begin with once upon a time, but it does have a happily ever
after—not because it will all be perfect, but because it will all be held
together by a perfect God.

MY STRONGEST CONVICTION FOR WRITING THIS BOOK IS TO
encourage those who feel pulled apart—pulled one way between
the person they love, or want to love, and the calling and leading
of Jesus. That pull is strong. That constant tug is demanding and
exhausting, and I will never forget how it left me feeling. If that
describes how you are feeling, I have good news. Every time in my
life when I felt God's will pulling me away from my own will, the
most glorious parts of my story unfolded. You'll see.

John 10:1 describes God as "The Good Shepherd" for a reason.
He sees things we cannot. He knows our future, and best of all,
He writes our story. Having that understanding makes His guidance

seem like a no-brainer. Why wouldn't we follow the only one with the map?

But a lot of times, this is easier said than done, especially when following God requires an act of blind obedience. The simplicity becomes less simple. Do not give up faith! God holds you together, even when you feel pulled apart.

Maybe you picked up this book for another reason. Maybe you are not in a relationship at all, but looking for one. Maybe you are not interested in anything other than God's will for your relationship. This book will encourage you to continue in that passion for God's will and help you recognize His signposts as they appear in your life.

It is easy to become discouraged in the wait. The time between trusting God and receiving your promise can be a constant struggle between what you believe and what you see. Do not give up hope! God has a happily ever after written just for you too.

This book was written from my personal experiences and perspective, although some names have been changed to protect the privacy of the "characters"—names that were not changed have given me permission to include their part, whether large or small, in my story.

Chapter One

Not looking for Mr. Right

"It's making me sick. I can't even talk about it without getting all worked up," I vented.

"Why do you think that is?" Dad rarely asked questions he didn't already know the answer to.

"Well, I have a lot going on. I can't tell what's *really* bothering me anymore." I kept my eyes on the yellow turning signs as we drove around curve after curve, all the way up the mountain on the way home from the hospital.

"No. You're the only one who will ever know what's really bothering you. You're also the only one who can hide it." He knew exactly what the problem was, and he was trying to let me figure it out.

"I don't know what to do! I just can't keep doing this." I looked down at my tightened hands. I had to consciously lower my shoulders away from my ears. I had forgotten how to relax; I was so tired.

"Are you worried about your mom?" The cloudiness of his voice proved that he was.

"I mean, maybe, but I'm not afraid. I know she's going to be all right. Maybe I'm just overthinking everything." That was my go-to excuse. If I was overthinking, I could convince myself I wasn't choosing not to think about it. But when something so devious, so vast and so apparent, plagues your thoughts with every blink of the eye—it becomes a war with the mind not to pause there.

"Overthinking isn't always a bad thing," he answered.

I knew what he meant. He was right. This relationship with my boyfriend was tearing me apart, not that he had done anything wrong. I couldn't just leave. I had no concrete reason to leave. He was a good guy, bought me flowers, and told me he loved me. We rarely ever fought, and things looked so good. Good, except…

Dad and I didn't say anything else for a while. My thoughts were screaming loud enough to make the silence unnoticeable. After I blinked back into reality, all the yellow signs were gone, and the curvy mountain had disappeared. We were almost home.

"Dad…"

It seemed he flickered back too at the sound of my voice. He had other concerns to get lost in. Mom had been in the hospital a few days. Doctors thought she might have ovarian cancer and were going to operate soon. God had given me so much peace for her situation. He kept telling me, "*It's okay.*" Those two simple words spoken to my soul over and over again gave me a confidence that God was going to come through. Every time I began to doubt, gently and faithfully I heard the words, "*It's okay.*" How could I have so much peace in this monumental storm, and still feel an avalanche of worry rushing at my mind in another part of me?

"What do I do?" I asked after a long pause.

My dad always knew what to say. I was begging for an answer

that maybe I just had not thought of yet. My question was heavy with hope that he would solve all my problems. And I suppose he did. It just wasn't the solution I wanted to hear.

He answered me without hesitation, "Follow peace."

We pulled in the driveway.

I was in a typical high school relationship with a nice guy. He played sports, knew everyone, said sweet things, and made me feel wanted. He seemed to have the right qualities I thought I wanted. He was comfortable. And *that* was dangerous.

Typically, when the word "comfortable" is used, it's a good thing. I love comfortable blankets. Snuggling up into a warm, bouncy, comfortable bed at night is one of the highlights of my day. I love being comfortable—we all do.

So, my "comfortable" relationship with my boyfriend was dangerous, since comfortable tends to lead to this thing called settling. And once you've settled, it's no longer good. A lot of the blessings God has for us first require a little discomfort.

Confusing, right? Well, it was for me, during this internal struggle. The Biblical example that comes to mind is when God led the Israelites to the Promised Land. Before they were able to participate in all the luxuries, they had to go through the wilderness for forty years. During those years, they didn't do everything right. But God was still faithful to hold up His end of the deal.

Psalm 16:2 (NIV) states, "You are my Lord; apart from you I have no good thing." So when we settle for less than God's best, we pull away from His blessings. And worse, we pull away from Him. Apart from him, there is no good thing; that's a fairly simple concept. The hard part was realizing what was pulling me away.

Please don't get the wrong idea. I'm not saying I was too good for this guy because that was not the case. But if he wasn't the one God planned for me, then it was a "no good thing." So, what's the opposite of good? Bad. Even though everything looked fine on the outside, God sees things below the surface. He already knew the future plans He had in store for me, and this boy wasn't in them.

After all, I wasn't looking for Mr. Right—I was searching for Mr. Man of God. The difference is immeasurably vital. I could have fallen in love with a lot of boys, but my heart wanted more than just a good guy. I wanted the man who would help me walk out the calling God had placed on my life. I wanted the man who God knew would help me fulfill my destiny better than the others. I wanted the man from God's plan for my life, not the guy the fairytales told me to look for.

The awesome part was that God loved me enough to warn me about it. The problem was, I wasn't listening. Psalm 10 says, "In all his thoughts there is no room for God." Following peace was way harder than it needed to be, because I didn't want to go where it was leading me. It wasn't a cloud in the sky spelling out *END THIS RELATIONSHIP.* It wasn't a thunderous voice ordering me to abandon someone I thought I loved. It was just peace, or better yet, a lack of peace. I just knew God had other plans—better plans.

That "peace" my dad was talking about would be my most useful tool in the journey to come. It would be my compass and my road map, so I didn't get lost in this crazy thing called love. I ran from peace, and for a while I was doing just fine. The beauty of it all was that it didn't relent. That perfect peace chased me down until I couldn't run anymore. I knew what I had to do. I knew what I was going to do. But the fact that I didn't want to did not change.

March 11th. I've been sixteen for a total of twelve hours now. As a "Thank You" letter to the guy who just threw me a surprise birthday party, I'm going to end our relationship.

Great.

Mom has been out the hospital for a few days now. It wasn't cancer, and she's going to be okay. When we got the news that the mass was benign and everything was fine, I couldn't help but think back to those two words God kept speaking to my soul: *"It's okay."* I was so glad I chose to believe what God was telling me over what my fears were trying to tell me. Once it was all said and done, God was right. He always is. And that thought nudged me closer to trusting Him with this relationship issue.

Mom sat in her chair, and Dad in his. I hadn't realized how much I loved this simple routine of us coming home, changing into our pj's and just relaxing as a family. After everything that happened over the past month, I wouldn't take that for granted anymore. As relieving as that was though, I still felt terrible inside. So I guess that narrowed down the problem, huh? I felt a single tear fall into my lap, then another, and then splashes of them.

"Honey, what's the matter?" Mom looked at me, surprised by my sudden outburst of silent tears.

"I'm not exactly sure," I choked out through the crying. "I just feel chaos in me. I think it's because of Peter. I think I need to break up with him, but I have no idea how. I don't even really know why!" I was frustrated that I didn't know why. I was borderline angry about it. If only I had a reason; if only I could see how this would benefit me.

"You'll never go wrong doing what God tells you," my dad chimed in.

"I just really don't want to do it. I'm afraid I'm going to do something wrong. I don't want him to be mad at God. I'm going to sound crazy if I tell him why I'm leaving." I hadn't said any of these thoughts out loud until this very moment. I was crumbling quicker than I thought. "What do I tell people at school? I can't explain this."

"You don't worry about that. You obey God, and God does the rest," Mom assured.

She was right. I knew she was right. I would have told anyone else the same thing if they asked me for advice on this situation. I knew what the right answers were, but they were just so hard to put into practice right now. But getting it all out into the open gave me a small sense of relief. It was like someone cracked a window in a smoke-filled kitchen. I gave into the feeling of relief, and I walked up to my room to make the phone call.

"Hey, what's up?" He had no clue this would be one of the last phone calls we ever shared. I wanted to do this in person; honestly, I did. But I couldn't. There was a sense of urgency that had been bottled up far too long. After saying the words out loud, it all just exploded. It had to be done immediately. But nothing negative had happened between us, so why should he expect anything?

"Hey..." I was desperately trying to choke down the tears and hold my voice steady. "We need to talk, and I'm probably going to start crying, but just hear me out." That was it—tears.

"Okay, what's wrong?" His voice was still light, and it made me feel even worse. Everything in me wished we were in a fight. I want- ed so badly to have an easy explanation or an excuse that made sense to any other teenager in the world, but I didn't. Nothing about this was easy. But for the first time, I had no doubt that it was right.

"I need you to know that I'm not saying this because you've done anything wrong. But I've been praying about us, and I just don't have peace anymore." It took me an unbearably long amount of time to squeeze out those words through the thunderstorm pouring out of my eyes. "It's not because I want to break up. But more than all the things I don't want to do, I do want to follow God. This isn't your fault, and I don't think God is disapproving of you. But if I'm not right for you, I don't want to get in the way."

Did that even make sense? I hoped that didn't sound like I was blaming God. Though at this point, I would settle with just getting the words out.

Silence. He wasn't saying anything. Was he crying? Did he hang up?

"I understand," was all he said.

"You do?" The tears took a break. I began to focus all of visual attention on a single black fly on the wall above me. The fly didn't care how bad this would hurt tomorrow and the next day. The fly didn't think about tomorrow at all. It didn't have emotions. What a lucky fly.

"You're really committed to doing what God says, so I believe you." His voice didn't even shake.

"So, you're not mad?"

"No, who am I to disagree with God? It's okay." He was making this easier on me than I thought.

"Thank you." I stopped crying. I knew this was right. And for the moment, I was as the fly—numb and still.

9

That was one of the hardest things I've ever done. Ending a good relationship the day after my birthday doesn't tend to make anyone "happy." I'm not going to pretend like it was effortless. So here is what God had to explain to me—before I understood why He was asking me to do this—the difference between *happiness* and *joy*.

Happiness is an emotion. It is strictly based on circumstance and situation. It is constantly changing and shifting. Joy, on the other hand, is a fruit of the Spirit. In Galatians 5:22–23 (NIV) it says, "But the fruit of the Spirit is love, *joy*, peace, patience, kindness, goodness, faithfulness, gentleness and self-control." The cool thing about joy is that it isn't based on circumstance. You can have joy even when everything is falling down around you.

Here's why.

Psalm 16:11 (NIV) says, "You will fill me with joy in your presence, with eternal pleasures at your right hand." Joy is found by simply spending time with God, doing the things He asks you to do. Little did I know that learning about joy was just the first step. God would show me how to obtain all nine of those fruits throughout my journey.

I learned that with joy comes happiness, not the other way around. I resolved to run to God and depend on Him for my joy, because He never changes. And I trusted that He could fix my circumstance to then make me happy. Sometimes, we even have to do things that make us unhappy in order to receive joy.

Now I know, I know, this is not sounding too fun anymore, but stick with me. It'll all prove to be worth it. Please know that God will never ask you to give something up, if He doesn't already have something better than you could ever imagine in store for you.

Psalm 30:5 (NKJV) says, "…weeping may endure for a night, but joy comes in the morning." When I read that verse, I realized all this pain was only temporary. But the joy that was to come would be worth it.

Chapter Two

Knock Knock

BEEP BEEP BEEP BEEP!

"Is it six a.m. already? Okay, no more midnight crying sessions for this girl; they took up too much sleeping time." I pulled the mascara-stained pillow over my face. I thought back to the conversation I had with Peter last night. He swore he wasn't "talking" to her, but I knew he was. The hard part though was I knew it wasn't just her.

It had been one week since we broke up, and I could see that moving on was not quite as hard for him as it was for me, and I'm the one that broke up with him! *Come on, pull yourself together. This is ridiculous,* I coached myself. It still hurt though, I couldn't help it. I've heard that breaking up is kind of like pulling off a Band-Aid. If you do it quickly and all at once, it wouldn't hurt so badly. And yeah, that's probably true, but I didn't have any emotional attachment to the Band-Aid. It wasn't quite that simple.

I eased my way out of my comforter and into an abnormally steaming shower. *Good morning, God.* I didn't even say the words out loud today. Maybe I was angrier at God than my ex-boyfriend, or maybe God was mad at me? *No, shake it off, Jo. God isn't punishing you.*

Out loud this time, I said, "Good morning, God."

I turned off the water and felt the offensive cold rush of air as I reached for my towel. Monday, March 18th, our anniversary. *Happy anniversary.* I wasn't even going to pretend to be "okay" today.

"Keep smiling, honey. God knows what He's doing." Mom dropped me off at school and squeezed in some encouraging words right before I slammed the door. I really didn't want to be here.

God knows what He's doing… Yeah, I'd love if you'd fill me in, God. If this is really what You wanted, then why does it hurt so badly?

No answer. Nope. None… awesome.

I walked into the hallway, lost in my consultation with God. As distant as I felt from God, I had to admit, I was somehow more at ease now than I had been in months. That is, until certain things rocked my world, like flickering back into reality and seeing my ex-boyfriend with her. *Her.* It didn't matter what her name was, how old she was, her social status, how she looked, or even if she knew that I existed. She was inevitably the new thorn in my paw.

Walk by or make a scene? Walk by… Make a scene… My heart stomped against my chest. *Keep walking, Jo. You know it's not her fault. Keep walking, Jo.*

Romans 8:28 (NIV) states, "And we know that in all things God works for the good of those who love him, who have been called according to his purpose." *ALL THINGS.* The good, the bad, the *her,* the ex, the obedience, the tears, the memories… all of it. God

promised He would work it all out for my good. He promised. At this point, I will admit I was beyond confused and frustrated, but I did know about this one particular promise that kept me standing just a little while longer.

I wondered what I had to do to qualify for such a promise. The end of the verse says "called according to his purpose." So, I figured I had to be doing something for God for good things to happen. It wasn't until I was hurting and unable to do anything on my own that I realized that part of the promise wasn't at all about what I had to do for God, but all about what I had to allow God to do *in* me.

"Who have been called..." I couldn't make God call me. There was nothing I could do to make God pick me; that was His choice. He chose to make all things work for my good, because He chose to call me. Just like He chose to call you. He chose to make your mistakes an ingredient for your good. I did have a crucial decision to make with this new information.

I now knew God had called me, chosen me, and had a plan and a purpose for me. But God is a gentleman. He will not force himself where He is not welcome. Revelation 3:20 (NIV) says, "Here I am! I stand at the door and knock. If anyone hears my voice and opens the door, I will come in and eat with that person, and they with me."

God wasn't going to barge into the dinner party of my life and begin rearranging, perfecting, or cleaning anything unless I let him. He was knocking on my heart. But I had to choose to let Him in to do the work that only God can do. I had to choose to do this whole adventure His way and with His map. I had to choose His will, even when sometimes it differed from mine. But I knew it was a safe choice, because He promised that if I did, He would perfect every step of the way.

One day God showed me a different way to read it. He explained to me that yes, *all things* is very important, but at this particular time, *all things*, isn't what I needed to focus on. He told me to stop focusing on the "things" around me and to change the emphasis. He told me to read the verse again like this: "And we know that in all things *God works* for the good…"

God! The Creator of the Heavens and the Earth, the all-powerful miracle maker is working for *you*! God! The same God that moves mountains and paints the sunsets every morning. The same God that breathes thunder, fills His hands with lightning, and then tells it where to go. The same God who keeps lilies clothed in color and beauty. The same God that watches over the sparrows in the sky—that incredible God was working for me.

When you know who you are working for, it changes your perspective. But when you know who is working in you, it changes everything else.

God is knocking, trust me. You should let Him in.

Chapter Three

Only Temporary

"WHAT HAPPENED?" SHE WAS SINCERELY CONCERNED—NOT THAT I could tell her what actually happened, because I was crying so hard. She was the only person I didn't feel stupid crying around, so I figured I should get it all out now. "Did y'all fight?"

I nodded my head in a pitiful yes. "When we broke up, he said he wouldn't talk to other girls for a while. He said we'd still be close." Of course he didn't know he couldn't keep that promise at the time, but I still held him accountable. "He's moving on, and I'm the one that broke up with him!" I sniffled, as if Peter's adjustment to the single life was somehow a betrayal. My head knew he had every right, but my heart protested.

This Band-Aid was stickier than I thought.

A minute or two passed before she announced, "I'm gonna break up with my boyfriend." She said it with a blank stare. I stopped crying and looked at her in shock. "What you're doing is hard, but we both know it's right. I know it's what I need to do too." Her smile was weak, but still a smile.

"Julia…" I wasn't even sure what to say. She saw this tearing me apart, and she was still going to go through with her it herself. God must have been talking to her about this stuff too. "Why?" I asked, knowing the answer to that question.

I had silently asked God that same question so many times, rationalizing that it would be wrong to say it out loud. I thought it would be wrong to question God, as if He didn't already know what I was thinking.

But questioning Julia was easy. "Why?" I asked again.

"Because it's gonna be worth it, right? That's what you told me when you said you were breaking up with him. God knows what He's doing."

Oh, yeah. All my faith seemed to be so far away these past couple days. *Worth it.* I felt my own weak smile. *Worth it.*

"I know," I said. I didn't feel like I knew it. But I did.

"And it's not about how you feel. It's about the facts. You might be sad right now, but this is only temporary, remember?"

I nodded. That's why she was my best friend. She reminded me I wasn't alone. All those words had come out of my mouth not even a week before, and now I needed her to repeat them back to me. She was a blessing. *Thanks, God, for my best friend.*

It was March 19th, and after that talk with her, I realized I needed something more than a bowl of chocolate ice cream. I needed answers as to why exactly God was taking me down this road.

"Then let's do this," I stopped crying.

She made the phone call.

WHY?

That was the haunting question. I went out on my porch on March 19th. I sat down and decided that day would be *the* day I stopped being helpless. I stopped being afraid to ask God all my questions, and I simply came to Him as His beloved baby girl. I realized that asking God questions was a different conversation than questioning God. Asking Him for direction, for understanding, and for comfort was a humbled approach to His mercy seat. This is not at all like questioning His faithfulness when the plan stings a little more than I expected. I wasn't approaching God questioning His goodness, like maybe He had forgotten me. I was coming to Him broken and in need of a lot of answers I didn't have.

God loves it when we run to Him. In fact, Proverbs 4:7 (NIV) says, "The beginning of wisdom is this: Get wisdom. Though it cost all you have, get understanding." That verse felt exactly like what this exchange between God and me was. I had given up what seemed very valuable to me. And here I was not asking for it back, but asking for understanding on how to move forward.

Then, I opened my Bible— and it had never seemed so heavy. Every page seemed like a thousand pounds to my flesh, but somehow each verse lifted a weight off of me.

I understand that reading your Bible isn't always easy. Trust me, I know. But just do it. If you're looking for answers, that's where you'll find them. If you're looking for freedom, there's your key. If you're looking for peace, that's the map. God told me about the plans He had for my life. He showed me His way, and promised it was better than my way.

James 1:2–4 (MSG) says, "Consider it pure joy, my brothers and sisters, whenever you face trials of many kinds, because you know that the testing of your faith develops perseverance. Let perseverance finish its work so you may be mature and complete, not lacking anything." This verse is such a paradox. Joy in trials, doing things that are uncomfortable, yet acknowledging it as joy.

We have trials so we can develop perseverance, endurance, and strength. According to this verse, without perseverance we aren't complete. We're lacking. To know you're no longer going to be incomplete is enough to make anyone happy, right? But that's not where the joy comes from. There's a reason God wants us to be complete; so we don't miss the blessings He's so desperately trying to give us! It literally says, "…not lacking anything."

I knew God had a man set apart for me, my own personal man of God, who would help me accomplish all the plans He had for my life. I saw then that He was only trying to give me a blessing. He wasn't taking anything away. He was completing me.

I knew in that moment, as I stared down my empty driveway, that one day my man of God would be walking there. I knew in that moment that one day, this would only be a memory, and I would be more than happy again. I knew in that moment on my porch that I'd remember this moment forever.

Chapter Four

What If?

MY THOUGHTS WERE ALL TANGLED UP IN EACH OTHER. *YOU CAN'T get back with him, you've got too much to do. Stick to God's plan,* was quickly tied in a knot with, *It would be so easy… one conversation and this could all be over. You wouldn't have to worry about other girls anymore.* The only reason the later thought didn't win every time was because deep down, I knew no matter what, I'd always have to worry about other girls, regardless of our relationship status. That's just how it was. Worry was never far when I was with him.

But today was different. April 19th, one month down. The pain was still there and obviously I still cared, but today was different. *Okay, but God, what if I didn't really get back with him, but we just hung out still and I…*

What if?

My bargaining was interrupted by the bell. First period was over, and if I walked fast enough I could meet him at the end of the hall before he left me. We had originally agreed to meet there after first period. That was, until he had other girls to meet in that amount of time, and every day I became less and less of a priority.

There he is. "Hey! Wh—"

A few more steps revealed he wasn't alone. *Her.* I honestly wanted to think she wasn't as pretty as me. Or I hoped she'd be dumb, so I could at least have something on her. But she wasn't. She was beautiful and on the honor roll, just like all the other girls I saw him with. Her hair was longer than mine and had some curl to it. Her eyes were bright, and her lip gloss had never been so shiny. I wonder if he could feel that he was standing on my heart. He looked up at me and nodded. He just head nodded me. Me! A month ago, he swore I was his whole world, and there was no one else out there for him. And all it took was a matter of days to forget who I was and replace all that affection with a *head nod!*

Incessant laughter was followed by, "Wow, that's so funny. That movie was hilarious! I would even watch it again. Maybe we could this weekend…"

They went on a date! I had just stopped crying every night, and he was already going out on dates! To top it all off, it was the movie I had been talking about since before we broke up. That was supposed to be "our thing."

I zoned out after that. He was really going to make me stand here and wait for him to finish making dinner reservations for this girl before even saying so much as hello.

Wait, why am I still here? I asked myself. After all, today was different. I wasn't helpless today. God had plans for me, and they didn't involve standing around unnoticed and embarrassed.

"Bye."

They both stopped talking and stared at me. She looked as though I just popped out of the wall. She never even saw me walk up to them. To her, I was just another face. I instantly wondered what her perspective of me was at that moment. My whole body wanted to be in her place, if for just a little while. I wanted him to look at me like that just one more time, and she wouldn't even remember my presence by the end of the day. He stood confused, while I walked away. Truth be told, he probably wouldn't remember either.

Thank You, God, for convincing me I'm worth something, I silently prayed. I could finally breathe. I wasn't alone today, and that made all the difference.

Philippians 4:6–7 (MSG) states, "Don't fret or worry. Instead of worrying, pray. Let petitions and praises shape your worries into prayers, letting God know your concerns. Before you know it, a sense of God's wholeness, everything coming together for good, will come and settle you down. It's wonderful what happens when Christ displaces worry at the center of your life."

Why would the verse say, "Let God know what you need?"

If God knows all our thoughts, why do we have to tell Him? I learned that when we tell God what we need, we are consciously giving that situation over to Him to take care of. Then, when we see the problem solved, we know who to thank.

That day wasn't different because my feelings had changed at all. My emotions were still running rampant and destroying every positive thought I attempted to have. That day was different, because I gave my situation to God, regardless of how I felt about it. Emotions are irrelevant. We don't need them for survival. What's so amazing about God is, He even cares about the irrelevant parts of our lives. He loves us enough to fix those emotions with His peace; all we are required to do is ask.

God didn't take away my sadness that day; he replaced it with gladness. I put my heart in God's hands, knowing He would make sure it didn't break.

When you make God smile, He wants to do the same for you.

Chapter Five

A Calling

HER BALLET SHOES WERE ALWAYS WHITER THAN MINE, BECAUSE SHE
didn't shuffle her feet when she walked. She never wore them
outside, and she always put them back in the box after practice. She
was so much more organized than me. I took mine out of the box,
comparing the three black scuffs on the front of mine to her pristine
leather pair. She saw me looking, and laughed. I looked up at her
and laughed with her.

Laughter. I had almost forgotten the sound of it. It felt good to
be laughing again.

"Don't judge!" I shoved her shoulders and snickered. She
slipped on her left shoe and then her right, while I stretched my
arms out before rehearsal.

"Are you nervous?" She wasn't asking because I seemed nervous, she was asking because she was. It was our third performance
together. We had come so far.

"Are you?" I pinned my hair back out of my face and stuck out
my tongue at her in the mirror.

"A little bit. I always am before we get on stage." We were on a church dance team. It was unlike any dance team I had ever been on. I wasn't dancing for points or personal pride. Now I was dancing for a purpose, for Jesus.

"Me too. It's all good. You better hurry up. We're doing our team prayer in a few minutes in the other building." I reached down and pulled her up with one of those giant tugs that makes you fumble forward a little. I found it peculiar that she was the nervous one. Out of the two of us, she was the one who was put together. She was handling this whole break up thing much better than I was.

Julia knew what she wanted to do. She knew her calling. God had laid it on her heart to be a neonatal nurse, to help babies. She was excited about her future and well on her way to getting there. I wanted so badly to know where I was going, what God wanted me to do. After all, I had broken up with my boyfriend because of that calling. I just wished I knew what that calling was.

"All right, ladies, let's get in a circle around the front." The dance instructor called us over. Six girls, sparkled and primped, gathered around and held hands. The white gowns flowed into each other, and all together we made a sea of satin. *We make a pretty picture*, I thought.

"I'll start the prayer, and we'll go around," said our instructor. "Julia, will you close out the prayer for us?" Julia had been dancing with her longest and helped her out with things like this. She nodded, and the head of the dance department went around and prayed for each girl individually. Every girl had a different need and desire, and every prayer was customized.

This particular prayer was one of those life-changing moments. After it happens, you need to write it down somewhere. It was one of those moments that needed to be recorded in time with details and illustrations, so you don't forget anything. She prayed for Julia and her man of God. She prophesied about how blessed they would be and do great things. I knew Julia and I had been praying about that more than anything, and I was excited for her to get to me and say something about my future relationship.

Well, she got to me and began to pray; and she didn't mention any man. She said nothing about a relationship. But what she did say was so life changing that a man seemed like a small detail in a big plan.

Her prayer described things to come. It was passionate about how God's plan for me was designed far beyond my hometown. I would go farther. I would reach the world.

"You're going to change the world," added our dance instructor.

As she prayed, I began to see why God had me do what I did. She was fervent about the weight this calling consisted of. I knew every detail of my life had to be in line with this calling for it to reach the magnitude God had in mind. She finished the prayer and hugged me. That prayer went far beyond the dance, traveled past the performance, and flew through the worries, the doubt, and the confusion. It hit me straight in the heart and became an *instant*. An instant in my whole life that I could stand on and build from.

No instructions, no specifics. It wasn't a career, being a world changer. I still knew no more about what classes I needed to take, where to go next, or how to get there. But I knew I would. If need be, God would carry me there.

"As for God, his way is perfect: the Lord's word is flawless; he is a shield for all who take refuge in him..." Psalm 18:30 (NIV) showed me that God had a plan for my life, a special destination to reach, and I could only get there one way—*His* way. Instead of peace that news was supposed to bring me, it kind of freaked me out. I was so afraid if I messed up any minute part, I would somehow flaw the whole plan.

So, I kept reading. Two verses down, God explained how to accomplish this monumental task. "It is God who arms me with strength and makes my way perfect" (Psalm18:32 NIV). My ways become His ways; and therefore, all because of God, I become perfect.

Perfection. What a difficult label to live up to. But I didn't have to accomplish perfection. All I had to do was hide behind it. All I had to do was rest in it. Perfection. That was God's job, because Psalm 55:22 says God will never let the righteous person stumble. He won't let us mess up the call. After all, we just have to answer it.

Pick up, perfection is calling you.

Chapter Six

Not Just Friends

EVERYTHING WOULD BE BACK TO NORMAL. IT'D BE EASY AGAIN, right? What would Mom say?

I'm so close to just getting back together with him.

We were practically still together anyway. This whole trying to be "friends" wasn't working too hot. All the old feelings were still there. I needed to just get away—or get just as close as I was before.

My thoughts were broken by the vibration of my phone. Mom texted me back.

> *Calm down. Just wait it out. God knows what He's doing, and He's working all things out for your good. You need only be still.*

I knew she would say that. That's why I texted her in the first place. I wanted someone to talk me down, because I knew it was wrong. Wrong, but easy.

The girls across the room were all whispering, and I was fairly positive they were talking about the football players standing in the hallway.

I walked in the door to a hallway filled with perfectly normal teenage smiles; easy, light, thoughtless smiles. I envied those smiles instantly and tried to reflect them back at the few people I knew enough to glance at. Eventually, my fake reflected smile met his. It quickly withered away into a puddle of my real emotions.

"Hi." I mouthed the word and looked away.

He followed me. "Hey! Good morning?" He twisted his voice back into a reflected happiness, sounding like all the other voices in the hall.

"Yeah, good morning." I hadn't had a "good" morning in a while, but that's not what he was supposed to hear. He was supposed to think remaining "friends" was working. It was my idea, after all. My classroom was only a few more feet away, and the bell was about to ring. I could pretend to not be miserable for a few more seconds. "I guess I'll see you later." I threw in a tiny pitiful grin with the words.

"Wait." His word was muffled by the sound of the ringing bell. Before I could do or say anything, he kissed me goodbye. It wasn't a "goodbye kiss" though. Not like the "this is the last time" kind of kiss. It was more like the kind of kiss you use when saying, "I'll see you later." It was the kind of kiss that happens again.

"Uhh…" I didn't care to think of a real sentence. I just walked inside my class to notice all the gaping mouths who just saw what happened.

Why would he kiss me? It's like nothing changed, but needed to. *Okay, Jo, pull it together. Either tell him it's completely over or that you're back on. This floating in between isn't going to get you anywhere.*

I felt just as anxious as I did before any of this happened, and I pulled out my phone to text him and tell him this wasn't working like I thought. I had a whole paragraph planned out in my head as to what I would say.

I clicked on the phone.

I shouldn't have kissed you, right?

He knew, just as well as I did, this wasn't going to work. The kiss was proof. We didn't know how to be "just friends."

"Just friends," aye? Word to the wise—that *never* works. When God asks you to give something to Him, He's not asking for a piece of it. He doesn't only want half, especially when it comes to matters like this. The reason for this is because we were never meant to handle these relationships on our own, anyway. When it comes to your heart, God is not interested in sharing the burden with you. He wants it all and for good reason too. Out of all of the people in the world you could choose from, God has certain people He has designed for your life.

Not only did this mean the man I chose to involve myself with, but also the friends I chose to spend valuable time with. Proverbs 27:17 (MSG) states, "You use steel to sharpen steel, and one friend sharpens another."

I had a great God-sent friend who was sharpening me in the way of the God's will. But there were also some other friends who had been sharpening me in other matters that were not beneficial to the calling. I didn't want to be sharpened in gossip or drama. I didn't want to become sharp in drinking alcohol or sneaking out late at night. I wanted to be sharpened in the Word. I wanted to become sharp in patience, in kindness, in generosity.

You are being sharpened by the friends you surround yourself with whether you want to be or not. You are being molded, whether good or bad. Make sure you find godly sharpeners.

Just like I had to let go of Peter, there were some friends I had to let go of as well. To be honest, I had to let go of almost all of them. I had friends I talked to in class at school. And friends I invited to church. I had friends who texted me happy birthday and all of that good stuff.

But, I only had the one friend I allowed to sharpen me. Julia was the one I spent my time with. She was the one I poured my heart out to; but most importantly, Julia was the only friend that I let build me. While my other friends were great people, Julia was the only other one as focused on following God's will as I was. A lot of other people my age would have called me crazy if I told them I was breaking up with a boy because God told me to. And that's okay. They didn't understand. But it is so important that you find and surround yourself with those who embrace the same faith and values. That way, you can help pull each other along. When times get trying, you can encourage each other to keep the faith.

I'm not saying you have to have only one close friend. That's just how it happened for me. But I can say that I would have traded all the popularity in school for my one best friend who did devotions with me on the weekends. I would have exchanged all the high school parties in the world for the prayer time Julia and I had together. And I knew that if God could provide such a quality best friend to do life with, then once I received the one I was supposed to marry, I would trade all the summer flings and high school boyfriends for my Mr. Man of God in a heartbeat.

Now, please don't get confused when I say "The One" regarding who you're supposed to marry. God has a "perfect will" for your life, as well as a "permissible will." And by that I mean I think there are plans A, B, C, so on for your life. You can never mess up so much that God can't put it back together.

But I wanted plan A. I wanted God's perfect will. I wanted the best of the best. And that's what God wants for you. He wants you to walk out His best possible plan, the one with the least hurt and the most blessing. The chances of us finding and executing that plan perfectly on our own is impossible. So, when He put it on my heart to end this relationship, because it wasn't the right one, He wasn't just telling me to change my *Facebook* relationship status.

This didn't mean we had to be enemies, but it did mean I had to step back. I had to get away for a little while. I had to give the entire relationship to God, because He was the only one who knew how to handle it. But letting go of this relationship completely meant I was going to be completely alone.

That's what we're all afraid of, right? Being alone. Or worse, having to wait! I was afraid of the in-between stages from broken to better. But that "in-between" time was more beneficial to me than anything. That "alone" stage showed me that I was not alone after all. It showed me that God loved me. It showed me that before I could be happy with another human being, I had to be happy alone. Psalm 9:10 (NIV) says, "Those who know your name will trust in you, for you, Lord, have never forsaken those who seek you." I was going to have to seek God now. He's the only one who could promise to never forsake me.

The beautiful part was, the more I sought out God, the more I trusted Him. The more I trusted Him, the less afraid I was. The reason God wants all of you is because if you *truly* know who God is, trusting Him will come naturally.

I'm okay. I am A-okay. Don't do it, Jo. I was doing everything I could not to text that boy back. I kept checking the time, waiting for it to be a somewhat acceptable hour to go to sleep, so I didn't have to think anymore. I toppled across my cluttered bed. The abundance of unmade sheets and pillows were the perfect place for me to muffle my sighs. I found some mild comfort in my sea of unkempt fabric and fluff.

But I still just kept staring at the screen of my phone.

I probably shouldn't tell you this… but I miss you.

Oh. No. He. Didn't. I was finally starting to get some distance, and this is what he says to me. Part of me wanted to turn off the phone. But the louder, more convincing part of me wanted to lay out my every thought and feeling about the past month in one long, book-like response. I was convincing myself that I did not have to vent everything to him for me to feel better. But Julia wasn't answering the phone, and there was a civil war crashing around in my head. My purple nest of pillows wasn't sheltering my desperation anymore.

Before I knew it, my fingers were running away from my brain, and I was typing, let's just say, a long response. I told him I was angry and hurt, and that I missed him. I told him I hated that I missed him. I was flying through every emotion, as the word vomit flowed.

Send. I immediately regretted that decision. *What. Did. I. Just. Do.*

My heart was beating in my ears and every second that went by without a response felt like a gaping hole into eternity. My phone vibrated to end the torment.

> *I know. I'm sorry. But you were right. I can see that you love God so much, and I loved that about you. But from day one, I knew that I wasn't as dedicated as you are. I just thought we could work around that. But I'm not ready to put in 110% to God like you. I really want you to be the person I kiss good night every night, but… it's not right. I don't care how much I miss you I won't let this happen. You have way more potential with someone else other than me. You'll find that man that willingly wants to put 120% of his time into God and you.*

My head stopped whirling. The war stopped raging. The time stood still. Even he knew this was right for me. Even he knew I was going to be okay.

> *Thank you.*

I closed my eyes, and with a huge breath of release, I whispered a tiny prayer, "Thank you."

"I have told you these things, so that in me you may have peace. In this world you will have trouble. But take heart! I have overcome the world." (John 16:33 NIV). God gave me a glimpse of his plan in the middle of my chaos. God showed me something that night. Love doesn't hurt. Loving the wrong person does. He had overcome this situation already. He didn't say it wasn't going to be trying. He didn't say that once I handed over the relationship to Him, all my feelings would cease to exist. But He told me not to worry, because He had already taken care of it.

I made the decision to turn over my wants and submit to God's ways. My feelings, my circumstance, and my position had not changed, or at least not right away—not in any way I could see. The world kept going on as usual, which made it hard to keep standing in faith. You might feel that way right now—like it's hard to keep standing faith.

Sometimes your next step of faith is to just keep standing. Sometimes you have to stay where you are and let God show you things, let God love you right there in the midst of your mess.

Matthew 26:41 (NIV) says, "Watch and pray so that you will not fall into temptation. The spirit is willing, but the flesh is weak." This verse showed me that I needed to be right where I was. My spirit was willing to do whatever it took to follow God's will, but my flesh did not like it one bit. I needed to be there, in my messy room, on my messy bed, reading a text message that said everything I needed to hear to keep me going.

All this was teaching me, preparing me, and setting me up for what was yet to come. Take heart! This is just training you. You'll thank Him for it later.

Chapter Seven

Insecurities

"Do you want to go over that intro one more time?" Mom asked as she placed the next practice song on the stand of my keyboard. "It sounded great. Just want to make sure you feel comfortable with it."

I was going to be playing an intro on the keyboard to one of the songs on the set list for Sunday morning worship. I hadn't played an intro alone yet.

"Um, yeah. Just one more time." I nodded.

She motioned for Sterling, our drummer, to begin the beat again. I smiled at how easily we all flowed together. He knew what the wave of her hand meant, and he executed the request skillfully. This was our third year together as a band. We made a great team.

The team consisted of six of us. My mom was the worship leader. Not only were we all a team, we were friends. We bonded over the common interest of the love of music and the love of Jesus.

Sterling began the beat again, and I completely blanked on when to come in. Seth, the bass player, saw my look of panic and walked over beside my instrument. Seth and Sterling were twin brothers who had played together for years. Their sound flowed without them even trying. I, on the other hand, had to try plenty hard. "Here, watch my fingers. I'll play the intro so you can see when to come in. Then you try it on your own." Seth guided me. Truth be told, it sounded better with him playing it. He was excellent at just about every instrument, and I was still learning this one.

"Thanks." I mouthed the word, as I picked up where he stopped and began to play. He walked back to the other side of the stage. Everyone joined in at their scheduled time. It was a beautiful sound, and I thought it must sound even more pleasing to God. After all, it was all for Him.

"Good job. Let's move on to the next song," Mom said, and we all flipped our pages to the next one. "Seth, how about you sing with me on the bridge?" she asked with a smirk on her face.

"Oh, I don't sing." Seth looked at the ground, and I almost thought I saw him blush. He wasn't wrong. He didn't sing. In front of people, anyway. Mom caught him singing before practice started when he thought he was the only one there. He sounded amazing. I wasn't sure if it was just because I didn't know he could sing, or because I knew he was always entirely too shy to. But for one reason or another, this secret was too hard to keep. It was perfect irony—a fantastic voice wrapped up in a man too shy to use it.

"Oh, yes you do. I heard you before practice. You sounded great." His eyes widened as he realized he'd been discovered.

"Come on, just sing backup on the bridge." Mom was always trying to inch us out of our comfort zone. She always succeeded.

"No, I don't think so."

"PLEEAASSSEEEE!" she jokingly pleaded with him. "Just try

it in practice."

And so, we did. The sound of their voices together, and everyone as a whole, was like complete harmony. Like everything was in place now that he was singing too. I smiled at the sound of it. I found it even more precious due to how humble he was about it. Maybe that's what made it so good, so sweet.

"Duuuude! Yes!" The guitarist motioned for Seth to high five him. And of course, Seth played it off like it was nothing special.

Worship that day was extravagantly deep—just what I needed.

That day I saw something I had heard about my whole life. But still, I very clearly needed a revelation of a lack of confidence in self, replaced with a complete confidence in Christ. I was so nervous to play the piano that morning, because I felt inadequate, like I wasn't good enough to be on the platform or in the melodies of worship at all. Every other musician on that team was excellent. They had played since young ages, practiced their craft, and knew the ins and outs of it all. I, on the other hand, had not. I only been playing for about four years.

I saw how confident Seth was while playing the bass and how shy he was about singing. Both of which he was great at. That's how I felt with this whole adventure to find my life partner, like I was so confident in the parts of life that I had experienced, practiced, and walked out. I was confident in the areas of the situation I understood. But, I was so shy, so uncomfortable, in the areas I had not yet walked through. God was showing me that if I would just walk with him, I would be great at those areas too.

With the humbleness that accompanies "I don't know" comes

a beautiful reliance on God. 2 Corinthians 12:10 (MSG) words this concept gracefully: "…My grace is enough; it's all you need. My strength comes into its own in your weakness."

When I started feeling overwhelmed by the journey, the wait, and the anticipation, I reviewed this repeatedly. The times when I feel most inadequate were the same times God was taking over the majority. In that, I found great peace.

Just as worship was noticeably deeper that day, not only Seth, but also I, stepped out even in our insecurity. So my relationship with God grew deeper and deeper when I began to give over my "not good enough" to Him. He did the most miraculous act and turned it into His "more than enough." That's what God does. That's what He wants to do for you. All He requires of us is that we step out when He directs to. That we sing even when we feel shy. That we play even when we feel unskilled. And that we follow Him, even when we don't where He's leading us.

I made up my mind then that I was going to see this through until the end just as David said in Psalm 119:112 (NIV), "My heart is set on keeping your decrees to the very end." I was excited with the melodies God was going to make out of me through this adventure.

In your life, when you begin feeling not good enough, afraid, or incapable of walking into what God is leading you to, get excited. Because at those times of weakness, God is up to the most good. Your story is progressing leaps and bounds when you give yourself over to the Author and Finisher of our faith (Hebrews 12:2).

Chapter Eight

Playing With Fire

BEFORE THE EX, BEFORE THE BREAK-UP, AND BEFORE THE PAIN, there was someone else. Julia was dating this guy, and his best friend, Ben, was looking for a "good girl." That's where I came in. It was one blind date. What could it hurt? It was a chance to hang out with my best friend and her boyfriend for the night without being the awkward third wheel I often was. I agreed to meet up with them. Little did I know, this guy, would be the one God used to teach me a lot of things I had to experience before I would listen.

The date went terrible. We went to the park, because Julia had to referee a little league soccer game. It was only supposed to take an hour, but that hour turned into three. And we were stuck outside with nothing to do. We played soccer for a while. We talked for a while. We starred at the ground for a while, and then finally, she was done. So instead of going to a nice restaurant to eat dinner, we went to McDonalds. The guys tried to bounce nickels down my shirt when I wasn't looking, and there was an abundance of empty, space-filling conversation.

Finally, it was over, and Julia and I went back to her house. We both agreed it was awful. A few days later we hilariously agreed to do it again. We went on another double date, and then another. Somewhere in between the painfully uncomfortable conversations, I started liking this guy. But, even though he wanted a good girl, he didn't want to be a good guy. And bad boys were way off Julia's radar and mine. We never even gave them the time of day, and somehow, we were both going on dates with them.

"He has a good heart, he just makes poor decisions. I just don't think he knows any better." Julia and I said these words on a daily basis in order to convince ourselves we weren't being careless. We were just helping people, right? We were "helping" them because we didn't want to walk away from them. Finally, one day Julia was ready to walk away. So she did. Part of me thought I just stayed with this boy because it was an excuse to hang out with Julia. But even after she ended it with her guy, I stayed. I kept playing with fire. I kept going out with him on dates. I kept staying up late on the phone with him every night. I kept giving in just a little bit at a time.

I got him to come to church with me and stop cussing around me. Instead of partying on the weekends, he hung out with me. I thought he was really changing.

Finally, the day came when he wanted to make it "official." He asked me to be his girlfriend one day after church. I knew it was coming. I just wasn't expecting it so soon. I thought as long as we weren't "official," I wasn't doing anything wrong. So, when he popped the question I'm pretty sure my immediate response was, "Crap! Uh, not now—maybe one day but…" And then he walked away, wordless.

He just walked away.

People will constantly be waltzing in your life. Each one is important, whether they were there to teach you, help you, leave, or stay. We can't help who dances in, but we can choose who we dance with. This guy was no good for me, and I knew that. I used the "I'm just being a teenage girl" excuse and brushed off the little voice inside that said, "No, wait for my timing." I danced with danger. And then when he glided off the dance floor, I should've just let that be the end of our song. So I did, for a while.

I saw that his actions were changing because I told him to. I thought I was really helping him. But in this was a very important lesson that took me a very long time to learn. People will change because you ask them to, but only for a little while. Eventually the monster of habit will consume them again, because people cannot change people. The only way anyone really changes is through the grace and love of Jesus Christ. Romans 2:4 (NIV) talks about repentance and turning from old ways: "…God's kindness is intended to lead you to repentance".

It's the goodness of God that draws men to repentance, not other men. Ladies, men will pretty much become whoever you want them to be in hopes of a future relationship. Because we're all people. We long to be accepted. In order to blend in, we cover up all the parts that we assume will be deemed unfavorable. But this covering only lasts for a short while. Permanent change requires grace and a heart transformation. The only One capable of such a shift is Jesus.

Until this boy fell in love with Jesus on his own, there was nothing I could say or do to make him want to be any different.

My ex and I had been broken up for some time now, and I couldn't get that fire dancing fella out of my head. I did have a lot of fun with him, and I even sometimes missed him. Maybe it was because I just ended a relationship and wanted a rebound. Maybe I felt the need to be with someone so I wasn't alone. Maybe I didn't want to face the fact that I was alone, and God's answer for all the relationship questions I was asking Him was "Wait."

Either way, I decided I was just going to text him. We ended things pretty badly, so the chance of him even acknowledging me were slim.

Hey, Ben, I miss you…

An immediate twinge hit my heart strings. "Why did I just do that?!" I asked myself in a panic. A few minutes went by. I was starring over the railing on my front porch. The yard seemed to stretch out for a thousand miles, and the time seemed to slow down. I felt so little in that moment. The whole world was right off that front porch step. My future, my greatest fears, and my biggest accomplishments—they were out there. I was just a teenage girl. Still, I had friends, amazing parents, a close relationship with God. And yet I felt so far away from everything except myself, all because I didn't know how long it would be before another guy told me I was pretty.

Before now, I had never needed a guy's approval. I had never once been "that girl" who was boy crazy and completely dependent on a having a boyfriend to make me happy. So where did I go wrong?

I miss you too … :(

He texted me back! I wondered if he thought I was just trying to talk to him again because I just got out of a relationship. It didn't matter though, because he texted me back.

Fear of the fall, or fear of the landing? I've heard many times before, "I'm not afraid of falling, I'm afraid of what happens when you land." I guess there's truth to that, but I think everyone is just a little bit afraid of the in-between. That space when you float. That moment where your whole body is being held up by nothing but time. The time it takes you to reach the bottom. You know what I mean—that space that allows your brain to evaluate how badly it will hurt when you land. You know, that moment of nothing.

That was scarier to me than hitting the bottom. That stage between happy and sad—that hollow moment. It was the worst of all. Because when you become hollow, you naturally desire to fill the void. The correct thing to do would be to get so close to God that He fills that space for you. And in all reality, He's really the only one that can. But God is rarely ever our first choice for void-filling. We tend to choose easier tangible things, such as sex, relationships, drugs, partying, self-gratification, or work.

I knew that eventually, there would be a bottom to the fall. I knew sooner or later, I would touch the ground. Maybe I would hit hard, or maybe land on my feet. But somehow or another, I'd get there. I knew that! Yet, I couldn't bear the suspension that time was holding me in. I couldn't handle the hollowness. God even told me specifically, "Don't get an 'in-between' guy."

I never stopped doing my daily devotions. I went to church every time the doors opened, and I talked to God probably more at this point than ever. But that didn't mean I was choosing God to be my void-filler. I refused to let God be enough. And even though I knew exactly what I was doing, I chose to play with fire as my void-filler.

In Psalms 13 (NIV), David writes down this exact feeling when he asks the Lord, "How long, Lord? Will you forget me forever? How long... must I wrestle with my thoughts and day after day have sorrow in my heart?" I guess I wasn't the only one afraid of "how long?"

Chapter Nine

Lover of Your Soul

CHRISTMAS EVE. THIS CHRISTMAS WAS DIFFERENT THAN THE others. I wasn't excited about the packages a downward flight of stairs away. The excitement that was keeping me awake tonight was the boy who promised to have Christmas dinner with me and my family. Little did I know, not only was Ben not going to show up, he wasn't going to so much as notify me our plans were off.

I felt like I was constantly fighting to keep him close, but not this time. I thought, surely he wouldn't bail on me at Christmas. We used to talk on the phone every night, but now we hardly talked at all. If he did call, our conversation that used to stretch out for hours upon hours was always summed up in about twenty minutes, tops.

Since it's Christmas Eve, can we pleeeeeaasse talk tonight?

I wasn't expecting a gift from him this Christmas, so much so that I didn't get him one either. All I wanted tonight was to simply talk to him.

Yeah, I'll call later, promise.

Relief flooded through me. He was at least going to appease me for Christmas.

But hours went by, and he didn't call. We didn't talk. I wasn't angry this time though. I didn't want to get him back. I was just hurt. He promised! I realized he just really didn't care to speak to me. I was by no means a priority to him. He wasn't even trying to let me down easy. I was being ignored on Christmas. I felt tears swelling, not in my eyes yet, but in my chest. They were creeping up my throat soon to come leaking down my face.

But they were interrupted by a sudden thought that God could be asking me the same question: *Hey, baby girl, since its Christmas Eve, can we talk tonight?*

What have I been doing? I was so busy chasing a boy who didn't even care to speak to me that I had forgotten about the Lover of my soul. The One that chases me even when I don't care to talk to Him. The One who watches over me to ensure that I'm safe and cared for. I had forgotten my Heavenly Daddy. I realized that night that the way I felt waiting for the phone to ring, desperately waiting, was how God felt about me. God showed me that no matter what I did, He couldn't help but want to talk to me. No matter how many promises I broke, no matter how many days had gone by since we last spoke, no matter what—God wanted to just talk to me.

That night I sat on my bed, turned my silent phone off, and just talked to my Daddy, the One who loves me. I talked about life, about future plans, about my feelings. It wasn't some spiritual prayer time, it was simply a talk with my Daddy.

I had never felt more loved than I did that night. Who am I that God Himself desperately wanted to spend time with me?! How unfathomable is that love. Regardless of the phone call I never received, I got a clear picture of the way God loved me. Desperately, hopelessly, and unconditionally. Even when I was faithless, God remained faithful.

As God and I spent time together, He began to give me a mental picture of how to come closest to Mr. Man of God. And the way to do that was by first getting close to God. I had a visual image in mind of a triangle. The three points represented the three characters of my most important story: God, myself, and the man I was going to marry. God was the top point, I was the left point, and the man, the right. While in the shape of a triangle, we were all an equal distance away from each other. But God showed me that the closer the two bottom points moved toward the top point, the smaller the triangle became. And as the two bottom points rose closer to the center, they came closer to each other.

God explained it to me like this: The closer we each came to Christ, by default, the closer we also became to each other. The smaller the triangle became, the smaller the gap between us became. God showed me that you cannot find the right significant other if you don't first find your Father.

I was so consumed in chasing the blessing, that I had lost sight of the Giver of the blessing. I needed to readjust my focus. You will not be able to love someone else the way God intended, if you do not first know how God loves you. How can we give unconditional love to someone else, if we have never experienced it ourselves? 1 John 4:19 (AMP) states, "We love because he [God] first loved us."

This concept is not just for finding your spouse; it will also be crucial in keeping him. A marriage with God as it's foundation will be strong and fortified. That constant seeking of God will also keep you and your spouse close to each other. Even after the "I do's," don't forget the Lover of your soul.

For anyone who is currently married and reading this book, if you are feeling distant from your spouse or having issues, I also encourage you to begin passionately seeking God. That comes by reading the Bible, listening to His teachings, praying, and dedicating time for just you and your Creator. Most importantly, follow the directions He begins placing on your heart. Do this and watch, as that mending of your spiritual relationship will also mend your marital one. You will find forgiveness easier; you will find peace more attainable. You will find perfect love.

Ben came, and he left every time the wind blew. His heart was a dandelion. A dandelion, the most spectacular weed, yet a weed, nonetheless. You cannot keep a dandelion. You can't carry a bouquet of them to your mother. You can't wear them proudly in your hair. You can't even savor them in a vase; because no matter how tight you hold the stem, the whimsical bed of petals will always float away from your fingertips. But they will dance off in such a way that you could never object. They float so peacefully away that it verges on the point of enchanting.

Who am I to tell beauty not to be beautiful? No matter how tight I held onto him, his heart danced away from me, long before I left. As hypnotizing and majestic as that summer was, it had to sail away too. It seemed the only time the wind stood still was those few summer months. That was the only time we really ever got along.

I'd let him ride away on the breeze, and I'd let him drift right back. I waited for days when the wind would return him to me. Once at an oven-heated day at the fair, he was late, as usual. His tardiness was another imperfection on his oh-so-perfect petals that I continuously overlooked. Sometimes, he wouldn't show up at all. I would forget my frustration, because of the way his excuses slid off his tongue and sang to me.

On this particular day, I heard the words of my friends, Seth and Sterling, running through my mind in a specifically foreshadowing tone: "Stay away from those kinds of boys. They're all trouble. Trust me."

I laughed. They were older than me, so I assumed they were speaking from experience. Those brothers were always so protective of me. I never exactly understood why. I knew they were good friends with not only me but also my parents. I wondered if my mom occasionally paid them to keep an eye on me. But I always knew if I needed anything, I could call on those Smith boys. I liked the idea of that. I am an only child, but I imagine that feeling is what it's like to have older brothers.

Today though, Ben showed up. He arrived with a harmonious song for being late, and I smiled at the sound of it. I waltzed my way through the dense cloud of heat and twirled into his passenger seat.

"Hey, Beautiful," he purred the words. Those words were hypnosis to my ears. My head knew he meant nothing by them, but my ears giggled with each syllable. He did not look at me when he used that trick. To him, "beautiful" was a title, a label, not a description. If I asked him what color my shirt was, he would not have been able to answer correctly. He didn't really look at me. He more looked through me, as though I were his mirror, and he wanted to see himself solely. I was aware of that reality even then. I didn't care.

To this day, I cannot say what was so infectious about him; but there was something. Something that spread, flourished, and surrounded me. Maybe it was the way he never completely smiled, enough though you could tell he wanted to. Maybe that was why I stuck around—to be the only person in his world that could coax that expression. Or maybe it was the way I understood what he actually meant when he spoke, simply by the way he emphasized the words. He lied incessantly, but because I always knew it wasn't true, it didn't register in my mind as a lie. To me it was just like him using different words to tell the truth. Maybe it was the appeal of the forbidden. Either way, he was a disease. He spread quickly. And for such a disease as deceit, the only cure is unforgiving truth.

The kind of truth that spares no feelings. It isn't sugar-coated to make the delivery any sweeter. It's the kind of truth that hits you in the gut, that dispels everything you were hoping to be true. I remembered feeling that kind of truth when I realized Peter felt like Mr. Right, but he wasn't Mr. Man of God. I feared feeling that truth again. So I tried my best not to listen. I wanted to be comfortably deceived by every lie Ben ever told.

I often thought about "love." I came up with two definitions. One type of love was a diseased misconception—the "I love you as long as everything is going good" conditional breed of love. It's only based on feelings and emotions. The other was the strong, long-suffering type. It recites, "No matter what, I'll be here." That's the kind of love God shows us. That's the kind of love we are incapable of without God. In my mind, real love was not an emotion, but an action. "For God so loved the world, He gave…" (John 3:16).

That's an action-giving love.

This boy though, he poisoned me with first option. That's how he loved me anyway. He spoke of love-like actions, but never carried through. He promised happily-ever-after, but not once did he move towards it. That shattering actuality took time to figure out.

On the way to the fair, he turned on the radio to music he was completely aware I hated. He didn't acknowledge the fact, and I didn't say a word. After a while, he looked at me, smiled, and put in a CD. He said nothing. There was no introduction, no explanation. He let the music speak. The songs were by no means beautiful, and I will not describe them as such. I won't say they were perfect, and I probably wasn't the first girl he dedicated them to. In spite of it all, it was me in that car. In spite of it all, I loved it. I read into every lyric and clung strongly to every note. He never told me how he felt.

This was our second try at romance. The first time, he treated me like a princess, and I turned him down. I think he was afraid to care that much again. I think he was afraid of me. So now, these songs were the only window to his heart that I knew of.

In the middle of the last song, he shut off the car and awoke me from my trance. I blinked owlishly, and realized we were there. He got out of the car and leaning his head in his opened door said, "You comin'? I didn't drive all the way here for you to sit in that car."

I giggled my passive tone and skated out of the opened door. I'm not passive by nature. I don't know why I was with him. It was less like passiveness and more like fear of confrontation. I was afraid to confront him about my issues with the way he treated me, because I was afraid he would leave. I remember never wanting to feel that way again, like needing to sacrifice my feelings in order to make him love me.

Honestly, to be fair to him, I never told him what hurt me. I didn't try to "fix" any of our problems that he probably never knew we had. I was too afraid. His affections for me were too fragile.

We walked in close, a hand's distance apart. My fingertips tingled with expectation of meeting his. They never did. He was not very tall, or very broad, or very anything but average. He avoided things like holding hands. Little did he know, I had been studying his hands every time we were together. I watched the way they glided over things. I followed his fingers when he spoke. I paid close attention to such details, because I loved them; they enthralled me. I wouldn't dare tell him that.

Chapter Ten

Petals and Wind

WE MET UP WITH SOME FRIENDS, MINE AND HIS. MY FRIENDS AND his did not mix. They did not get along yet, and they didn't struggle either. They simply kept their distance and dared not to cross the defined invisible barrier that kept them apart. It was so defined that you could almost feel a tingling when they got too close. Almost like a reminder, "Step back! You're not allowed here."

We were a large group, but we were not together. The only strings attaching any of his friends to mine were him and me. We all knew that fact which, in silent moments, became unbearably awkward. I stayed on my side of that invisible barrier with the exception of him. Our friends definitely did not care to mix. I definitely did not either. Until recently, I could not see that he was just like his group of sidekicks. Maybe that's why I couldn't stand them; they had all his faults, all his stains. Only difference was, they were not infectious like him, and he was not ordinary like them.

It was hot. Everyone complained. All of the others seemed to be terrorized by the unbroken fever; yet, I only noticed when it would form an unflattering droplet above my lip. Water became a common interest. No matter how different we all were, we could agree we were thirsty. So we paused from our romping and went in search.

A slight tinge touched my hand, so light I almost thought of it as accident. Then, an undeniable excitement formed its way into my palm. We were behind the crowd, and finally, he decided to hold my hand. I tried my best not to express my feelings. I don't think I did very well on account his smirk and the light "Ha!" he let out after looking at my face. Soon, the heat made the airless space between our palms sweaty, and he let go.

"I'll be right back!" He waved his hands at me while being dragged in a different direction by one of his minions. But he did not come right back. I waited for him. I waited for an unforgiving time limit, and then decided to search him out. Surely, something was wrong. Why else would he have left this long? All of my friends agreed this was an unusual time lapse. I refused to think he had run away without me.

I found him and his friends a fair distance in the background, giggling like monkeys and pointing the way only immature kids can do. I approached him. Again, his floral-like alibi floated off his tongue. This time, I earnestly tried to fight the trance. He noticed my resistance and quickly changed his tune.

"Let's ride the Ferris wheel. Just the four of us!" He was referring to the only other "couple" there. We hesitantly agreed, and the others wandered away.

He slithered his arm around my shoulders and nudged me into him. I stopped trying to fight his virus and gave into his lure. I gently reclined against his chest and breathed in the summer air and his contaminating scent. The breeze was soft, and I rested easy in that fact. I feared if the breeze became wind, it might tear him away from me. This moment was too perfect. The wind couldn't have him. At one point, I even lounged heavier on him to hold him down from drifting away on the air.

I knew at that moment, it was our peak. Just as the Ferris wheel would descend eventually after this night, our relationship would too. Even though I knew it, I was also alert that it would be a slow fade. The wind would only take him a few petals at a time. I knew I could hold on for a while. I intended to. I would admit this guilty truth to myself, but never aloud. I was afraid the wind would hear my voice and sweep him away all at once.

He wasn't right for me, this was easy to see. But I was right for him, and he needed me. Right? He needed *me*. Otherwise, he'd do bad things. Without me constantly nagging and instructing him to not do this, or stop doing that, he'd be a bad person; and it would be my fault. At least, that was my justification for carrying around the ugly empty stem. That was his illusion. He knew I felt responsible for his character. His illusion disease only worked on me.

We left that night with new inside jokes, a smaller group, and a further forgotten boundary. We held hands on the way to the car, even inside on the way home, as the CD eased my worries in the background.

We got to my car, and I got out of his. I knew what he was going to do, but I wasn't going to make it easy on him. We'd been through so much, and not once had he kissed me in fear that I might take offense. Tonight, he knew where I stood. His weed-like roots had finally been made secure.

He got out of the car, something unusual for him to do. Even though I was totally aware of what he was trying to do, I turned and began to walk to my car. I knew that after that night, I would be the one chasing him. So for that one moment, I longed to be hunted.

A nervous hand touched my wrist and twisted me around.

"It's been too long..." he breathed and kissed me.

I would love to report that it was enchanting, but I cannot. At that moment, I wished I could say it was confirmation we were supposed to be together, but it was not. It was as if his hold on me was drained. And if anything, it was a sign to run away immediately. The kiss was clumsy, awkward; I loved it. It didn't matter that it wasn't perfect. The fact was, he kissed me. First kisses were never good anyway, right?

For the remainder of the summer, his abracadabra wand held me tight. Little did I know, the longer I let it, the more his infection infected. I had now fallen for him. Hard. I would do anything for him, I would stick around and work through whatever obstacle was thrown at us. Only problem was, I was the only one. He said he loved me, he swore he did. Yet he continued to leave me un-announced, and lied about the biggest of things to hide his fallen petals.

I knew he didn't love me right. I knew he didn't treat me right. I wanted to leave. I can honestly say I did; but I couldn't. I was too weak, and his tactics were well played. I tried to run. I tried every antidote and every cure. My heart argued with my brain that this would be justified, although my brain knew better. I had every reason to run. But I was so afraid to feel the pain of walking away from the thing I wanted most, like I did with Peter.

Ben nor Peter themselves were what I wanted most. What I wanted more than anything was the security of knowing I was with the right man. I wanted the release of being in God's will while still being in my own. I knew better than that. Yet still, I wanted to not feel tugged in two directions by the callings of Jesus and my own fleshly desires.

Memories of the hurt of leaving Peter chilled and put a pit in my stomach. *Please God, don't make me leave again,* I would repeat, silently bargaining with God. I wouldn't say it out loud, because I knew the answer to this one. I knew I was never supposed to fall for Ben in the first place. I knew I ignored every caution sign up to this point. God didn't lead me to him—I walked here all on my own. But once again, I could feel God leading me away. Every time I tried, Ben would find a new smooth excuse for me to stay, just one more day. Every time. His words were wonderfully poisonous.

It wasn't even Ben's fault for my unhappiness. I wanted him to be something he was never designed to be. I wanted him to be "the one." Not even Ben could make that happen. It wasn't his fault that I had developed feelings for him. It wasn't his fault that he wasn't my Mr. Man of God.

And then, in the back of my mind, I heard God say, "It's not my fault either."

We had history. We had been through so much, and I felt like I couldn't just walk away. I felt some deranged sense of obligation to him. It was almost as if he was the only person in the world who connected with me. He had at some point convinced me that I was the broken one. My "standards were too high," and I'd "never find anyone that can live up to your expectations." I believed him. I felt like he was doing me a favor for sticking around, because I had "commitment issues." And no one else would put up with me. I think that's why I was so afraid to let go of him completely. I prayed and prayed about Ben, who I fiercely wanted to be good. I wanted him to be good, because if he was, he could be my man of God. If he could just start living the way I thought he should, I could mold him into being the one God wanted for me.

Now looking back, I see how I had deliriously muddled everything in my mind. But that's what these relationships will do to you. They blur everything. They force you to twist things you know to be false in order to find your storybook ending. We try to make people fit in our lives, because to us, they look like the right candidate. But God often has other plans. And until you give up trying to figure them out, you're going to be a confused little girl, alone on Christmas, chasing the breeze.

Isaiah 55:9 (MSG) explains why we are to let God handle these important areas of our life, "As the heavens are higher than the earth, so are my ways higher than your ways and my thoughts than your thoughts."

God knows what He's doing. I never found my Mr. Man of God, until the day I stopped looking.

Chapter Eleven

You're Already There

I FINALLY GOT THE CHANCE TO ESCAPE FOR A BRIEF TIME ON A mission trip to Costa Rica. I had to leave his words for a week. We said our sweet farewells, and he promised to "behave" while I was gone. Even then, I didn't trust any of those venom-dripping promises.

While I was gone, I had no way of contacting him. I missed him. He often visited me in times of solitude, but only in my thoughts. I imagined moments when I would return to him, and he'd miss me so much that he'd finally shape up. He'd see he really loved me.

Julia and I decided that while we were away, we weren't going to worry about finding or figuring out our man of God issues. We were simply going to focus on Jesus, if for just this week.

We all gathered into the church building, which was mostly just a slab of concrete with what looked like barn doors and walls. We were staying with an Indian tribe on top of a mountain. This place was remote. Its simplicity was decorated in natural beauty.

There wasn't paint on the walls, but the huge flowering tree limbs that peeped through the open window frame colored the room. The chairs weren't covered in fabric, but the ornate wood design in the long benches attracted attention. It was all beautifully simple. We didn't have a sound system, huge speakers, or even a microphone for that matter. We were all just gathered together to worship. And I imagine God found our simple worship quite beautiful too.

Seth led a song, which in itself was wonderful to watch. We had known Seth for five years. But he was so shy and quiet, it was difficult to actually "get to know" him. Mom tried coaxing him to sing for months, and it was satisfying to watch him finally step out of his comfort zone and lead us in a few songs there on top of the mountain.

It was like watching God work. I could see the progress from day one to now. In that moment, Seth's life was a testimony to me that God is working. It was like confirmation that God isn't just sitting on His hands, waiting for me to be perfect, so that He will do what He promised. In that moment, Seth's example produced a new song of praise in me.

I was just so thankful that God was good, and that He was faithful. And even though I couldn't see it yet, I knew God was marvelously and fiercely working on my behalf. I just began to take all my attention off of me and what my circumstances were. I stepped into this revelation that this life is all about Jesus. I just wanted to be close to the Lover of my soul.

Something happened while I was there focusing on Jesus. I saw what real love looked like, while I was gone. Then, I didn't notice it. It wasn't infectious like the dandelion at home, it wasn't forced and feared like that "dancing-with-fire" kind of love. It was simple. It was light and optional. It was a choice. It wasn't rushed, because it couldn't blow away. I didn't have to scamper to capture it. This was planted love. This was grounded affection. This was right. This was real. And to be honest, it was so distinct, so finite, and so impossibly positioned, that I almost missed it.

I think I found it, because I finally stopped looking. Or maybe I didn't find. Maybe I was found, out there in the open somewhere away from the dandelion field. I was praying about the next step. Where do I go from here? I wasn't expecting the answer to be, "You're already here."

So David, to answer your question of "how long?"—the answer was now. Today. The very moment you say, "God, I'll accept whatever it is YOU have planned for me." The time it takes you to go from knowing God *can* do this for you to knowing that He loves you enough that He *will*—that's how long.

It's kind of like being pregnant. There's a baby in there. You can't see it, you can't hold it, you can't give it a bath or sing it to sleep. But nonetheless, it's still a baby. And every day, the baby is growing, and every second it's getting closer and closer to coming out to see you. Even though you haven't had the baby, doesn't mean it's not there.

This was the same case with my man of God. I couldn't call him my husband. I couldn't change my *Facebook* status to "in a relationship." I couldn't call him every night, and I wasn't receiving flowers for an anniversary. But that didn't change the fact that later down the road, God promised he would be. Once you claim your promise, it starts growing. It starts working. It comes alive, even when you don't see anything happening right then.

Every day, I woke up one day closer. Every day, God was moving one more obstacle out of the way. The wait was over when I asked God to work in my life and let Him fill my void of time. TODAY is the day. Right NOW is the time. So get excited. God doesn't disappoint.

Amazing. Nothing shy of it either. The light was slowly drifting into His pastel-painted chamber for the night. The sun would soon be long gone to wherever it hides at night. But its warmth will linger in the air, until the sun returns with the morning. Mountains danced along the edge of it all. Perfectly in place, clouds hung just above the scene. Pink, then peach, then gone. Sunset.

Everything living sings a melody here in this jungle, but as for now, they're all silenced by the rain. It's the good kind of rain—the wet kind. The kind that falls straight down, because it's too heavy to be tossed by the wind. The kind that gets you instantly drenched when you stand in it. The good kind of rain—the wet kind. It leaves a white misty fog as it parades to the ground. No birds chirp, no bugs hum, nothing breathes, but the sound of the thumping rain. It demands all attention and glaciates everything outside of the shelter I'm in. Plans get cancelled because of this rain. You almost feel a sense of being trapped, at the mercy of the duration of the storm. But then all of a sudden, in just a short breath away, it will be gone; everything will come back to life again. This time, even more alive than before.

The sun shines brighter after this kind of rain, and it's relieved to be the commander of the sky again. The grass turns greener, and the bugs throb louder, in response to the refreshment of the rain. Because the harder it rains, the faster it leaves. It's the good kind of rain—the wet kind.

Today, we all visited a park area and spent time playing with the Costa Rican children. I spoke more Spanish than most of the people with me, so I was given the job of learning everyone's name and giving them a name tag. Julia and I performed a dance for everyone. I didn't have to think about the next move; my body knew what it was doing, as it followed the music's every instruction. Every note was its own command, and my limbs obeyed them. We had practiced in the airport, in the studio, in the bus, and in the house. Julia and I were ready for this dance, for this time, for now. The song was in Spanish; but by the end of it, even those who didn't know a bit of Spanish understood the song. The movements told the story that the words could not.

Regardless of the bruises from the uneven terrain and the dirty hands and feet, I loved everything about it. The way polished ballet toes felt pushing the dirt side to side with every spin of the body. The way clean hands perceived dry grass, as they pressed deeply into the ground to uphold a whole person upside down. The way hot, humid, and gummy air felt passing deeply in through the nose to fuel the next move. It was unlike any dance I'd ever performed. It was such a graceful movement in such a rusty display. The contrast was resplendent.

"In the morning, O Lord, you hear my voice; in the morning I lay my requests before you and wait in expectation" (Psalm 5:3 NIV).

In the morning, the time when all the darkness goes away, and you can feel the light ease in on your face. The time when all the rain has stopped, and everything is better for it. The time when you realize you're out of the storm, and everything is going to be okay. The morning… I wait in expectation.

Don't worry, your morning is coming. Just remember, this is the good kind of rain—the wet kind. The wet kind that passes quickly, even though you feel stuck wherever you are because of the downpour. When it's done, you're instantly elated by the sun. Just remember, without rain, everything dies. You need rain in your life sometimes in order to grow, thrive, and live.

There came a point somewhere up on that mountain, I realized I couldn't do anything to bring my man of God to me any faster. I could not think up a scheme. There were no words that if properly strung together, could coax him to fall in love with me. There was nothing I could do but simply follow God's direction. Every day would be a new note my body would obey. And together, God and I would dance to a language unknown to me.

Together, God and I—the God who moves mountains with a simple word and holds all the stars in place. The God who tells the oceans, *This is as far as you can come.* The God who knows my every thought, my entire future, and every doubt, fear, and worry that I held on to. That God would take care of me. Me, the paltry, unable girl that couldn't even so much as fathom how big God's plan was for me. Me, the girl who had to have an "in between guy" in order to have some finite grip, some backup plan, for her future. Together, the graceful God and the rusty I would dance together. The contrast was resplendent.

The view itself is worth the plane ride—the boat ride, the hike, and the sand-filled shoes. I stopped for a moment to take a picture, but quickly put my camera down. The picture would never do this landscape justice. This was meant to be an experience for the human eye to interpret, not replicated on a piece of paper. It wasn't the colors or the flowers that made this place so beautiful. It was the breeze that whispered lullabies, while you stopped to look over the horizon. It was the sound of the birds zipping through the trees above and below. It was the feeling of being completely and undoubtedly minuscule in this giant tree-wrapped universe. It was the thousand words that the picture would be worth. It was all the things that a camera could never capture.

Costa Rica had not disappointed. Every part of the trip was a wonderful adventure. There was one night, though, that was wilder than the others. There was one night more beautiful than the rest. I couldn't shake it out of my head. I had this dream. But, I had dreams every night. They are filled with attempted impossibilities. Our mind just tries to figure out a way to instantly change things that are completely out of our reach. Dreams are just dreams, right?

This dream felt different though. It was like I was watching myself through someone else's eyes. I wasn't wondering what was happening next. It was like a knowing. In this dream, I just knew.

The dream went like this:

We were sitting next to a tall over-hanging lamp in a big green chair in an otherwise empty off-white room. I was positioned right in the middle of his folded legs. It was like I was watching us from someone else's point of view. I could see us from behind, as if I was standing over the chair directly behind it. Light leaked onto our faces, just enough to show the buried dimples underneath his light-mudded beard. And enough to show the red letters on the pages of the book in his hands. We were reading the Bible; we were reading the Bible together, in a green chair—together. We didn't say a word. We barely even moved. It was almost less of a dream and more of a glimpse.

Who was that man in the chair with me? My outside-of-body point of view knew exactly who it was, before I even saw his face. And, as if the camera pivoted around to the front of the chair, I saw there, plainly and wonderfully, *him*. I knew exactly who "he" was. For just a moment in time, my mind rested easy knowing this was the way things were supposed to be. For the first time in forever, it was right. Yet, as right as it was, it was even more impossible.

"He" was eight years older than me. He was my parent's friend and referred to me as "kid." I had never in my life thought of him in a romantic kind of way. The thought was so impossible, it never even crossed my mind. So, how could I dream such a thought. Surely, it couldn't have been mine.

I woke up and instantly tried to forget. My mind played through a million different scenarios, and in none of them could I figure out how this was going to work. This was impossible. This was ridiculous. This was out of reach. This was Jesus answering my prayer.

As excited as I was for the insight, I had no idea how to ever make the man in my dream fall in love with me. I realized this was something God was going to have to do. And even though I knew the "who," I was still left waiting on the "when.'

Chapter Twelve

Impossible is God's Specialty

SOME THINGS IN LIFE AREN'T MEANT TO BE CAPTURED, UNDERSTOOD, or replicated. Your future relationship with your spouse isn't supposed to be a Cinderella story or a fiction novel. It's not about the cute butterfly feelings or the romantic dates—this is real life. This is to be experienced. I wanted a mapped-out picture of what God wanted me to do. But even if He would've given me one, it wouldn't have done any good. There were things I didn't understand, things that only God could see in me. Things a camera could never capture.

"'Do not be afraid, Daniel. Since the first day that you set your mind to gain understanding and to humble yourself before your God, you words were heard, and I have come in response to them. But the prince of the Persian kingdom resisted me twenty-one days... Now I have come to explain to you what will happen to your people in the future, for the vision concerns a time yet to come.'" (Daniel 10:12–14 NIV).

So, Daniel prays to God for an answer, and for twenty-one

days hears nothing. Finally, an angel comes to Daniel and explains that immediately when he sought out God, God sent an answer. But, some things were in the way of Daniel receiving that answer. This is the explanation of what God means when He says, "Today is the day!"

The day I sat out on my porch and prayed, "God, I give my relationship to You," He heard me and *immediately* sent me my man of God. He didn't come riding in on his white horse to carry me back to the palace that day, because there were some things in the way of him and me. For one, age. I was sixteen years old, and he was twenty-four. That didn't mean it wouldn't happen, it just meant some time had to pass before it could. Another being our personal relationships with God. We had to be happy being alone, before we could be happy with someone else.

The same goes for you and your life. It might not be age in your case, but maybe God has to teach you some things, before you're ready to love another person the right way. Whatever the holdup is, remember this: God is working every day to move obstacles out of the way. That is why it is so crucial for you to give this area of your life totally over to God. Because in most cases, those dilemmas in the way of you and your future spouse are often too big for you to overcome alone.

Good news is nothing is too big for God. Those mountains in the way are nothing but ant hills to God. So even when you can't see your answer coming, just know that it is. The important thing for you to do in the meantime is get as close to God as you can. It makes the waiting easier. God loves you. He is working.

"God is rarely ever early, but He is never late."
—Dillion Burroghs

When I got back to the U.S., Ben called me immediately. It was three o'clock in the morning, and he had waited up for me. I swooned at the fact. But right as his once-hypnotic voice materialized through the phone, I realized I had found the cure to him. He spoke of plans we would make for me returning home, yet he wanted to hear nothing of what happened while I was gone. At that time, I finally saw I was just his mirror. I hung up. Wordless.

I saw what real love looked like while I was away. I met someone—someone truly spectacular. I became aware that I didn't want anything shy of authentic. I wanted a flower to bloom. Not a weed. Weeds grow when they're not planted. They are easy to procure. Real flowers, must be cared for, grown, and worked on.

I can't say why I hung up the phone that day. I wasn't angry or upset; I wasn't miserable or lonely. I was detached. All his puffy petals had long since floated off to reweed someone else. I let go of the exposed stem that day. I wasn't under his imaginary spell anymore. Real love never promised to be easy, real love never promised to be fair. Real love never even promised to be possible. But real love was promised. Real love kept the promises it made.

The odd thing was, he didn't call back. He must have known I had broken his curse, or maybe he just didn't care. It did not matter; because either way, he was a disease. He spread quickly. And for such a disease as indifference, the only cure is impossible. And impossible is God's specialty.

"Julia, I've got to tell you something. You can't tell anyone, and you can't judge me for it." We were giggling down the aisles of Walmart after our first day back from Costa Rica.

She gave me a tilted smile and raised brow. "Ooookay…"

"While we were on the trip, I had this dream…" I almost stopped talking, because I knew once I said the words out loud, it was going to sound even more ridiculous than it did in my head. "I had this dream about my man of God."

Her eyebrows lowered, as her expression became unsuspicious. This is why she was the only person I could tell. Saying things like "I had a dream about my man of God," was normal to her. This was part of our everyday conversation.

"Aaannndd…" She motioned her hands for me to continue.

"Um, well, we were in this chair reading the Bible together. But I saw his face. I know who it is. And this is going to sound crazy, but the man in my dreams was…"

Before I could finish the sentence, my phone rang. Seth had texted me.

> Hey, you. I just wanted to say you were really awesome on the trip. To see you doing things for Jesus and being so passionate about it was inspiring. You're a true baller.

My eyes got as big as my face, and I could feel the blood flooding to my cheeks. I looked up at Julia, who was completely confused by my *I-just-saw-a-ghost* expression.

"What?! What just happened?!"

"It's Seth." I handed her the phone to read the message. "Seth was the man in my dream."

This was it! The very thing I had been praying for was the very definition of "too good to be true." He was everything that everyone told me I would never find. He was everything I wanted, and then some. My mind couldn't wrap around it. It was so hard for me to believe. This man saw me as nothing but my father's daughter, or so I thought. There are a couple verses in Galatians 3:4–5 (GW) that said exactly what I need to hear: "Did you suffer so much for nothing? I doubt it was for nothing! Does God supply you with the Spirit and worked miracles amount you through your own efforts or through believing what you heard?"

I did what God said by giving my relationship over to Him. God promised to turn that pain into blessing, and now He was laying out the puzzle pieces right before my eyes. It was time for my faith to take the next step. I had been begging God to show me some answers, to give me some direction. Now that He finally did, I was terrified of it. I was scared, because I knew it was 100% impossible. I couldn't win Seth over with a hair flip and a flirty pick-up line. I could not figure out how on earth this was going to happen. But that's exactly what God needed—room to work. I couldn't do anything, so God had to do everything.

Sometimes, you get to that point in your life and feel desperate or helpless. But often times, that's when God can do His best work. After all, impossible is His specialty. Just like it says in Galatians, God doesn't work miracles by anything we can do. By faith, just stand and believe God's promise are going to come to pass.

Here I am again, outside on my porch bundled in a huge crimson blanket, picturing the day my future husband would pull in the drive way with a ring in his pocket and a question on his mind. The rain is coming down hard, and it reminds me so much of the rainstorm in Costa Rica. I'm trying to determine the way this thunderstorm makes me feel. I think I like it. I didn't even decide to come out here until I heard it storming. For some reason, I feel so comfortable out here underneath the chaos in the clouds. I want to be a part of the symphony in the sky.

I don't quite understand thunderstorms, though. How does something that gravity can't even hold, so loose and light, make such a monstrous bellow?

Cloud impinging upon cloud. Drum, drum, drum across the entire sky. And even though I know the loud sound is not the response of some tragic collision, I still cannot help but jump when the thunder thumps along with my heartbeat. I can't help but tense up when awakened at night by the familiar summer storm. Maybe that's what is so attractive about this storm. Even though I know it cannot hurt, it cannot reach me. It cannot break me. Something inside me still whispers, *Respect it.*

My dad walked out onto the porch and sat down beside me. "It's nice out here, huh?" He bundled up in the blanket with me. As if he was reading my thoughts, he added, "You'll find the right one, honey." He knew what was on my mind. "Don't stress it too much. Remember what I always say to look for in a man?"

At the same time, we said, "Find a man who is kind, gentle, and selfless."

He said that all the time. When I brought a guy home, he'd ask me if I thought the guy was those three things. I always said, "I wasn't sure yet," or "Maybe." Dad somehow always knew right away. Let's just say, so far, none of them had met the checklist.

"I know. I remember," I said nodding my head.

"You know, if I could handpick a man for you, it would be a man like Seth Smith. He's a good guy. Find a man like him."

I blinked my eyes a few times to see if this was real, or if I was imagining it. Julia was the only person I had told about my dream. I hadn't said a word to either of my parents.

"What makes you say that?" I asked, trying to hide the shock on my face. He did say find a man *like* him, which made me think that Dad thought he was too old for me. Or maybe that's just what I thought, and I was assuming Dad would think that same thing.

"Your mom told me he took good care of you in Costa Rica. I asked him to keep an eye on you and your mom before you guys left."

Did Dad already know?

"Yeah, I think he's great too. Too bad he's eight years older than me." I laughed and shrugged off the idea.

"Eight years is nothing, when you get older. You might just have to wait."

That word. *Wait.* Oh, I hated it. On the one hand, it was incredible to me that my dad just walked out here to confirm what God had already told me. But on the other hand, the thought of waiting for years and years was almost sickening. I was going to have to learn to *wait* on God's timing.

I was excited and disappointed all at the same time. I felt like an upset toddler, and wasn't proud of it. But I didn't know how not to feel impatient. *God, help me with the wait.*

Thunderstorms lead me to believe it's acceptable to feel more than one way about a situation in life sometimes, even when those feelings are completely contrasting. I loved the storm, but the lightening and loud sounds still made me jump. That's how I felt while I was in the waiting process. I was falling more in love with God every day, but there was still a small part of me whispering, "What if it doesn't work?"

But just like the storm, those whispers couldn't hurt me, couldn't reach me, and couldn't break me. That poisonous thought was just like the hot air. It could sound really big. But that's all it could do—sound. It was acceptable to feel both ways. Not because I was fearful, but because I respected the process. I respected the wait, the fight, the storm.

And with storms, come rain. Oh, how we need rain.

Chapter Thirteen

Stuck in Seventeen

March 10th. my birthday. Almost a complete year has passed since the big breakup, and I almost can't believe how much has changed, not only in me, but in my surroundings. I'm sitting here at an impromptu birthday lunch with none other than Seth Smith. When God first told me he was the one I was going to marry, just two short months ago, I couldn't even imagine how to get him to have a conversation with me, other than small talk. Now, he's sitting here beside me—celebrating me.

Considering my parents, his best friend, and mine are the only other people in attendance, surely he's got to think *something* is up. It seems like ever since we got back from Costa Rice, one way or another, we have been together almost every day.

"Happy birthday to you, happy birthday to you..." My mom walked into the kitchen with a birthday cake. It had the most horrific display on the top—the thing I had been so desperately trying to sweep under the rug every chance I got. The biggest mountain between Seth and me, that I could see, sat on top of that cake. Two giant candles shaped into the numbers 1 and 7. And oh, how they glared at me. I tried my best to hide my embarrassment from spilling out onto my face.

I was hoping that maybe if it never got brought up how old I was, then maybe he wouldn't notice. But as the song went on, he sang along to the tune. He looked those candles in the eye and didn't flinch. I blew them out immediately as the song ended, and I tried my hardest to divert attention to *anything* else.

"Thanks, guys. Hey, is anyone else going to the Outcry concert next month?" I smiled and turned away from cake that was mocking my hope.

"Oh, yeah, I forgot that was coming up. We should all go!" Julia chimed in, totally picking up on my uncomfortable tone. "We can get tickets cheaper if we get a group rate."

"Yeah, I want to go." Seth nodded and looked at my mom. "You want to order tickets for everyone?"

At this point, I had told Mom about my hidden suspicion that I was going to spend the rest of my life with that gorgeous, long-haired, green-eyed, towering man. I didn't exactly describe him as such to her. Really, I didn't even have those thoughts about him until that dream. Now, every time he walked in a room, it was hard to breathe. His hair was so curly that it always looked perfect, like he had just come in from a walk on the beach in sea salt air. His teeth were unbelievably straight to never have had braces. Which made that dimpled smile of his swoon worthy. And my goodness, did he get taller since Costa Rica, or has he always been that broad and statuesque? He was so calm and caring all the time. He made whoever he spoke to feel like the most important person in the room. He was so good, so pure, and so genuine.

He was just… everything I never even knew I wanted.

"Yeah, I'll do it right now from my phone, and y'all can just give me cash." Mom smirked at me a tad too obviously for comfort, and then looked down at her phone. *Great! Now we have plans together next month too,* I thought to myself, trying to keep my excitement off my face and only in my head. As impossible as all this seemed, it was playing out incredibly effortlessly.

"Hey, how about tonight we all go catch a movie after we leave here." Mom had a way of making it a little easier too. Everyone nodded in agreement. Just like that, the whole day would be spent with Seth. As wonderful as that was, I hated that the focus of the day was around how old I was. I caught myself silently asking, *God, why am I stuck in seventeen?*

It seemed like God's promise to me was being guarded and blocked by a factor I could not change—my age. I hated that I was so much younger than him. I remember a few other girls trying to catch his attention who were two or three years older than me. He shrugged them off, which in one case made me glad. But I was also afraid he paid them no mind, because they were so much younger. And I was even younger than them. I felt like God had messed up a little detail in His plan. I had a sense of hopelessness, because I knew what God said. And I knew He had promised to work it all out, but I couldn't imagine how.

As soon as I finally stopped trying to hide this thought from God and brought my dilemma to Him, He so graciously gave me the answers I needed to rest.

Ecclesiastes 11:9 (MSG) states, "You who are young, be happy while you are young, and let your heart give you joy in the days of your youth ..."

There are multiple verses in the Bible that talk about enjoying your youth. When I found myself hating it, I realized something was twisted up in my thought pattern.

That night, I sat down and wrote myself a letter. It went like this:

> *Today I am 17. Today I am teenager. Today, I laughed with my friends. Today, I realized I don't get today back. Today, I decided to be happy where I am on the way to where I am going. You don't get to be this young ever again, enjoy it. God knew what He was doing when He decided when to bring me to life. Who am I to doubt what God set into motion many years ago?*

God knew how old I was when He spoke the dream of marrying Seth into my heart. He knew that Seth was eight years older than me. Most of all, He knew how to work that to my good. At the time though, I couldn't see it.

A lot of times, the same area in our life that we despise is the same area God wants to use. But first, there is a "handing over" that needs to take place. That night, I decided that my age would be God's responsibility. I decided to give that concern to Him. I was reminded of the verse in Isaiah 55:9 (ESV) "For as the heavens are higher than the earth, so are my ways higher than your ways and my thought than your thoughts."

And even though I didn't understand, I knew God did. Just because a circumstance doesn't make sense to you, doesn't mean that God messed up. His ways are so much higher, His thoughts so much greater than ours.

Even when it didn't make sense to me, I said, "God, you made me for such a time as this. Have Your way."

Looking back now, I realize that my testimony wouldn't be half as extraordinary if it wasn't for the age difference. I see now that the age gap made me depend on God to materialize the relationship and not rely on my own abilities. I see now that God's timing could not have been any more perfect. I am thankful it made me put it all in God's hands; and that is where every circumstance is safest.

Your situation is most likely different than mine. But we all have our own mountains that seem so big in our life. We have no idea how to get around them. Rest in the fact that God sees your mountains. They are but ant hills to Him. He is not only big enough to overcome them, but He is faithful enough to use the very same problem that plagued you as an ingredient for your good. He is a good, good Father.

"I love the salsa here. It's not too spicy," I said as the four of us sat down at our local Mexican restaurant. No one said it out loud, but I'm pretty sure this counted as a double date. It was just Seth and I, and our best friends. Just the four of us. Finally. Up until this point, we were always in big groups. And while I loved that, this was entirely more exciting.

"I like it spicy," Trevor, Seth's friend, responded to me from across the table. He was sitting next to Julia, which by default, left Seth to sit with me. I took my coat off and placed it behind my back. Seth left his on. I could tell he seemed a little uncomfortable. He pulled out his phone and started texting someone. It took all the self-control in my body to not look at the screen when it lit up beside me to see who he was talking to.

Don't do it, Jo. You're going to look desperate. I just smiled and kept staring at the chips in front of me.

"I don't know why I'm even looking at the menu, I always get the same thing." Julia laughed and put her menu to the side. She was a picky eater, and the taco salad was her go-to. I looked at the menu, too excited about the night to find anything remotely appetizing. I wasn't the least bit hungry. My stomach was too full of butterflies.

Buzz, Buzz. His phone vibrated on the table again. He picked up to type out a reply, and then looked up to me and said, "Your mom is hilarious, look at the picture she just sent." He flashed his screen in my direction. The photo was of a cute little kid rolling his eyes with what looked like chocolate ice cream all over his mouth.

I let out a little giggle and wondered why she sent that. Part of me was relieved it was just my mother he was texting, and not some other potential candidate for him to date. The other part of me couldn't wait to get home to read what their messages where about.

After we finished our food, we got up to pay. As we walked toward the cash register, Julia placed her hand on my arm to hold me back a couple steps behind the boys, and she whispered, "If they offer to pay, it classifies it as a date."

We both giggled and waited to see how they spilt the check.

"I'm going to buy everyone's," Seth told the man at the register, as he pointed to the three of us standing behind him.

"Oh, you don't have to do that." We all said in unison. Trevor probably wanted to pay for Julia's. Julia wanted Trevor to offer to pay for hers, and I couldn't get a clear reading on the situation if he paid for everyone's.

Well played, I thought to myself.

We had a great night. We laughed. We talked. We saw a movie that I couldn't tell you a single detail about, because Seth and I talked through the entire show. It was wonderful. Being with him was so easy. There was no awkward pauses, no unsettling obligation to hold hands or say all the right things. We all knew each other and weren't worried about impressions. We had been friends so long, it just came naturally.

We said our goodbyes, and Julia and I rode to my house together. As soon as I walked in the door, I asked Mom for her phone so I could see their conversation from earlier in the night. She reluctantly handed it over. By her expression, I could tell I wasn't about to like what I saw.

> *Hey, I hope you're cool with us hanging out with your daughter tonight. I didn't want you to think I was trying to date her or anything. We're just hanging out as friends.*

As my heart fell hard from cloud nine to the bottom of my stomach, I showed Julia the message. I then didn't find the picture of the little boy rolling his eyes too funny anymore. He was telling my mom it wasn't a date. He was clarifying that he just wanted to be friends. He proved that he was most definitely uncomfortable with the age gap.

And I silently asked God, *How are you going to work around this one, God?*

That night, I had no reason to keep hoping, and yet I still believed what God had spoken into my heart. Romans 4:18–21(NIV) tells a story of a great man in the Bible who believed, even when all the odds were against him:

"Against all hope, Abraham in hope believed and so became the father of many nations, just as it had been said to him, 'So shall your offspring be.' Without weakening in his faith, he faced the fact that his body was as good as dead—since he was about a hundred years old—and that Sarah's womb was also dead. Yet he did not waver through unbelief regarding the promise of God, but was strengthened in his faith and gave glory to God, being fully persuaded that God had the power to do what he had promised."

I love the beginning of this passage that says, "Against all hope... Abraham believed." Even when all the odds were stacked against him, he still trusted that God was stronger than the opposition. I want to encourage you today to retain that kind of faith in God. When you know what He has promised you, just rest in the fact that no power can stop what God has planned.

The passage also says, "...he faced the fact that his body was as good as dead...." Abraham didn't try to deny the realities of his life. He faced them. He looked the opposition in the eye. He stared down his circumstance and said, "I believe God in spite of you." God honors that kind of bravery in the face of trials. God loves that kind of faith.

I was having a hard time wrapping my mind around the fact that the night we had was so wonderful, it seemed like total confirmation that God was right and this man was perfect for me. And yet, he told my mom he didn't feel that way about me. How could that be? When all hope should have been dashed, I decided that I didn't need to understand. I didn't need to understand, because I knew God understood. I knew He could see me. I knew He was aware of my situation. I knew He had placed this desire in my heart in the first place, and He would be faithful to cash in on His promise.

No matter what a situation might look like, stand—knowing God is not caught off guard. This was all written into your story from the beginning.

Exchange service was in just a few hours. I could barely contain my excitement. Exchange was the services for young adults that Seth had started up in our church. I found the fact that he was interested in putting together a special service for a younger generation especially attractive. Not in the physical kind of way, but I was attracted to his heart for people. I was drawn more and more to him with every conversation we had about our heart for ministry work. Every word out of his mouth was either something I had prayed for or about. He didn't know it, but he was giving me increasing confirmation that I hadn't misinterpreted that dream in Costa Rica.

"What are you going to wear to Exchange?" Julia asked while rummaging through her closet, looking for the perfect outfit. She held up a long flowing shirt and smiled.

"I don't know yet, I have a couple different outfits in mind." If I already had an outfit planned, that meant it was a special occasion. We giggled about how excited we were just to go to a church service.

"I think I like the pink shirt with the light denim jeans." She pointed to the third picture I showed her on my phone. "Seth said 'casual' is his favorite style," which for me was difficult, because I always looked for any reason to put on anything with glitter and a pair of heels.

"Yeah, you're right. Pink one it is." I nodded in agreement

and pulled the outfit out of my bag. I had stayed the night at Julia's house and had packed all three outfit options. It was a big bag.

We listened to our favorite worship music and danced along while we got ready to go. On we went, to church on a Saturday night. We pulled in about fifteen minutes early to see if Seth needed any help setting anything up. I wanted to be as involved a possible, not only to spend more time with him, but also just to be a part of serving in the church.

I walked in expecting to be the only one early, but I wasn't. There, right before my eyes, was my fear I hadn't said out loud. Another *her.* You remember, like the *her* that was with Peter in the hall that day; the *her* who didn't matter who she actually was. All that mattered was she was there, also gunning for my man. I could see them talking over in the corner, as Seth was untangling some microphone cords. She wore almost the exact same top as me, except hers looked better. *Great...* I thought to myself.

I looked over to Julia in panic. Her eyes were wide, looking at me with the "uh-oh" expression on her face. This girl hadn't actually done anything. But I knew before Seth and I went to Costa Rica, they had texted back and forth some. The worst part of it all was she was older than me. I knew she would have the upper hand because of that.

What do I do? Come on, Jo, think fast.

Before I had a plan completely strung together, I found my feet moving towards them. "Hey guys," I squeezed out between a shaky smile. "Can I help you set up anything?" I was looking only at Seth.

"I'm just sitting here waiting for him to tell me what I need to do," she responded to my question.

"Jo, you can help me with these cords. Apparently there are

three in here." It was just a jumbled up ball of black. I smiled, because I knew it might take some time, and we would be doing it together.

"What do you want me to do?" she asked.

"Oh, um, you can go get the mic and music stands and bring them out here if you'd like." I could tell that was not what she was hoping to hear, but she got up and went to the back of the church to get the extra stands.

"How did this happen?" I laughed holding up the knots.

"I'm not sure. I've been meaning to untangle them for a while now. I just haven't done it." He laughed a little too, at the excessiveness of the tangles. Right about that time, Julia walked in the room carrying some soda cases alongside Trevor. They were laughing and talking about an inside joke between the two of them.

"Looks like they're getting along well." Seth nudged my arm a little and nodded for me to look over at them.

"Yeah, they've been texting every day." So had Seth and I—it just wasn't about anything romantic or even interesting, for that matter. I would just find an excuse to text him about anything. Some days he would do the same to me. We could tell we wanted to talk to each other, but we just weren't quite sure how honest we could be. I couldn't help but wonder if maybe God told him the same thing in Costa Rica. If in fact He did, Seth had not mentioned it. And I was far too afraid to ask.

"Ohhh, you know what that means..." He smiled and raised his eyebrows up and down. I wanted to point out that we had been texting every day as well, but I thought that would lead to some unbearably awkward silence. So I refrained.

Just as I was about to respond, *she* walked back in the room.

Don't get me wrong, she was a nice girl. She went to church with us, and we were all friends. I just had a hard time not viewing her as competition. She was beautiful, talented, and like I mentioned earlier, she was older than me. I felt so unsatisfactory next to her.

It was almost time for the service to start, and people were beginning to come into the sanctuary.

"Let's get this party started," Seth said, looking up from the still-mangled cords and grinning. His dimples danced on his face, and I had to focus not to stare at him for too long.

"But what about the cords?" I said, holding up the mess of them in my hands.

"I don't need them tonight," he whispered with a half grin on his face. He didn't even need that done for tonight, but he had me sit there with him and work on it while sending the other helpers on necessary errands. I thought I was going to squeal with excitement. That gesture seemed to be undeniably obvious. He wanted to spend some time with just me. Right?

And yet, after the night was over, I went to sleep tossing and turning with *her* invading my thoughts. Jealousy. Goodness, it was miserable.

Jealousy, inadequacy, and competition were some of the most draining emotions I began feeling that night. I felt like I had to protect what was mine, even though it wasn't mine yet. I knew what God promised me, and I still thought another girl could mess up God's perfect plan.

A verse I hung onto in this time was Song of Solomon 2:2 (NIV). It showed me how my man of God would and should view me:

"Like a lily among thorns is my darling among the young women." God had to keep reminding me that I was a lily. I would stand out; I would be different, not because I was better than anyone else, but because I was right for him and he for me. Just as Peter was not a bad guy, he just wasn't the right guy. Therefore, the other girl would be wrong for Seth.

We, as Christians, need to be careful when dealing with other people in relationships. We need to not cast blame or villainize the people we feel threatened by. I couldn't blame her for being attracted to Seth. He was wonderful, handsome, kind, and single. She had done nothing to me personally, nor was she trying to. She saw a good Christian man and was interested in him. I had to learn to fight the urge to make her the bad guy in my story. I had to realize that the urge to shift blame on her was a problem in me. I had lost confidence in my God, and the confidence in myself was challenged. I couldn't compete with her, but I was never supposed to.

We are called to love our neighbors, even the ones who seem to challenge the desires of our hearts. When we love them like God loves us, it gives God free reign to work on our behalf and theirs. Don't forget, God loves them too.

When I felt the need to compare myself, or the need to compete with *her* or anyone else for that matter, God calmed my fears with the reminder that if Seth was indeed the right man for me, then I would be a lily to him, and all others just thorns. I would also remember words that my mom instilled in me for years and years before this: "If someone else can take him from me, then he was never really mine." I believed God was drawing Seth and I together. So, because of that belief I had to stand in faith, knowing that no one else could take him away from me.

Just because I had this revelation didn't mean all my negative emotions just disappeared. It didn't make it easier when I would see her flirting with him. It didn't stop the pangs of hurt I felt when I saw them sit together. But it did give me hope. It gave me rest. And it gave the peace that I was patiently following throughout this entire journey.

No matter what a situation may appear to be now, remember, you are a lily. You are set apart. You are written into the story, and no man or woman can change God's plan. Romans 8:31 (ESV) states, "...If God is for us, who can be against us?"

You have the Miracle Maker orchestrating His plans for you. There is no person on earth that can top His power and authority. Rest in that.

Chapter Fourteen

Where Else Are You Going to Go?

WAVES SMASHING AGAINST ROCKS. SWISH, SMASH. ALL I COULD HEAR was the sound of the monster water storming into the cliffs and reluctantly being yanked back by the pull of the tide. I could see Seth at the end of the long beach with his back turned to me. He seemed fully undisturbed by the deafening roar of the waves. The distance between us was covered more with protruding rocks than sand.

I looked down at my aching feet and saw the pink water rushing over them, because it was mixed with blood. I had no shoes to walk across the jagged ocean floor. To my right were huge cliffs, so high I couldn't see the top. To my left, an angry tossing ocean. The beach behind me was fully submerged by the water. I knew moving forward would hurt my feet, and I knew the pounding waves would crash me to the ground. More intensely, I knew that if I stayed still, the tide would come closer to the rocks and soon swallow up the ground all together. Forward was my only option.

Seth was only about the size of my hand due to distance between us. He looked so far away, and it seemed like I would never be able to close the gap. I felt myself began to panic. I began to feel trapped in open air. I tried calling his name and waving my arms to get his attention, but he couldn't hear me. He didn't turn around.

Time was moving against me, and so was the nature of the ocean. What had I done to make it so angry with me? The sun that originally shined so bright I had to squint, was now turning dark and consumed by a blanket of clouds. "Move, Jordan," I yelled at myself, yet still, my feet ignored me.

"Why are you standing here?" I heard a low voice behind me, as if it was rising out of the water itself. As soon as the question entered the air, the ocean quieted and the tide swept back. Not out of sight, but away from my feet. I looked down at them without the cover of water and saw the gashes and cuts covering my toes. My eyes began to well with tears as I turned to face the voice. It was a man I had never seen, and yet I knew him.

"Why don't you move forward? Seth is over there. Don't you want to be on the safe side with him?" He moved toward me, balancing from one rock to another without looking down, as if he had walked this beach every day his whole life.

"Yes, but my feet," I pointed down to them, but didn't want to look at them again, "They hurt so bad, and the waves will knock me into the rocks." I motioned to where the waves were hammering just thirty seconds before.

"What waves?" He looked out on the calm sea and let out just a slight laugh.

"They were just here. They were crashing on the cliffs." I turned to look over at the mountains of rocks beside me. They weren't there. They were no higher than my head. It was a small ledge. I looked back at the man in shock. "I swear, they were right there."

"Well, it seems like the odds are no longer against you. You can go to him now." His words formed out of his smile, like he was in on some hidden camera show I didn't know about. I turned back around to look at Seth. His back was still turned to me. I wondered if he even knew I was out here. Did he even see the surrounding storm just moments ago?

"But what if the waters come back and cliffs get high again? What if I drown? What if I fall? What if I don't make it?" I felt the tears coming back to my eyes.

Then the man bent down and took the shoes off his feet. "Here, you can wear my shoes. I'll help you across the beach." He began tying them on my feet.

"But, what about your feet? They'll get cut up too." I didn't understand why he would do that for me.

"Don't worry about me, I know every rock and stone on this beach. I don't make wrong steps. I'll keep you from falling." How would he know every single rock? How could he say I wouldn't fall? I still didn't move. I was still so afraid. "Besides," he said while grabbing my hand into his, "Where else are you going to go?" We began to move forward.

I woke up in the safety of my room in the comfort of my bed with sweat clinging to my back. I could feel the heaviness of my breath. It was only just a dream, but it was so real.

I looked at the clock on my phone that read *5:03 a.m.* I immediately realized this was no ordinary dream. God was telling me something. I reached over to my painted-chipped nightstand and grabbed my Bible. I flipped it open, and the verse already underlined on the page was Psalm 121:3–8 (NIV): "He will not let your foot slip—he who watches over you will not slumber; indeed, he who watches over Israel will neither slumber nor sleep. The Lord watches over you—the Lord is your shade at your right hand; the sun will not harm you by day, nor the moon by night. The Lord will keep you from all harm—he will watch over your life; the Lord will watch over your coming and going both now and forevermore."

"Okay, God," I prayed out loud. "How do I move forward? What do you want me to do?"

God was the man in my dream. He was urging me to move forward. But I was so beyond afraid. I was afraid of the "what-ifs." I was afraid I wouldn't make it. I was afraid of the chaos around me. I was afraid of the pain that might come with pushing ahead. I was so afraid.

When God walked into the scene though, the waters relaxed, and the mountains sunk low. All God had to do was show up, and the wild world around me hushed low. He gave me His shoes. He handed over protection for my feet. What I loved about the dream was when He told me that He didn't need them. He knew the way. God knew exactly which steps to take to make this journey to Seth the least painful.

He knew the way, because He had already been there. The Bible says in Isaiah 45:2 (MSG), "I will go ahead of you, clearing and paving the road..."

The Bible also refers to God many times as the Good Shepherd. A shepherd leads and protects his sheep. That's what God wanted to do for me. He wanted to guide me, to take my hand and lead me on the best possible path to the man He had prepared for me.

Even though He had given me His shoes, taken me by the hand, pushed the waves back into the sea, and lowered the mountains in my way, I was still hesitant to do my part and just move. That's all He was asking me to do. Just follow where He was leading. And still, I stood still.

That last question in my dream rang in my ears time and time again: *Where else are you going to go?* I couldn't walk to my left. I couldn't walk to my right. I couldn't turn around, and I couldn't stand still. He was right. Trusting God's lead was my only viable option. And for that, I had never been more grateful. I saw this lack of options as complete and total grace.

God was ensuring I didn't go the wrong way. He was showing me that His option was the only option with a future. He was directing me onward in the most merciful way. With God Himself at my side, I couldn't mess this up. All I had to do was walk. Before, I was so afraid of making the wrong choices. I was constantly praying that God wouldn't let me mess this up. I was practically begging God to keep me on the right track. This dream was showing me that He heard my prayers and was so lovingly answering them.

As all the revelation of my dream swept in, another wave of thought came with it. There were still rocks in the path, and Seth never turned around. This dream wasn't telling me this was going to be easy. If anything, it was telling me to not be afraid when it gets hard. I also had a sinking feeling in my gut that it meant Seth didn't even know I was trying to get to him. He didn't hear what I heard up on that mountain in Costa Rica.

And what God told me to do next was going to take some guidance.

"Hey honey." Mom lightly knocked on my bedroom door, as she walked in. "I want to talk to you for a minute." Those words always seemed to give me that mild panic feeling in the bottom of my stomach. *Uh-oh,* I thought.

"Okay." I closed my laptop on my lap and looked up at her with curious eyes. My heart was already beating a little faster.

"I've been praying about you and Seth, and I think you should tell him that your dad and I are cool with you two being together." She sat down on the end of my bed. My heart now beat much faster.

Without hesitation or even thinking the words, "No way," rolled out my mouth.

"Why not?"

"Telling Seth that you guys are 'cool with it' means I have to be the one to admit that there is something to be cool about. He hasn't given me any indication that he knows I'm even female. I'm not telling him that."

"Well, you do what you want. I'm just saying, I think he's afraid of what we think. That's why he texted me the night you all went out. He's afraid we will be mad."

She had a point. Seth thought the absolute world of my parents. He and my dad were forming an especially close "bro-mance." He probably was afraid of what they would think, but there was no way I could say anything about it to him.

"I'm afraid if I say it out loud to him then he will completely shut down the whole idea. And then everything will be so awkward between us. At least this way, I have a little hope." It had only been four months since Costa Rica. And while our relationship was definitely closer than it had ever been previously, we still weren't at the "admitting our feelings" stage.

"Jordan, a man doesn't call you on your way home to tell you to flip to a radio station playing *Hey, Pretty Girl* if he doesn't like you." She smiled really big when making that statement. That had happened last night.

I was on my way home from worship practice, and he called me to tell me to flip the station to 94.9. It was a country station, which I don't ever listen to; so I thought it was an odd request. Before I found the station, he said, "This song reminds me of you," and hung up the phone. Julia was in the car with me, and when we began to listen to the words of the song, we both began squealing like we had won the lottery. The song talked about being in love, getting married, starting a family. Oh, yeah, that meant something.

While Mom had a point there, he still hadn't actually *said* the words out loud. What if I was just reading into it all?

"I'll tell him if you want," Mom said with a mischievous smile. She was always matchmaking. I won't lie; she's pretty good at it. She had already set up Sterling with the perfect match, and they ended up getting married. She did know how to call them, but I can guarantee, even she didn't see Seth coming. He was the biggest plot twist I had ever experienced.

"NO!" I learned forward and grabbed her arm. "Do NOT tell him anything. We don't need another 'oops, I left my daughter moment.'"

A few days ago she had literally left me at church and called Seth to tell him he had to give me a ride home because she "forgot me." It would have been nice to be filled in on the plan ahead of time. I'm certain he didn't buy it for one second, but he graciously played along. The last thing I needed was my mom professing my love for him.

"Maybe God has already told him. That way, I don't have to. Besides, isn't it typically the guys job to chase the girl?" I was justifying my cowardice.

"Honey, nothing about this is typical." And with that, she went back downstairs and left me with a lot to chew on.

She was right. This whole idea from day one was utterly impossible. Four months in though, so much impossible had almost unnoticeably shifted to possible.

"God, I *really* don't want to have to do that," I prayed. As much as I wanted to ignore what God's answer to me was, I couldn't. It was so clear.

God said, *Baby girl, you need to move forward.*

All at once, the dream rushed back into my mind. I knew what I had to do.

Okay, God. You're going to have to lead me though, I silently agreed. I could hear my heartbeat in my ears.

Sometimes, following God's direction feels like stumbling around in a dark room. You know where you're trying to get, but you have no visual on how to do it. God will often give us the "what" before He gives us the "how." This is same thing God did to Abraham in Genesis 15. When Abraham was given the promise of many children, God told him to look up at the stars. As many stars as Abraham could see, God said that would be how vast and numerous his descendants would be. Abraham found this hard to believe because he and his wife were very old. God gave Abraham the promise, but He didn't instruct him on how to receive it.

Later, in Genesis 16, Abraham tries to figure out the "how" on his own. He and his wife cook up a plan to make a family on their own. Sarai, Abraham's wife, tells Abraham to sleep with her servant Hagar. Hagar and Abraham did indeed succeed in conceiving a child. But it wasn't the way God had planned, which in turn, produced a child named Ishmael. Verse 12 calls Ishmael a "wild donkey of a man."

I didn't want to take matters into my own hands and develop an "Ishmael" in my life.

If you continue reading the story of Abraham, Sarai does eventually get pregnant, even in her old age. Together, they have a son named Isaac. Isaac was the intended promise. He was dedicated to the Lord. I only wanted "Isaacs" in my life. I wanted to be sure that I was getting God's best.

Even though Abraham made some mistakes, God still came through on His promise. But I wanted to do this without all the mistakes. I wanted the least painful path. I wanted God's way or no way. I just felt helpless, because I didn't know what His way was.

I thought back to my dream on the beach. Each stone was its own path. Some stones were slick, some were steady. Some gave way if stepped on, while others held. But just by looking at them, there was no way to tell. That's why I needed God to tell me which stone to take, even if that meant He only told me one stone at a time.

Talking to Seth about my parents' views on our relationship seemed to be the next stepping stone. But to my mind, that wasn't the logical decision. I went back and forth about every possible scenario I could muster up on how this would go. Still, I knew that God had a way that I could never envision. He always does.

When it seems like all resources and options have been exhausted, God always has a way of pulling out the exact blessing you had no idea you needed. He has possibilities around every corner that you could never guess, no matter how long you tried. He simply knows more than we do. He has a bird's eye view of our lives, while we see everything through a keyhole.

God knows exactly which stones will hold you up in the walk across the beach. He knows the "how" from the "what." One of the reasons we don't get it all at one time is because He wants us to trust Him.

Another reason—it sincerely just wouldn't make sense. If you tried to tell a young child how to do division before ever teaching them subtraction, it would never work. The whole concept of division would not make sense without the basis of multiplication, addition, and subtraction.

Frequently, we ask God for information we would not understand, even if He gave it to us. Because of this, we just trust God and learn the addition and subtraction fully first. When it seems like you have been in a particular season of your life for too long, or longer than you expected, just know that God is trying to instill in you the basics you need to know for your next season. He won't send you into the season unprepared. Instead of trying to fight where you are, like Abraham and Hagar, find out what God is trying to show and teach you while you're here.

Chapter Fifteen

You're in Good Hands

I saw Seth's name on pop up on my cellphone.

> Hey :) Would you do me the biggest favor in the world?

He didn't know it, but I would have followed that man out of a moving airplane if he asked me to.

> Of course! What ya need?

I put my phone in my front pocket, as Julia and I got in my car to leave school. I was heading straight to worship practice. I had been excited for it all day, because Seth and I were going to work on a song together. We were already getting there early to put the music books together.

> If you bring me some coffee, I'd love you forever.

I am almost certain my heart jumped out of my chest and landed on my steering wheel. Julia laughed at my wide-open mouth, as I handed her the phone to read his message.

Her expression then perfectly mirrored mine. "Did he just say the 'L' word?!" She snickered in a high-pitched tone.

I had heard him say this before to random people. It was just an expression he used, but I was going to read into it as deeply as humanly possible.

"What are you going to say back?" Her fingers were ready to type out my response for me.

"I don't know." I could have easily said some generic response like, "Sure." But we both knew that wasn't going to happen. I was going to take *full* advantage of the use of the "L" word in our conversation. "Type back, 'I don't know, forever is a long time.'" I hid my mouth in my hands, after I said it out loud. It was so risky. This felt like actual flirting—something we hadn't quite gotten to yet.

All of Julia's face was a semblance of awe. "You really want me to type that?" She was already writing the words. Before I could even reaffirm my decision, she sent it. We both squealed in anticipation of his response.

The past few months had been a prime opportunity for us to get to know each other. And the "just being friends" twist hadn't been all disappointing. I was able to see the real person as opposed to all the fluff that is put into flirting. I didn't have to try to find the authentic Seth through the muddled clouds of unrealistic expressions of love. To make a long story short, we were not what I referred to as "cup-caking."

Cup-caking is that feeling a brand new relationship gives you. It's where the two people are so "in love" that it annoys everyone else in the room. We weren't trying to win the other person over or be someone other than ourselves. We got to know each other without the pull of physical contact that so dangerously obscures judgement. We were real with each other, and that had been nice.

The time in between sending my response and waiting for his was unbearable. I had my lips pushed together, and my stomach was pulling into my ribs so tight it hurt. I felt like I wanted to pull the car over and get into the fetal position. I was so nervous.

I heard the phone vibrate in Julia's hands. "Ahh! What did he say?!" She read it and didn't even answer my question. She just smiled. "WHAT DOES IT SAY?!" This time the question was desperate.

I pulled up to a red light, and she handed me the phone.

I know. I can handle it.

The irony in that message was profound. I knew he was going to love me forever, because God had told me. That text made me wonder if maybe God had told him too. That was, after all, the million dollar question. Did he know we were supposed to be together?

Needless to say, I got him the biggest cup of coffee I could find, and I couldn't hardly wait to bring to him. I walked into the church doors, coffee in hand and butterflies in stomach. There he was, sitting on the couch, fiddling with a song I didn't know on his guitar. He didn't stop lightly strumming the strings when I walked in.

"Hey."

He nodded up at me. Goodness, he was perfect. Butterflies practically lifted me up and carried me across the room.

I handed him his coffee that was a binding agreement he had to marry me (at least in my head). Best four dollars I ever spent.

"Thanks so much for bringing this. I haven't had any all day."

"My pleasure. I brought you something else too." I pulled a

five pound bag of Sour Patch Kids out of my purse. They were his favorite. I pretended like they were mine too.

"Whoa! Where did you find this? I've never seen a bag this big before!" I knew candy was his weakness, and so I went searching for the largest bag of weakness I could find.

"I thought we could keep it here in the bottom drawer of the desk, and it can be our secret stash." I giggled.

"Yeah! You're awesome."

Those words were more melodious than the tune he was playing on the guitar. I felt myself blushing. I just knew if I tried to reply to him in that moment, my words would come out clumsy and wrong. So, I just smiled at him and tried my best to keep the red cheeks to a minimum. He smiled back at me, and for the first time we had this moment.

In this connective moment, we both knew what we wanted to say, and we both understood why we weren't saying it. Neither of us looked away too quickly.

"Hey, you guys, I wa…" Mom walked into the room. "Uh…" She could sense we were having a moment, too, because as soon as it was disturbed, the room became terribly uncomfortable. It was comical. "I was just going to say, we are going to start practice soon."

"Okay, we're coming right now," Seth said, as he got up off the couch, pulling his guitar strap over his arm and head. "Jo, will you grab those music books beside you?"

I looked down and realized we were so busy talking, we didn't actually finish putting all the papers together.

"Um, yeah." I looked at him with a slight smile on my face to point out that they weren't finished. He grabbed the remaining papers off the table in front of us that were supposed to be in the book sleeves and carried them into the sanctuary with his head tucked low, so my mom wouldn't see the silly dimpled grin he was hiding.

In that moment, it was like we had our own inside conversation. Just in our heads. But as I walked into the sanctuary where all the other musicians were setting up their instruments, it was as if all the connection between us had been drained. He wouldn't even look at me. He put the papers down on my keyboard stand and wouldn't match my eye contact. He didn't want anyone to notice anything between us.

Ugh! I thought to myself. *God, are you going to tell him to get on board anytime soon?* It had been four months of this back and forth. *Come on, God. When will we finally get together?* As if I needed to remind God about His plan He had let me in on.

Then I heard God speak to my heart in a gentle loving whisper, *When I say so.*

We've established that God will often provide the "what" without the "how." There was yet another lesson I had to learn about walking out God's will. Sometimes, He will also give the "what," all while leaving out the "when," which for me was even harder to cope with than the "how." I didn't like not knowing when. It made me feel like I was losing, wandering, or maybe even flailing.

When what God promised me wasn't coming to pass on my time table, it made me feel immensely frustrated. Frustrated at Seth, at myself, and worst of all, I felt frustrated with God. I felt like He forgot. I felt forgotten. Looking back, I understand that this time before the "when" was so necessary. I see now how I needed that in between time. That time allowed for me to receive strength, the kind of strength that comes only from trusting God.

Without the "how" or the "when," we are required to stay a step behind God. This order is important. Since God is the Good Shepherd, that means He is leading the way. Because out of the two of us, He is the only one who knows where we are going. If I try to get ahead of God, I will be wandering around lost, walking aimlessly, and at best, guessing for direction.

Those times when I felt frustrated, it was not because God was refusing to come through for me. I was frustrated because I was jumping ahead of the Shepherd. Proverbs 3:5–6 (MSG) states, "Trust God from the bottom of your heart; don't try to figure out everything on your own. Listen for God's voice in everything you do, everywhere you go; he's the one who will keep you on track."

When you try to make things happen in the timeline that you deem acceptable, it pulls you out of the correct lineup, just like Abraham did with Hagar. If you are feeling frustrated with the timing of your promise, it's because you've stopped trusting that God's way is better than yours—even if that's not a conscious thought.

Feelings of chaos, strife, stress, worry, and impatience are all signs of unrest. Those feelings all point to the same source—a lack of trust. Please always remember that God can be trusted in *all* His ways. That means even the ones that don't make sense to you yet.

Even when you don't see "when" in sight, God's plan is still God's plan. I was so excited when God first told me about Seth. And every time I'd see a glimpse that maybe he felt the same way about me, I would chalk it up to God's plan coming to pass. I was all in. But as time went on, and it got harder to see the glimpses, I started to lose hope. This verse in Hebrews 10:35 (MSG) addresses that exact feeling, "...So don't throw it all away now. You were sure of yourselves then. It's still a sure thing! But you need to stick it out, staying with God's plan so you'll be there for the promised completion."

I asked God how I was to "stick with it." I didn't know what else I could possibly do. I felt like I had done everything in my power, and it still wasn't enough. Quite frankly, it wasn't. It couldn't be. This was a God promise, and that meant God had to do it. Over and over again, when I began to feel uneasy, God would simply tell me to rest.

There is a skill to rest. Resting is not as easy as it sounds. It takes strength to rest when every part of you wants to steamroll forward. Hebrews 4:11 (NIV) even says to "... make every effort to enter that rest..." It clearly states that it takes effort to rest. True rest calls us to lay down our need to *do,* and give it to God. Resting bubbles out of trusting. We have to trust Him before we will be willing to hand over any area of our life.

The time it takes to get to the "when" is where you learn to rest. It's how you hone the skill of trusting God. Hebrews 10:39 (MSG) states, "But we're not quitters who lose out. Oh, no! We'll stay with it and survive, trusting all the way."

The most luxurious effect of resting is relaxing. Relaxing into God's timing. Sliding and forming into His ways. That peace I've mentioned quite a few times in this book, is found in this place of rest. Proverbs 1:33 (MSG) states, "First pay attention to me, and then relax. Now you can take it easy—you're in good hands." You can relax in God's will, timing, and ways.

You're in good hands.

Chapter Sixteen

Selflessness

WITH THE TWIRL OF HER WRIST, THE WHOLE ROOM HANDED OVER their attention. "All right, everyone," she started to further everyone's concentration on her, "I'm going to show you how to walk in from the back to the front. I'll be telling you the order and timing in which you are to come in. Please, pay attention. If you mess up here, the whole routine won't flow correctly."

Julia was instructing the little girls we taught in dance class. We'd been teaching dance classes at the church for almost two years now, and we had it down to a science. We loved it.

Julia lined up each girl to match the layout she had written down in her binder. Because she did things like keep a binder. I never did. She did things like keep timing. I just started dancing and hoped for the best. She did the things I was never good at. I was thankful for her and her binder. I wondered why I wasn't like that too. I supposed it was necessary to have the whimsical freestyler I was, in combination with the formulated order she was.

The little girl in the back of the line extensively missed her cue—for the third time. Julia laughed and graciously realigned the entire team, so they could try again. I, on the other hand, was ready to throw in the towel. The performance was in two days, and we were—less than ready. Then again, it felt like this every time we had a performance; and every time, it went on without a hitch.

I walked over to the corner of the room and checked my phone to kill some time while Julia instructed the very beginning of the dance—again. My breath stopped for a millisecond when I saw Seth's name on my screen. Julia and I had pretty much begged Seth and Trevor to go see a Christian rap concert with us.

Seth's response was less than exciting.

I'm really not into rap music. Sorry!

Ouch.

Seth could have asked me to go caged-shark diving, and I would have said *yes*, solely because he asked. Obviously, that was not the case for him.

He had sent me like five country music songs that he liked, and I pretended to like them too. One, because I wanted a common interest to talk about. But more emphatically because two, *she* liked country. You remember, the *her* who had her eyes on Seth too. She couldn't have more in common with him than I did! He didn't need to like rap. I just wanted him to like me!

I wanted to take back ever asking him. I wanted to not like Christian rap either. I wanted to agree with Seth. I felt like if we had something that wasn't in common, there was something wrong.

My phone vibrated again before I had time to respond.

But while you're there, stay away from boys.

Ha! There wasn't a boy on the planet that I was more interested in than him. But I absolutely *loved* the fact that he felt the need to tell me that. It meant he was concerned with me finding someone else. At least, that's how I was going to interpret it.

I ran over to Julia to show her the message. First, she gave me a look of disappointment. Then as she read the next message, she smiled. Good, she interpreted it the same way I did. I put my phone down. I'd respond after dance. That gave me time to concoct a reply that didn't make me look so desperate.

I danced to the beat of the music, while Julia counted the time. I noticed we worked best as opposites. Maybe it was okay if Seth and I didn't have everything in common.

Ever heard the saying, "opposites attract"? Yeah, me too. Yet, I still felt like I couldn't have any part of me opposing to Seth. I felt like we were supposed to be totally the same, and that would be confirmation that we were supposed to be together.

While it's great to have interests you both enjoy, believe it or not, you don't have to be exactly the same. Maybe you're thinking, "Duh, I knew that." But so many times in life, we sell ourselves as something different than we are to make people, more specifically love interests, find us more appealing. We try to become who we think they want us to be, sometimes unconsciously. I found myself changing my style in clothes to fit what I thought Seth liked. I tried to listen to the music he liked and watch the shows he watched. I wanted to get more into music because he was so amazing at it.

That is—until God revealed information to me that I had not noticed before. Your spouse is made to balance you, not equal you.

If you had all the same qualities, you wouldn't need each other. Just as Julia and I made a terrific dance team together, because she was strong where I wasn't; and I had strengths that she didn't. It was all right for Seth and me to have different opinions, ideas, and desires, as long as the main focus was the same—Jesus. Our goal was the same.

I felt the call on my life to go into ministry; so I knew it would be imperative for my spouse to line up with that call. But that didn't mean the way we executed ministry had to be the same.

I tend to be loud. I am outgoing and by no means shy. Sometimes, I wish I were, because sometimes that "not shyness" will let out thoughts I meant to hold in. Seth, on the other hand, is quiet. When he does talk, it is always words of consideration, which is most of the time a great thing. But both qualities can be helpers and hurters. Sometimes, Seth will be passive, when he shouldn't. Sometimes, I'll be controversial, when I shouldn't. But together, we balance and harmonize with one another. As a team, I make sure what needs to be said gets said, while Seth makes sure it gets said right.

You can be right and wrong at the same time. Right in what you said, but wrong in how you said it. That's just one of the examples where Seth and my differences help make each other better.

God also showed me that if I was truly supposed to be with Seth, I had to be me. The real me. Not the me I thought he wanted me to be. When you are in the process of getting to know your potential spouse, it is important to be who you really are. If the two personalities don't mesh, you weren't supposed to be with them anyway.

God knew what He was doing when He constructed you. He

made me loud for a reason, and Seth quiet for a reason. You are to complement your spouse's qualities, not mirror them.

Concert night. The night we planned on my birthday. Eight of us were going to see the Outcry concert. Most importantly, Seth was going to the concert. I was already putting my outfit together when I heard my phone ring. It was a text message from Seth.

> What time are we meeting up tonight? Are we taking separate cars or the big van?

One of our friends had volunteered their van, which would have been nice and all, but I was looking forward to being in a car with Seth. I suppose riding together in a van would work too. I knew it was silly, but I'd lose sleep thinking about ways to get a seat beside him without wreaking of total and all-consuming desperation to be with him. I just wanted him to notice me, and I didn't trust his desire for me enough to wait and see if he would sit with me first. The van had three rows of seats. Too many options for my liking.

> I think we're meeting at 6. Taking the van.

I did notice that he could have asked anyone else who was going that question, but he still asked me. I knew it was going to be cold, and so I was trying to find a way to wear a big coat and still look cute. It wasn't working.

Hmm, I thought to myself, *cold and cute, or warm and frumpy?* Cold and cute won. I opted to wear a light jacket rather than my big, lumpy coat.

My phone rang again.

Dress warm, it's supposed to be 30 degrees and raining tonight. We will probably be standing outside in line for awhile.

It's almost like he was reading my mind!

Sure will!

I did not.

We all met up together and said our hellos and got in the van.

"I have to ride up front or I will get car sick," Seth said, and my expectation level for the night descended. I wasn't driving; so that meant I wasn't going to be next to him. I went for the next best thing and jumped in the first row of seats. Julia hopped in beside me. I tried my best to listen to his conversation and add in, but it was so hard to keep leaning forward with my seatbelt tugging on my neck. I eventually gave up the effort and sat back.

"Well, I guess I'm going to take a nap," I said to Julia. We had about another hour to go until we arrived at the concert hall.

"I'm surprised you've made it this long without falling asleep," she remarked, and then laughed. I did have a track record for falling asleep every time I got in a car for longer than thirty minutes. "Just don't do your sleeping face. Seth might not like that," she whispered and nudged my arm jokingly. She had a point. I tend to sleep with my mouth wide open, with full speed ahead on the drool. It wasn't my most attractive quality.

"You're right! Never mind! I'll stay awake." We both laughed. It was going to be hard to fall asleep anyway, considering how cold

I was. Everyone else had on winter coats, and so the AC was blasting in the van.

Seth noticed my shivering and turned to me. "I see you didn't dress warm." He laughed, but he was shivering too.

"Hey, you're shaking." I pointed out to the chills on his arm.

"Yeah, I think I might have a fever." He laughed.

"What?! Are you sick?" I couldn't believe he would still come to the concert if he had a fever.

"Nah, I don't get sick. I'm a Christian." He gave me a slanted smile. That was his go to line, and he stood by it. Sick or not, he always did whatever he had planned to do. This was one man I had never seen have a "man cold."

I laughed with him. "I'm a Christian too, but if I had a fever, I would not be going out." Just as I finished my sentence, we heard rain beating on the hood of the van. It began to downpour.

"I sure hope we don't have to stand in line in this rain," Julia said.

We did.

We arrived at the concert venue an hour before show time. The line wrapped so far around the building, I couldn't even see the end of it. A few people in our group brought umbrellas, me not being one of them. We all huddled together closely, as many as could fit under one umbrella. I noticed Seth's shivering was getting much worse. I felt bad for him.

"AHHH!" I squealed. Water from the edge of the umbrella dripped down my shirt. If I made it out of this night without catching pneumonia, I was going to be proud. Seth turned and saw the water draining out the bottom of shirt and handed me his umbrella.

"Here, you and Julia can share mine." He motioned for me to

take his umbrella, as he pulled his hood up over his head.

"No way, you need it. You're sick, and you shouldn't be in the cold and the rain." Plus, there was no reason he couldn't get under the umbrella with us.

"I have a hood, you don't." He put the umbrella in my hand. "I'll be fine. We're almost through the line anyway."

I couldn't help but think of him as the stereotypical knight in shining armor. Even though it was a small gesture, it was a meaningful one. He was sick and still handed over his umbrella.

"What are you sick with?" I asked, expecting him to say he had a cold.

"The flu, I think." Homeboy had the flu! And he was still here!

"Seth! You really shouldn't be out if you have the flu!" He didn't even complain about anything the whole drive here.

We finally got into the building and tried to shake off some of the water, like dogs who had been jumping around in the sprinklers. I was trying my best to stay right behind Seth, so when we all went to find a seat, I'd be beside him. But against my most valiant efforts, it wasn't working. The line had turned into a blob, and there was no rhyme or reason to how everyone was filtering in.

It came time to hand over our tickets and walk through the carousel. Seth moved forward, and a guy beside me stepped in front of me. Then a girl, then another guy, and just like that, I lost sight of Seth.

Great, I'm going to be sitting through a three-hour concert and not be with Seth the whole time, I thought to myself. But just as I handed over my ticket, I saw Seth standing to the side, waiting for me to go through the line.

He smiled at me and motioned for me to go in the door.

"Ladies first," he said. Even though he wasn't complaining a bit, I could tell he wasn't feeling good. I walked down the row and took a seat. Seth followed right behind. I'm pretty sure this counted as him sitting with me, not the other way around.

Despite the fact that the chances of me catching the flu were substantially raised, I was willing to risk those odds. I was just happy to be near him.

The concert started. Everyone stood except Seth.

"Are you okay?" I yelled so he could hear me over the loud music.

"Yeah, I just need to sit." He gave me a thumbs up.

After two and a half hours, the concert ended, and we got up to go home. I could tell Seth was feeling worse than before. I so badly wanted to be able to help him, but I didn't know what I could do.

Once we stepped outside, an instant smack of cold burst into me. The temperature had dropped so much my nose went almost immediately numb. I knew that if I was this cold, Seth had to be utterly freezing. We all walked briskly to the van and piled in fast to defrost ourselves. Julia and I huddled together to try to get warm, and they cranked up the heat.

Finally, I warmed up from frigid, but I still wasn't classified as warm. I laid my head in the empty seat next to me and curled up into the fetal position. I knew I was going to fall asleep and look hilarious, but I didn't care at this point. It was late, and I was cold.

Just as I was almost asleep, I heard Seth whisper to Julia, "Is she asleep?" Julia nodded in reply. "She's still shivering. I told her to dress warm."

"She never does." Julia whispered back to him and laughed.

I heard him moving. But I didn't want to open my eyes, in case he wanted to say anything else, while he thought I was sleeping. (Like confess his deep love for me.) Then, I felt him put his jacket over me. It smelled like menthol and cologne. Butterflies flooded through me. He just put his jacket on me! In front of people! That means something, right?

He was sick and still gave me his jacket, which then made me think I was almost guaranteed to get sick, but I still didn't care. I felt like I was cuddled up in a canopy of confirmation. Surely, he had feelings for me. I wasn't the only one shivering in the car.

First the umbrella, then the jacket. He was taking care of me, even though he was the one who needed taking care of that day. He was being selfless. That made me want to rush out all the words I'd ever thought about him, but never had the courage to say out loud. But—he thought I was sleeping. So, I kept silent with a small grin on my face, and my eyes closed.

Selfless. That word has a heavy weight to it. To be truly selfless means to prefer another over one's self. But to just do something for someone else when there are no negative effects for you, isn't true selflessness. It's when putting the other person first actually takes something from you. Sacrifice—that's when you're being selfless. That's also one of the key elements of how the Bible describes love. 1 Corinthians 13 lists multiple qualities that love has, and a lot that it does not have. Verse five says, "Love is not rude, is not selfish..."

In order to love someone, you can't be selfish.

Ladies, there is a very important reason to find a man who is not selfish. A passage in Ephesians used to bother me. It talks about wives submitting to their husbands. That concept just didn't sit well with me for awhile. I had a hard time imagining myself trusting another person that much. Submitting means following their instructions, even if you don't agree with it. To submit is to allow the other person to have the final say. For awhile, I just didn't see how that could be what God wanted me to do. After all, what if they were wrong?

Ephesians 5:24 (NIV) states, "Now as the church submits to Christ, so also wives should submit to their husbands in everything." That verse used to tear me up. The thought of blind submission to whatever my husband decided gnarled in me. *But*, it is imperative to read the next verse to understand the full revelation God was trying to give. Ephesians 5:25 (KJV) expresses this act of selfless love. "Husbands, love your wives, even as Christ also loved the church, and gave himself for it." It says to love like Christ loved the church. Christ died for the church. Christ gave himself, handed over his "jacket" so to speak, even though it was going to cost him everything.

This idea of being selfless means even when it costs you something, prefer the other person. I understood why my dad used to tell me to find a man who wasn't selfish once I saw it in action. I could trust Seth.

I could submit like the Bible says to do to your husband, because I knew he would always have my best interest in mind. When decisions would come up in our married life, I could rest easy knowing he wasn't thinking about what would be best for him. He would be thinking of me first, and I would do the same for him. That way, even if I didn't agree with every decision he made, I could still follow him, because I would know he was trying his hardest to do right by me.

Knowing your spouse has your best interest in mind first, makes submitting a whole lot easier to do. On the other hand, if you thought your spouse was only thinking of himself, submitting to him would be frustrating. It would cause a division in the marriage, and that was never what God intended.

From day one, even in Costa Rica, Seth took care of me. He didn't have to. He had no obligation to me. But he did. He preferred me, even before there was anything in it for him. It wasn't just me that he had taken care of, however. While hiking up a very steep, very long path to the top of the mountain we were staying on while in Costa Rica, Seth had to carry all his clothes and necessities for the week, as well as his bulky guitar and guitar case. He had more stuff to lug around than anyone else on the trip.

A woman on the trip had some health issues, and the hike was proving to be just a tad too difficult for her. So Seth, being the selfless man he is, took her bags and began to lug those up the mountain too. No one asked him to; no one expected him to. That's just the kind of person he was, and is. You can't fake that kind of love for people.

This is a quality you cannot see in someone right away. It is easy to be selfless once, or for a little while. Time will test the trueness of a person's selflessness. I could see why on a list of only three things to find in a spouse, selflessness made the cut.

Chapter Seventeen

Freely Given

I FILED THROUGH MY STACK OF IMPORTANT DOCUMENTS, LOOKING for my plane ticket. I was going to Florida for a week to visit my grandmother. I was super excited not only to see family, but also because Julia was coming with me. We had beach plans, pool plans, pretty much anything in the sun plans. While digging through the unorganized drawer, I picked up my passport laying right on top of the ticket I was searching for. I held it up and smiled.

That passport meant more to me than just a way to get in and out of the country. I flipped to the page of stamps that showed the countries I had visited. I had been on a few mission trips, but remembering back to Costa Rica was my favorite. It was where my promise took shape. It was where I found an answer to the most daunting question I'd ever had… *Who?* I smiled and ran my thumb over the Costa Rica stamp.

"Jordan, are you ready?" Mom's distant voice came from downstairs. I closed my passport and grabbed my ticket and bag off my bed.

"Sure am." I said, as I made my way down the steps. Julia was already by the door with all her bags ready to go. I was truly excited about going. But in the back of my mind, I was mildly concerned about what Seth would be doing while I was gone. We were texting every day, but it normally started because we were talking about plans for the church events we had that day. This week, if we texted, it was going to have to be comprehensively unveiled. We couldn't hide behind excuses this week. It was going to be telling, for sure.

"Already looking at that phone to see if Seth is going to text you?" Julia nudged my arm and smiled. "We haven't even made it to the airport yet."

"I know. I'm insufferable. How am I going to hold my sanity all week?" I rolled my eyes at myself. I did not want my whole week to be ruined if he didn't end up texting me. "Promise me that if I get all upset if he doesn't text me, you WON'T let me text him more than twice in a row without a response. PROMISE IT!" I was too awkward for my own good. I didn't need to add clingy to the list. Julia laughed and promised to throw my phone in the ocean upon the third unrequited text.

Once we arrived at the airport, and checked in and accessed our gate, I checked my phone screen one more time. Still no messages, and it was time to turn the phone in airplane mode. *Okay, God. I'm not going to stress this. You promised, I believe You,* I prayed under my breath. Mom followed behind me as we got on the plane.

We all got to sit together, which was pleasant considering we didn't pay for seat assignments. The plane ride was only about two hours, but being together made the time fly by. We were already having fun, and the more we had our "girl time," the more I was forgetting about the pressure of keeping contact with Seth. This week was going to be great. I made up my mind I was going to enjoy it, no matter what. I was going to relax and let God sort out the details.

We landed and turned our phones back on. Right away, a message came across my screen.

Let me know when you get there, killa. Safe travels!

"HE TEXTED ME!" I practically announced to the entire Florida airport. Julia and Mom laughed at my choice of vocal volume. So did a few other people not in our group, which made us laugh even more.

"There's Nana over there." Mom pointed to her mom over near the waiting area, waving for us to notice her. We all said our hello's and loaded up her car to go to her house. We were here, and Seth had made contact. Now all I had to do was not start worrying if he would do it again tomorrow...

There is some deep-rooted part of my brain that thinks if I don't do something, it won't get done. In school, if there was ever a group project, I was the kid everyone wanted in their group, because I felt an obligation to do about ninety percent of the work and let everyone else do ten percent, just so we could say it was a team effort. I knew if I did the work, it would be done right, and I wouldn't have to depend on anyone else for my grade.

The problem is, I was the same way with God. I felt if I didn't make things happen between Seth and me, then it just wouldn't happen. If it were any other regular relationship, that might be true. But this one wasn't just another guy I liked. This was my

Mr. Man of God. This was my promise. This was supposed to be a gift to me, but I was trying to forcefully grab what God was trying to freely give.

The moment I released my grip and said, "Okay, God. You do this," God did what He always does, and comes through just like He said He would.

According to James 1:17 (NIV), "Every good and perfect gift is from above, coming down from the Father of the heavenly lights, who does not change like shifting shadows." God isn't fickle or flaky. He won't halfway fulfill His promises. He doesn't need to be reminded to be faithful. And He isn't in need of motivation to move on your behalf.

I often felt like God was dangling a blessing out in front me. As if He would let me have it, only if I worked hard or begged enough for it. But that's not His heart for us at all! This was a misconception that I made up all by myself. I had always been taught that God is good. That He is faithful. That He is kind. But that didn't stop me from feeling like I had to persuade Him to be all those things to me.

Matthew 7:7–11 (NIV) states, "Ask and it will be given to you; seek and you will find; knock and the door will be opened to you. For everyone who asks receives; he who seeks finds; and to him who knocks, the door will be opened. Which of you, if his son asks for bread, will give him a stone? Or if he asks for a fish, will give him a snake? If you, then, though you are evil, know how to give good gifts to your children, how much more will your Father in heaven give good gifts to those who ask him!"

When we ask, God hears. He moves on our behalf. It might not be in the time we expected or in the way we thought, but He is always faithful to bring your perfect gift right when you need it. So release the control to the One who is capable and faithful.

Birds were chirping from high up in the palm trees towering over the open-sided veranda. The air was thick with morning dew. You could taste the warmth oozing from sunrise. The miniature waterfall trickling into the pool created the perfect harmony with buzzing bugs and the rasping of the frogs. Morning devotions poolside were quickly becoming the favorite part of the vacation for Julia and me.

Peace just came naturally here. All the beauty of nature operated like a megaphone for God's voice to my heart. I was getting so much revelation in just the four days we had been there. There was something special about being away from all the distraction of everyday life.

Julia and I sat out there, side by side, in the white-slatted pool chairs and shared our devotions with each other. We would have stayed out there all day, if Nanna didn't call us in for breakfast. This was our idea of a good time, and I cherished our friendship even more because of it. She was a God-send. I recognized how important having a godly best friend was. I spent all my time with her. I often thought how different my story would be, if I hadn't joined that dance team and met her.

She encouraged me to keep going. To stay strong in the faith. And I did the same for her. It was much easier to stay the course God was leading me on without having bad friends to distract me away from it. She was essential.

"Girls! Breakfast is ready!" Nana popped her head out of the sliding glass door and motioned for us to come and eat. We closed our Bibles and notebooks, and got up to go inside. My phone lit up in my full hands. I could see the text was from Seth. Julia turned to look at me.

Every time my phone rang since we got to Florida, everyone around me waited to see if it was Seth. And every once in a while, it was. We talked every day. Not all day, but at least every day. Seth had done a surprisingly good job at finding a good excuse to text me without it being solely "just to talk."

The first day, his reason was that a Christian artist we both liked was releasing a new album, and his words were, "So pumped about this." That conversation quickly led to us talking about all the worship music we liked, and what it meant to us. The second day, he had a question for my mom that he so smoothly relayed through me. The third day, he was buying an outfit for his upcoming college graduation and asked for a "female's opinion" on a skinny tie versus a regular one.

I told him, "Neither. Go with a bow tie. They're classier."

He then proceeded to send me pictures of every nerd he could find on the internet. Tragically, they were all wearing bowties.

Ironically, I was getting to know him so much better since I'd been in Florida. He was funny. The witty kind of funny that I always loved and never knew Seth had. He was so quiet all the time, I don't think anyone really knew he had such a great sense of humor. When I prayed, I thanked God a little extra because even though none of us knew Seth was just my flavor of funny, God did. Before I even knew I had anything in common with Seth at all, God did. And I looked forward to all the other characteristics of Seth that I never even knew I wanted, but God did.

This morning was different though. This text just said *Hey!* And

I knew it was dumb, but those three letters made me so excited. There was no reason for him to text me this time. This one was just to talk. I was so happy, I didn't even want to eat. I hadn't been hungry in months. I was too overwhelmed. Overwhelmed with anticipation, with excitement, with wonder, with doubt, but the most prominent one was relief. For the first time in a long time, I felt found. I didn't feel like I was free falling anymore.

When God told me to break up with Peter, it felt like a never-ending trust fall. I knew, eventually, I would land safe and sound wherever God was leading me. But I'd be lying if I said I hadn't felt lost in the chaos of mind.

After I finished moving the food around my plate to look like I ate more than three bites, I cleaned my plate into the trash and went over to the piano Nana had in her front living room.

Her piano emanated class. The keys were weighted, which gave them a pressure that lightly pushed back on your fingertips when you played. The sounds rolled out smooth and even. The deep ebony wood was glossed without a speck of dust in sight. Every note rolled out pure.

I just sat down and began to play. Not anything in particular, just whatever felt right. Before I even knew what was happening, a song came out of me and that piano. Effortlessly.

It went like this:

> A grace like no other
> A love from the Father
> Wrapped in His mercy
> Consumed by His love
> Watching His plans
> Unfold like a present

Watching the past
Just pass away
I've been found by You
I've been found by You
With grace that surrounds
Love that astounds
I've been found by You
A redemption story
A beautiful masterpiece
The God of everything
Chose me
That perfect plan
And that perfect peace
That perfect love
Is from perfect blood

Those words described exactly what my heart was feeling. Like the night was over, morning had come, and I had been found. I sang the song over and over. It was my thank you letter to God. I even told Seth I had written it.

He loved playing and writing music, so it was the perfect topic to bond over. He even sent me some video clips of songs he was working on. I could finally see everything God told me, wrapped up with a nice little bow. So neat and tidy. Without blemish or wrinkle. This was plan A. I was finally experiencing the part I had been waiting for.

I had been found. Those words meant a flood of various values to me. It was never that God had lost me and just now figured out what to do with me. It was that... I had lost me.

Galatians 5:16–17 (NIV) states, "So I say, walk by the Spirit, and you will not gratify the desires of the flesh. For the flesh desires what is contrary to the Spirit, and the Spirit what is contrary to the flesh. They are in conflict with each other, so that you are not to do whatever you want." My flesh and my Spirit had been in some serious conflict as of late. My heart wanted more than anything to do things God's way. My head, on the other hand, wanted what was easy, what was comfortable, and what was in reach.

I had been wrestling with myself for what seemed like a century. But now, finally, I felt like I wanted what God wanted. All of me. My heart, my head, my soul, and my spirit had all lined up and accepted whatever God was handing out.

If you keep reading that passage in Galatians, verses 24–25 says, "Those who belong to Christ Jesus have crucified the flesh with its passions and desires. Since we live by the Spirit, let us keep in step with the Spirit." My flesh had finally been put down. The word "crucify," is not a pretty word. It doesn't just mean to kill it. It is a violent death. It is painful. It is brutal. The flesh is not going to die without a fight. It hurt breaking up with Peter. It hurt walking away from Ben. It hurt when God told me to wait. It even hurt when God told me about Seth, because I knew that meant I would have to fully rely on God.

That dependence, at first, hurt. That patience, at first, hurt. That trust, *at first*, hurt because all those things were opposing to my flesh. They created war. Remember, God didn't bring the pain, but He sure did use it for my good. But all those hurts crucified my flesh. Just like the crucifixion of Christ was necessary for salvation to be available to the whole human race, the crucifixion of your flesh (meaning anything that is an opposition with the will and purposes of God), will be necessary for the restoration of your story.

My Spirit man had, as the scripture says, kept "in step with the Spirit." I had decisively chosen God's plan. And it had graciously led me home. I had found my true passion—and that was Christ. I had found my honest desires—and that was His ways.

It also meant that the God of all perfection, The Way-Maker, the God of the Impossible, the great I AM, the Alpha and Omega, the Beginning and the End, the Author and the Finisher of our faith, THAT God—had found me from the very beginning. Found me in my mess. Found me at my worst. Found me in the darkness I had put myself in. He reached in, without a glint of reservation or remorse, and brought me into the glory of His promise. He found me when I was hiding. He was so gracious to me. I could feel it now more than ever.

I looked back on the journey thus far, and it seemed like every day His mercy became more and more real to me. His plan was unfolding right before my eyes, exactly like He said it would. I was just sitting back, watching in amazement. There is a sense of comfort that comes from realizing even when you lost yourself, God knew exactly where you were and precisely how to get you where you needed to be.

I finally, for the first time in a long time, felt like I was right where I needed to be. Found—in the arms of the Savior.

Chapter Eighteen

You Have to Bring a Date

"Jo, your phone just went off." Julia popped her head into the bathroom door where I was brushing my teeth. "Do you want me to bring it to you?" It was still hooked up to the charger from last night.

"Is it Seth?!" I mumbled through the toothpaste in my mouth. If this was the long-awaited "good morning" text, I was going to faint.

"Umm, hang on, I'll check." She walked back into the bedroom to get the phone. "It's not him..." she said with disappointment. "It's a number you don't have saved in your phone."

"Okay," I answered back, "I'll check it in a minute." Bummer. Still not at the "Good morning, sweetie" stage yet.

I finished brushing my teeth and went into the bedroom to see who the unknown number was. It was a girl in my church who was getting married. I was good friends with the groom and his family my whole life. They wanted me to assist people at the guest book when you first walk into the wedding venue. I thought it was really sweet they thought to have me involved in their wedding. I responded and told her I would love to help.

> *Oh, and you have to bring a date. ;)*

That was a surprise. I swallowed hard. Did she know about Seth and me? Did anyone know about us? Did Seth even know about us? Were we *that* obvious? Part of me hoped we were. That would mean that all this wasn't just in my head, and Seth really did have feelings for me. Another part of me was afraid that if Seth got wind that people thought we might be liking each other, he'd completely shut down and run.

I showed Julia the text. She laughed.

"So, are you going to ask him now, or are you going to freak out about it for three hours first?" She was so right. We both knew I was going to ask him to go. We also both knew that I would overthink it first.

"I'm going to ask him right now. I'm just going to type it. I'm just going to do it." I was trying to hype myself up.

Julia gave me a little eye roll and grunted, "Uh huh."

Her disbelief encouraged me even more. Before I could think about what I was doing, I prepared a text.

> *Hey, I'm helping out a friend with their wedding. Doing the guest book. She said I have to bring a date. Sooo, you're coming with me. Okay?*

Before I let myself even proofread it, I sent it. Then, like only a seventeen-year-old girl can, I face planted into the still unmade bed and screamed, "WHAT DID I JUST DO?!"

Julia laughed and picked up my phone to see what I had sent. She then buried her face too. And we stayed like that, laughing until the phone dinged again.

We both looked up at each other and then at the phone. "I'm too afraid to read it. You tell me what it says," I said as I handed her the phone with my hand covering my eyes.

"It's not him." She laughed and handed the phone back to me. It was my mom texting me from the other room wanting to know why she heard muffled screaming.

Julia and I ran into Mom's room to tell her everything that had just happened. Even her jaw dropped. "I can't believe you actually did it. What did he say?" she asked.

"Well, he hasn't responded yet. And it's been like, five minutes." Which to me, was a lifetime right now. I felt if he took too much longer, my heart would explode.

Mom's phone buzzed on the nightstand beside the bed. She picked it up to look at it, and said, "Your daddy just sent me this." She flipped the screen around to show me his message. It was a screenshot from Dad's phone. It was a text from Seth. He was asking Dad if it was all right that he take me to the wedding.

> Hey, man, Jo said she has to bring someone to this wedding you guys are going to. I want to help her out cause I'd do anything for you guys but I want to make sure it isn't weird with you. I don't want to do anything to disrespect you.

I didn't know how to feel about it. It was partly sweet that he was asking Dad's permission. And it was partly disappointing, because it sounded like he was just doing me favor. I knew he was concerned about what my parent's opinion was with us hanging out. After all, he texted my mom the first time we hung out. It was like a punch to the gut then, and this was feeling all too familiar again.

Mom called Dad. "What are you going to tell him?" Dad and Mom both knew how I felt about Seth. They loved him. I knew that. But Seth didn't. I was trying to give him the benefit of the doubt with this one and say Seth chose those words, because he was trying to feel out how my dad would respond. I couldn't hear what Dad was saying. But whatever he was going to say back, I needed him to do it fast, because the suspense was killing me.

"Well, make sure he knows you are happy about it," said Mom.

She got off the phone and told me Dad was going to tell him he didn't mind one bit. It didn't take more than two minutes before Seth texted me.

> *Okay. Sounds like a plan. But I'm not wearing a bow tie.*

He had no idea my parents and I were close enough to tell each other what he was saying. I decided to pretend like I didn't know his answer to me completely hinged on my dad's answer to him.

I jumped on top of the bed. I didn't even care if Seth was still afraid of what my parents thought. We were going to a public event. Together. All three of us squealed with excitement.

Asking for permission. Seth was asking my dad for permission to take me to a wedding I asked him to. It all felt backward to me. But a lot of times, that's exactly how we are with God. We ask permission to do, to go, or to accept something that He invited us to in the first place.

I can think of a dozen times God planted a dream in my heart, something that, without God, probably would never even cross my mind. And then, once I see it before me, I panic. I realize the magnitude or the practicality of the circumstance, and I question God's whole plan.

What Seth didn't know was that my dad had already said, "If I could pick a man for you to marry, it would be Seth." My dad had given Seth permission that Seth knew nothing about. But, there was no way for Seth to know that until he asked.

Just like that, God is often handing out permission and provision that we know nothing about. Not because God didn't tell us, but because we didn't ask. We sense the difficulty in the request, and so we don't bother requesting at all. 2 Corinthians 1:20–21 (MSG) says, "Whatever God has promised gets stamped with the *Yes* of Jesus. In him, this is what we preach and pray, the great Amen, God's *Yes* and our *Yes* together, gloriously evident." Whatever God promised you, He grants you permission to the provision.

God is not holding back anything you need. He has ample supply and is ready to pour provision all over you. Psalm 84:11–12 (KJV) states, "For the Lord is a sun and shield: the Lord will give grace and glory: no good thing will he withhold from them that walk uprightly. O Lord of hosts, blessed is the man that trusteth in thee." He is withholding no good thing. When you are walking uprightly or in other words, walking in the callings and leadings of Jesus, you have everything you need.

You no longer need to feel insufficient or inadequate. You don't have to shy away from the challenge anymore. Because all of heaven has granted you permission to all the necessary provision. Step into the call you have already been invited to.

Chapter Nineteen

Concrete Ballroom

THE DRESS WAS ALREADY PICKED OUT, THE HAIR WAS CURLED AND cascading, and the makeup was thoroughly applied. It was wedding time. I was sitting in the driveway of Seth and his roommate's house, trying to slow my breathing down. If I walked in now, it would seem like I ran here rather than drove. Butterflies were an understatement for what was swirling around in me. It felt more like full-grown birds. Not the little finches either. I'm talking hawks and eagles, the big ones. It felt like any moment now, they would carry me away.

I knew I had to go inside soon. They were going to notice my car outside and wonder why I hadn't come in. I said a little prayer, checked my makeup one last time, and got out of my car. "Okay, Jo, you can do this. Just try not to fall down." I was talking to myself out loud. It helped with the concentration. The six-inch heels I was wearing would combat that effort.

I knocked on the door. No answer. I knew the doorbell didn't work, so there was no point in trying that. I knocked again. I heard movement in the house. It sounded like footsteps coming toward the door, until the uniformity of the footsteps stopped, and three loud thuds followed. Then silence for a moment. *Did he just fall down the stairs?* I thought to myself. I even let out a little giggle.

The door swung open, and there stood Seth Smith in all his James Bond featured glory. I had never seen him so dressed up. I'll never forget the way he looked in that exact moment. He looked like everything I never knew I wanted.

"Hi," he said through his perfectly spruce grin.

"Hi." I wanted to tell him he looked nice, or that he smelled nice, or that he was nice. I wanted to tell him anything other than just *Hi*. But no other words were coming out.

"Come on in, I just need to tie my tie, and then we can go." He moved to the side so I could step into the house. Trevor was sitting on the couch, smirking up at me.

"Hey, Jo." He waved. "You look nice." Trevor and I had a sarcastic insult kind of friendship, so I thought it was strange that he gave me a normal compliment.

"Umm, thank you," I tried to say without seeming too puzzled. I turned to Seth. "Can I use your bathroom really quick before we leave?" I needed to check myself and make sure there wasn't something on my face or dress. Trevor's compliment had me paranoid.

I walked up the stairs to the bathroom, very carefully. The shoes were already hard enough to walk in on leveled ground, much less a staircase. Right as I went around the corner, I heard Trevor's voice, "You think she's hot, don't you?"

"Shut up." I could barely hear Seth's response, because he was whispering. Thankfully, for my eavesdropping, Trevor was not.

"I saw the way you looked at her when she came in. You like

her," Trevor said just loud enough for me to hear. I could hear Seth's voice, but I couldn't make out the words. "Good luck explaining that to Keith."

What did my dad have to do with this?

I needed to hurry before they wondered what was taking me so long. I went into the bathroom and turned the sink on high enough pressure that they could hear it downstairs. I wanted them to think I was actually in the bathroom and not crouching in the hallway, listening to their increasingly intriguing conversation. I shut the water off to give them notice that I was coming back downstairs.

Both of their voices stopped as soon as my high heel clicked onto the first step.

"Are you ready to go?" Seth asked, as I stepped down even more carefully than on the way up.

"Sure am." I smiled with a greater confidence than before. Thanks to Trevor, I knew what Seth was thinking about me tonight. Maybe this was the first time Seth ever looked at me like that, or maybe this was just the first time he was unable to hide it. It didn't matter, because tonight, he looked at me the way I had been looking at him for months—with careful consideration.

Deliberating what was to come of the person in front of us, we knew it was too risky to chance a relationship on a "maybe" it will work out. We had too much to lose. We both were going to hold our feelings in, until we were sure this was the real thing.

Confirmation. When God speaks something down in your heart, sometimes it's so soft and so tender that it's hard to tell if it was a God direction or a personal preference. I will be the first to tell you

I have missed it before. I have both ignored the voice and missed it. I've also taken a personal thought, assumed it was God, and missed it. This isn't uncommon, and it doesn't make you a failure. But I have found that there are ways to know before you go forward if it's God or not.

One of those ways is through confirmation. When something God told you is said by someone else, or a situation is manifested just like God said it would. And anything that lines that up with God's Word is confirmation.

This was one of the "firsts" in our relationship—even though, at this point, it didn't quite count as a relationship. This was not only a confirmation that Seth was beginning to feel the way I felt, but it was also confirmation that my mom was right. She said she felt like God had been telling her that Seth needed to know they were comfortable with us being together. That night, I noticed that every time we got close to some sort of actual progress, my parents would come up.

Like when Trevor said, "Good luck explaining that to Keith." Once again, my dad was thrilled with the idea of Seth; and yet, Seth was terrified of the idea of my dad finding out.

I was afraid to step out on that word that my mom gave me. I was afraid it would scare Seth away. But I've learned that God works through confirmation. He will always confirm His Word and His leadings. Confirmation is a fantastic tool when learning to navigate the leadings of Jesus.

Every instruction and detail God had laid before me was coming to pass. Every day I was more and more convinced that Seth was my Mr. Man of God. The confirmation was crucial encouragement.

Just as the confirmation pushed me to proceed, the lack of

it guided me also. Before Seth, I thought God was leading me to someone else. I thought that because that person, on paper, looked like the perfect candidate. But the more I pushed on that door, the more I realized I had made it out to be something it wasn't in my head. So, I then followed the lack of confirmation. And went back to the drawing board. I asked God to show me what I had missed and how to get back on track again. He is so faithful and did just that.

When God speaks, situations move. Isaiah 55:11 (NIV) says, "So is my word that goes out from my mouth: It will not return to me empty, but will accomplish what I desire and achieve the purpose for which I sent it."

Trust me in this, if God spoke to you, your situations and circumstances will bow to His instructions. His word will be confirmed by the manifested work.

"Do you guys want me to take your picture?" Mom asked as we walked over to meet them at the guest table area. I most certainly wanted to document this and share it with the whole world, but I wasn't sure if Seth wanted anyone to know he was my wedding "date." So, instead of answering, I just looked up at him to see what he'd say.

He looked back at me, probably hoping I would answer the question too. Instead, I just smiled.

"Yeah, sure. We do clean up pretty nice," he answered. He even put his arm around my waist to pose for the photo. We ended up having to take another, because I was smiling so hard in the first one that my eyes were closed by my cheeks. The second try, I contained my excitement slightly better.

Since we had to get there early, we had a little time to kill before the other guests starting arriving. This was the perfect time for Seth and me to get comfortable being around each other as actual "dates," before people starting seeing us. It was going great. There had been no awkward silences, neither of us had tripped, and to top it all off, no one had made any uncomfortable comments about us being there together.

That is, until someone did.

I'm sure they meant nothing by it; but nonetheless, they said it. Seth and I were looking for a seat before the ceremony began, and I heard someone from behind us say, "Oh, I didn't know you guys were here *together*." The comment itself wouldn't have been so bad if the emphasis wasn't put on that last word. But it was. I could feel the hairs on the back of my neck stand up. I didn't know if I should just pretend like I didn't hear it or try to address the remark.

Just as I was contemplating on how to respond, Seth spoke up.

"Yeah," he said as he bent his arm outward for me to hold on to. "Gotta love weddings, huh?" He nodded and kept on walking, with me on his arm—proud to be there with me. The blushing that had rushed into my face was immediately dispersed by his answer.

The ceremony was magical. All the talk of love and wedding vows really reassured everything I had been feeling about Seth this whole time. I wondered if the love in the air was making him think about me too.

Before I knew it, the ceremony ended, and it was time for the reception to begin. We ate at a table with my parents and two other people. We all talked like we always had for years. It was natural and easy. Nothing felt forced or strained. We laughed, joked, and had a great time. But then, they started the music. Out of the whole event, I was nervous about the dancing part; more in particular, the slow-dancing part. As soon as I heard that first note play, I became irrationally nervous. But this song was just the bride and groom's first dance, so there was no pressure on us. Not yet, anyway.

I was watching them dance and thinking how beautiful the whole image looked—the dress flowing gracefully side to side, the brisk evening air hugging in closer and closer as the sun set, the lanterns giving off just enough light to make a glow on their skin. It was all perfect. I looked over at Seth, who wasn't watching the first dance at all. He was looking at me with a gentle smile on his face, the same way I had been looking at them. He was looking at me like I was the only one in the room.

I smiled back at him and whispered, "What are you smiling at?" I could feel myself blushing a little.

"Just you," he said without a moment's pause. He was unapologetically giving into me. I smiled at the ground and looked back at the newlyweds. Their song was ending, and everyone else was invited to join them on the dance floor. I wasn't nervous anymore. I knew Seth was feeling everything I was feeling.

"Well," I turned to Seth, "Are we going to dance or what?" I stood up as an invitation for him to join me. Then I held out my hand for what felt like a solid ten minutes before he said anything.

"Oh, I can't dance. Like, not at all."

Uh oh. I didn't anticipate him saying *no*. I was already standing. I couldn't just sit back down; it would have been pitiful.

"I'm sure that's not true. All you have to do is move side to side. It's not even dancing, it's more like standing in motion." I wanted to stop speaking, but the words just kept coming.

To my rescue though, the song changed from the slow dance

kind, to the line dancing kind. I thank heavens that my mother was the queen of line dancing anything.

"This is our jam, let's go," she said excitedly.

Seth looked up at me from his still-seated position and said, "You go have fun."

I let the pulling of Mom's hand drag me out onto the dance floor. Normally, I would have kicked off my heels and danced ridiculously with my mom alongside, but this time, I knew Seth was watching. The stilettos stayed on through the whole electric slide. My feet were screaming, but hopefully, I was at least looking decent out there.

I could see Seth out of the corner of my eye comfortably leaning up against a large decorative post. He was talking to my dad. They were laughing and smiling. Occasionally, they looked over at us and waved.

Once the song ended, another began that, of course, we just *had* to dance to. This cycle repeated itself a few times, until I couldn't tell what was bothering me more—the fact that I could no longer feel my toes, or the fact that I was so out of breathe I could feel my heart beating in my head. Either way, we both agreed, it was time to take a dance break. We walked over to the guys and watched all the other guest dancing. Seth leaned into my ear so I could hear him above all the music. "You looked good out there," he said with a smile.

I leaned in to him too, "Thanks, now it's your turn." This was my final attempt to get him on the dance floor. The reception was almost over, and I was running out of time.

Just then, Mom said, "I think we're going to go soon. I'm worn out."

"We can go whenever you guys are ready," Seth responded.

We were leaving, and I still hadn't danced with Seth. *Maybe next time,* I thought to myself, hoping there would be a next time.

"Oh, wait! I left my bag inside," Mom said. "You guys go ahead, I'll be right behind y'all."

The gravel we had to walk through to get back to the car did not agree with my heels. Seth saw my immediate struggle and offered his arm out again for me, so I could steady myself. I gladly accepted his offer.

When I held onto his arm, I could smell his cologne lightly in the air. He was warm and comforting. He felt like home. I knew in that moment, it was all over for me. I couldn't go back now even if I wanted to. I had officially fallen for him. He looked over at me, almost like I had said those words aloud. Like he was thinking the exact same thing in the exact same moment. And just when I thought the moment couldn't get any more perfect, the music playing off in the distance changed to his favorite song. Not a sweet, sappy love song, but his favorite dance music song. And I couldn't believe my eyes, because the same man who just told me he was too shy to dance began to break out into this hilarious, uncoordinated, child-like dancing that people do when they're alone in their bedroom, singing into a hairbrush.

I laughed so hard my eyes watered. He started laughing, too, and we danced together, chaotically in the parking lot. Our very own concrete ballroom. It was perfect. He was perfect.

God saw that night long before I did. He knew about the blue dress I would pick out just days before. He knew which tie Seth would wear. He heard the conversation between Trevor and Seth before they spoke a word. He knew that song would play at just the right moment. He orchestrated our connection way before I asked him to. God saw to it that His promise was backed by His plans before He ever let me in on the blueprints.

God knew I wanted a "dance like a child in a parking lot" kind of man before I did. I didn't even know what I had been looking for until I found it. I didn't know what "home" felt like until I felt it. I didn't know anything, but God knew everything.

According to Proverbs 16:9 (NIV), "In their hearts humans plan their course, but the Lord establishes their steps." God not only planted the dream in me for Seth, but He also established the necessary steps I needed to take to get me there.

A lot of times, God's leadings and instructions don't always make sense to the human mind right away. They don't make sense because there are so many variables that God can see, and we simply can't. That's why it's imperative to trust that He knows the end from the beginning. Isaiah 46:10 (NIV) states, "I make known the end from the beginning, from ancient times, what is still to come..." God knows better. He sees more. He's a better planner than we could ever be.

I realized that night at the wedding that God saw my provision before He relayed His promise. And that's important to understand. Whatever promise God has planted in you, know that He has already established the steps. You don't have to stress the details, for God is the perfect coordinator.

Chapter Twenty

Movie Date

Buzz. Buzz. Seth hadn't texted me all day, but at least this text was worth the wait.

> Hey, some of us are going to go see a movie tonight.
> You in?

I needed to assess if this was a pairing off into couples kind of hang out, or just a bunch of friends. Typically, if the number of girls and guys wasn't equal, then it was truly just "some of us."

> Yeah! Who all is going?

> Not sure. I know Trevor is going. Think he asked Julia.

Hmm. That seemed odd. She would have told me by now. But just the four of us definitely felt more like a date.

I told him I'd see him there and made a mad dash to try to get ready in about thirty minutes. While trying to put an outfit together, all the clothes that didn't make the cut were exiled to the floor of my room. I'd pick those up later—probably. Powder was in the air, as I tried to put on a full face of perfectly polished makeup, only to sit in a dark theater for two hours. And the shoes...don't get me started on the shoes. My closet consisted of a giant mountain of unpaired and mismatched shoes. Even if I could find which style I wanted to wear, finding its mate proved to be the most time-consuming process of the night.

"AH HA!" I said out loud, as I held up the matching tan wedge to the one I already had on my foot.

I checked the time. I was going to be at least five minutes late. I figured I should let someone know that I was still coming. I texted Julia.

> *Hey, I'm about 5–10 mins late. Wait for me outside the theatre please! I would have texted Seth, but I didn't want him to think I was a late person just because I was late this time. Never mind the fact that I actually am a late person...*

> *Huh?*

> *Aren't you going to the movies with us tonight? Seth said Trevor asked you to go.*

I didn't have time to wait on her reply. I kissed my mom bye, and she gave me a smirk and told me to tell her all about it when I got home.

She even threw in a, "You sure you don't want me to come too?" joke, as I ran out the door. The theatre was only about five minutes from my house, so I'd just talk to Julia when I got there.

When I pulled in, I looked down at my phone. The screen said 6:59. I had one minute to get my ticket and find the group. That counted as on time, right? I also saw that Julia had texted me back, but there was no time to check it.

I made a sprint for the door...well, the best attempt I could make wearing six-inch wedges. You can probably imagine what that gallop looked like. Arms flailing, loud clumping of the heels on the pavement, and purse bouncing all around me. I pumped the brakes big time when I saw Seth standing outside waiting for me.

"Oh, Hi! I thought you'd be inside by now." I tried to regain some gracefulness. I flipped my hair out of my face...and my mouth. And smoothed my jacket down where it had gotten ruffled up in between my purse and my arm.

"Uh, yeah, about that. Everyone else bailed. Looks like it's just you and me. Is that weird? Do you still want to see the movie?" He fidgeted his ticket in his fingers.

"Oh. Those losers. Yeah, we're already here. Might as well watch the movie." I was actually pretty proud of how composed, even though slightly out of breath, my answer was. Because on the inside, I was dancing. This was totally going to go down in my book as a date.

Since the wedding, this was the first time Seth and I had hung out, just the two of us. We started walking in, and I reached into my bag to get my phone. I saw Julia's response.

I haven't heard anything about it.

Did everyone really bail, or did Seth just not ask anyone else to go?

Before I could type a response, Seth said, "I already bought your ticket, so we can go ahead and go in." Oh, yeah, this was a date. "Do you want anything to eat or drink?" He was offering to buy my food too. Check, check, and check. This met all date requirements, and I had just clumsily stumbled into it.

"Oh, no, I'm good. I don't want us to miss the movie. Besides, the previews beforehand are the best part." I smiled and stood next to him, while he handed the ticket-booth worker our tickets.

"Hey, man, how you doing today?" Seth made it a point to speak to everyone. He always asked how they were doing. A lot of times people would just nod and not even respond. But he always asked. I liked that about him. There he went again making everyone in the room feel important and seen.

"Are you a back-row sitter?" We had stepped into the theatre room and were standing at the bottom of the steps, deciding where we wanted to sit. We definitely had our pick, as the theater was almost empty.

"Actually, I like the front rows. No one walks in front of you or cares if you talk in the front row." I am that person who talks through movies. I was really hoping Seth could learn to love that about me.

"Whhhhat? The front row? Doesn't that hurt your neck looking up like that?"

"Okay, how about we sit in the middle. It's a good compromise."

"Sounds like a plan. After you." He motioned for me to walk ahead of him.

In my head I just kept thinking, *Please don't fall up these steps. Please don't fa—*

My thoughts were interrupted by Seth tripping up the steps behind me. I turned around quickly to make sure he was all right. Once I saw that he didn't actually hit the ground, I started laughing. Harder than I intended to.

"Shut up." He was laughing too. "I always fall up steps." I was so glad it was him and not me. I picked a seat just slightly off center of the row, and he followed in next to me. He took off his jacket and laid it on the other side of him. I assumed it was to ensure that no one else sat directly next to him. The lights dimmed down, and the previews started.

"Perfect timing," he leaned over and whispered to me.

Ha. You have no idea, I giggled in my head because I had praying for "perfect timing" to tell Seth that I thought we should be together, and my parents approved. Just as we settled in, I saw two more people filter into the room, looking up at the seats and deciding where they wanted to sit. I guess they had the same conversation that Seth and I just had, because they chose the exact same row that we were in.

The closer they got, the more I could see the girl's features. I knew her. Seth knew her. It was one of Seth's distant relatives. Now I wasn't positive, but I was fairly certain that Seth's twin was the last person he wanted finding out about me. I would have bet all the money I had to my name that Seth did not tell his brother he was on an accidental date with the seventeen-year-old keyboard player from church. I also wasn't positive, but fairly certain, that if Seth had told him, he would not have been exactly approving of it.

I turned to Seth and saw a look of sheer panic on his face. He leaned in and whispered, "You think they saw us?" He was tucking his head down low and trying to hide.

"Nah, they didn't wave or anything," I said to try and reassure him, but just as I said the words my phone screen lit up the room with a text from the girl sitting three seats down from us.

Are y'all dating?

Well, they saw us. I tilted my phone screen to show Seth the message. Even though it was dark in the room, I could still see him blushing.

"Just don't respond," he said.

That was not the answer I wanted to hear, but I guess it was better than him telling me to tell her no. I looked at her in the corner of my eye. She was not trying to be as discrete. She stared me down hard with a big grin on her face. I wasn't sure why, but I wanted to sink into the floor. I could see now a million more reasons why this relationship was going to be difficult. Even if I could somehow manage to get Seth to fall in love with me, how was I going to explain myself to the rest of the world? How would I go about this, and it not get weird?

I thought for sure this would scare Seth off. But once the movie began, his embarrassed shell melted away, and he acted like we were the only people in the room. He began cracking jokes through the whole movie. My favorite line was when he put his feet on the chair in front of him and leaned over to me and said, "I feel like I'm giving birth." I laughed much louder than socially acceptable for a movie theatre. Even he had the look of *why did I just say that* all over his face.

Before even considering the undertones of my reply, I said, "Does that line normally work on girls?"

But it didn't even faze him. "No. No it does not." He laughed it off.

I loved how easy being around him was. I couldn't tell you what the movie was about, because we made jokes and talked through the whole thing. It was my favorite movie ever.

At some point, I put my arm on the arm rest, and so did he.

Our arms were touching and that counted as flirting to me. Then, I felt him put his pinky right up next to mine. I could tell he clearly wanted to hold my hand. I had to fight everything in me not to reach for his hand, but I wanted him to come to me. I stayed still. Up until this point, I had made all the effort. I couldn't really tell if he was just too nice to shoot me down, or if he was genuinely enjoying talking to me. But tonight was genuine. He wanted to be around me. And if lightly grazing pinkies was all the courage he had worked up for today, it was enough for me.

The movie ended, and we waited for the other couple to get up and leave before we stood up. I was praying hard that she wouldn't come ask us the dating question face to face. I saw Seth's phone light up with a text from his brother, so I knew she had already spilled the news anyway.

"Did Sterling text you about us being here?" I asked when we got out into the parking lot.

"Yeah." He was looking down. "I'll deal with it later. I had a great time tonight."

We were standing at our cars. I didn't want to leave. "Yeah, me too. I'm glad you talk in movies too."

We both laughed. He opened my door for me to get in my car. "I'll see you at church tomorrow," he said just before he closed my door. I waved goodbye. Before I even pulled off the lot, I got a text.

Thanks for hanging out with me tonight.

I was on cloud nine, and I couldn't wait to tell Julia what had happened. But still, a small part of me had new doubts and questions about how we would face the rest of the world's questions once we really did start dating. But for tonight, I would just enjoy tonight.

I was en route and watching God's promises come to existence right before my eyes, and I still had a hard time fully giving into this hope that Seth and I would actually end up together. When one problem disappeared, it was like my mind could cook up three more to try to process through. God was consistently showing Himself faithful, and I was still afraid my "luck" might run out.

Often times, we have a hard time fully releasing ourselves to hope in God's promises, because we are afraid of disappointment. I know I was. I didn't want to fall in love with Seth, just to have another broken heart like before. It all seemed entirely too good to be true; and honestly, it seemed like it was happening too easily. I caught myself having these thoughts of *you haven't earned it* cross my mind. And although I knew they were not from God, it still wasn't easy to shut them up.

To look at my situation from the world's perceptive, there were far too many obstacles and too few solutions for this to happen. And I was often reminded of that when we saw someone we knew. Or every time someone asked me about Seth, I'd have to bury all my excitement and hope deep down and shrug it off, because if it didn't work out, I didn't want to look like a fool. I only halfway trusted God's promise, even as He was in the process of handing it to me.

Proverbs 13:12 (NIV) states, "Hope deferred makes the heart sick, but a longing fulfilled is a tree of life." That verse was a spot-on description of how I felt when I tried to play out this situation in my head—heart sick. I was growing tired of trying not to get my hopes up.

But then, I was lovingly reminded that this hope I was struggling to hold on to wasn't mine in the first place. I didn't even want Seth until God told me Seth was the one I was going to marry. Seth never even crossed my mind until God opened my eyes to him. But as soon as God placed the promise in my heart, I wanted it more than anything I had ever wanted before. I was truly only wanting what God wanted.

God will never plant a dream in your heart and not see it to completion. Philippians 1:6 (AMP) says, "I am convinced and confident of this very thing, that He who has begun a good work in you will [continue to] perfect and complete it until the day of Christ Jesus." Once I realized that, I saw that my hope wasn't supposed to be in Seth or our relationship. It was always supposed to be in God.

Psalm 42:11 (NIV) states, "Why, my soul, are you downcast? Why so disturbed within me? Put your hope in God, for I will yet praise him, my Savior and my God." I realized I was having a hard time hoping, because my hope had been misplaced. This verse says, "Put your hope in God..." Not in Seth, not in your marriage, not even in your promise. Put your hope in the One who makes the promises, who hold marriages together, the One who so faithfully comes through on His word. Every. Single. Time.

I remember that throughout this process, God kept telling me to *let go*. I got so irritated with that answer, because I had no clue how. I thought if I genuinely let it go, that meant I wouldn't care anymore. I wouldn't care if it happened or if it didn't, because I had "let it go." But that's not at all what God meant. Letting go doesn't mean you don't care anymore. I couldn't help that I cared. In fact, I didn't care until God told me to. Letting go means understanding that God cares about His promise to you, even more than you do. Letting go means trusting that God wants the best for you. Sometimes, we are even willing to settle for second best, but not God. He won't have second best for you. That's how much He cares.

I had to learn that when things didn't go exactly how I expected, it typically meant I was hoping for second best. And God was faithfully saving me for perfection. I had to see that God cared about me more than even I cared about me.

So I redirected my hope from hope in the promise, to hope in the Promiser. He would never fail, never walk off and leave me, never give up, and never ever not come through on His word. And in this new found location for my hope—it blossomed. My hope then became a force to be reckoned with. Every lie the world or the enemy tried to drop into my mind was quickly extinguished by the well-founded momentum of my hope. Hope is a powerful weapon if it's in the right place. It is safe to hope in God. You can fall in 110 percent. You can rest in it. You can relax, knowing God never disappoints. He will always come through. Put your hope in God.

Chapter Twenty-One

Cuantos Años Tienes?

"Hoy es miércoles," said my Spanish teacher.

The class clumsily repeated after her, "Hoy es miércoles."

It means "Today is Wednesday." And Wednesday had swiftly become my favorite day of the week. One, because Wednesdays were dance class days, and I always looked forward to those. And two, we had church on Wednesday nights, which meant I got to see Seth. I had a hard time focusing in class because the only thing on my mind was getting to church.

"Juju... hellllloooo, earth to Juju."

That's what William called me. I wasn't the biggest fan of it, but I never objected. "Do you want to partner up with someone else? It seems like I'm not entertaining enough for you." He waved his hand in front my face to try and snap me out of my daydreaming. Before Seth, I would have been thrilled to be partnered up with William in class. He was cute and witty. I was drawn to witty. But he was also the kind of guy who felt that belittling a girl would make her like him more.

He gave "insultpliments." That was my name for a half insult, half compliment. If I got an answer wrong, he'd say things like, "It's a good thing you're pretty." Meaning, if you're going to be dumb, at least you're attractive. And as much as I hated to admit it, it kind of worked on me. I knew his game. I had seen a dozen other guys do the same thing; but for some reason unbeknownst to me, I did feel like I wanted his approval.

Or at least I did until Seth came along. Now I felt silly for ever caring what William thought of me at all. He was just a high school boy, and I was desperately trying to be more than just a high school girl.

"Oh, sorry. What was the question?" I snapped back my focus onto him. Well, not really him, but his homework book. I didn't want him to question me anymore about Seth. Since our not-so-hidden outing to the movie, somehow some people at school had gotten wind of my twenty-five-year-old movie buddy. William was one of those people.

"Cuantos años tienes?" he repeated the Spanish question.

"Yo tengo diecisiete años." It means "I am seventeen."

William let out a light snicker under his breath.

"What?" I acknowledged his smirk. "Did I say something wrong?" I was pretty good at Spanish, so I didn't think I had made a mistake.

"No, it's just funny," he said quietly. "It's funny that you know you're seventeen, but don't have any problem going on dates with a grown man."

I rolled my eyes. I was really tired of hearing this. "Whatever, William. Can we please stay focused on the homework?" I tried to play it off.

"I just don't get it. For someone who is so strict on not having sex before you're married, you sure are dating a guy who can only want one thing."

This statement was particularly insulting, because it was the reason I gave William for not going on a date with him. He was far too physical for my liking.

I had made up my mind to save myself for marriage, and William constantly made fun of that decision. So much so that I almost believed my virginity was something to be embarrassed about.

"Seth isn't like that. You don't know him or anything about him. And I don't want to have this conversation with you anymore."

William could see he had just pressed the button to irritate me. "No twenty-five-year-old man wants to date a seventeen-year-old high school girl for any other reason than sex. If you think he's different, then you're naïve."

I knew William wouldn't even begin to understand the whole "God told me to marry him in a dream" concept, so there was really no point in trying to justify myself. Nor did I owe William any kind of explanation.

"Are you saying all this to try and protect me from something? Or are you just mad because I wouldn't go on a date with you?"

He wanted to be blunt, so two could play at that game.

"Ohhhh, she went there," Jacob chimed in beside us.

Jacob was my friend, and I could always count on him to either lighten the mood or change the subject. It was one of his redeeming qualities. Jacob wasn't a Christian, but he talked to me about God. He asked questions and listened to me talk about my church functions. He even knew the whole Seth story and didn't once mock me for following God. I didn't understand how someone who didn't believe in God could think that any of this made any sense whatsoever. But he supported the whole idea, and he always came to my rescue when William attacked my dream. It broke my heart knowing he had no idea how much God loved him.

"Shut up, Jacob," William snapped at him quickly. "You shouldn't encourage her. You would think you'd be on my side."

"There is no 'side' to take. My relationships are not up for debate," I leaned in to whisper because we were starting to draw attention from other class members.

"William, you just do you, man. Let her date whoever she wants." Jacob smiled up at me. "I'm happy for you, Jo."

Just as I was about to thank Jacob for defending me once again, our Spanish teacher came to our desks. "If you guys want to argue, just make sure you're doing it in Spanish." She winked at us. That was her very nice way of telling us to stop talking.

We all said together, "Lo siento, Señora."

William may have stopped hassling me, but his words were still swirling around in my mind. Did everyone think the same thing he did? Did everyone think Seth was only talking to me to sleep with me? That train of thought quickly turned into a train wreck of thoughts, and I began to panic a little. I didn't want anyone thinking that about either of us. Seth was so good, and I couldn't stand the thought of anyone thinking of him any differently. But if this is what people were already saying after just one movie, how much worse would it get when we did start dating?

Fear of man. It's probably the most common and pointless fear of them all. If you stopped and counted in a day how many times you didn't do something, or say something, because you were afraid of what another person would say, think, or do, the count would startle you. It's so common, in fact, that we don't even notice it. It's become a part of our daily thought pattern.

This could keep us from doing or saying something we shouldn't, like to a boss, a teacher, or someone in charge, for example. There's nothing wrong with self-control. But what about all the times we didn't tell someone about God, because we were afraid they might think we were crazy? What about all the times God was leading us to do something, and we shut Him down because what "man" would say about it.

Proverbs 29:25 (MSG) stated, "The fear of human opinion disables; trusting in God protects you from that." The fear of what people were going to say about Seth and me was truly disabling. It was disabling my faith. Crippled faith doesn't take you far. I needed to be reminded that only God's opinion of me was of any value, because God will always set the record straight in the end. I was going to have to trust Him to do that.

Galatians 1:10 (NIV) says, "Am I now trying to win the approval of men, or of God? Or am I trying to please men? If I were still trying to please men, I would not be a servant of Christ." In this verse, Paul even goes as far to say that if your rating with men is interfering with your standing with God, you aren't serving Christ properly.

When I read that verse, I realized there was going to be many more "Williams" before this was over, and I needed to be prepared to choose God's opinion of me. Otherwise, man's judgement on God's workings would cripple me.

Hebrews 13:6 (NIV) states, "So we say with confidence, 'The

Lord is my helper; I will not be afraid. What can man do to me?'" There was nothing William could do to stop God's plan. So, I had to stop letting his view of the situation determine my peace. I had to remember that God was the One setting the stage and choreographing all the pieces together. The Lord was doing it. Not man. Not William. Not Seth. And not even me.

When you begin to walk out the plans and purposes God has set for you, there will most likely be opposition. Sometimes, that opposition might even be from people close to you. But keep in mind that God is always right. God is the only One who can see your future and knows the best plan for your life. God even calls us "blessed" when this sort of opposition arises in our lives. According to Matthew 5:11–12 (NIV), "Blessed are you when people insult you, persecute you and falsely say all kinds of evil against you because of me. Rejoice and be glad, because great is your reward in heaven, for in the same way they persecuted the prophets who were before you."

I started viewing this particular brand of mockery as a gift. Because it meant I was edging closer and closer to receiving my promise. I began to relax into the picture God painted of the situation, rather than the one the world was trying to vandalize.

God's word is final. Man's word is fleeting. You pick which one you'll value.

Chapter Twenty-Two

A Tower of Towels

WORK WAS SLAMMED. I WAS THE ONLY ASSISTANT WORKING, AND there were three people at the shampoo bowl who needed to be washed. The tower of towels stacking up the corner needed to be folded. It was starting to look a sculpture, it was so high. I'd basically been working as an assistant in the hair salon where Mom worked since I was tall enough to reach the bowl. By now, I had enough experience to make even hectic days like this one go smoothly. But today, I was struggling.

I couldn't focus. I caught myself just staring off at nothing, with my mind running away to wherever Seth was. I was going over to his house tonight to watch movies. I was super excited, but also unbelievably nervous. There would be no buffer tonight. Julia wouldn't be there to step in if things got awkward, or I blabbed something that even I thought was weird.

Like last week when we all went to eat after church, Trevor said, "These potato skins are odd. It's like they're old or something."

And I, so eloquently blurted out much louder than I intended,

"That's how I like them. Nice and old." I then gave Seth the creepiest half smile to ever cross my face. It was only a half-smile, because I was in the process of debating whether to stick with what I just said and hope my confidence made it funny, or abandon ship and play it off, like I didn't just compare him to an old dried-up potato skin—considering he was only twenty-five.

Or the time Seth and everyone from the worship team came over to the house, and I tried to take a pill with coffee, instead of water, while in mid-conversation. Not only did the coffee seem to burn my lips clear off my face, but it also instantly dissolved the casing of the pill. It all just oozed out of my mouth in one big slime string. There was no covering that one up. Seth was talking right to me. Thankfully, he thought it was hilarious rather than disgusting; but I'm just about positive it didn't earn me any attractive points.

Thinking back on all my mortifying moments made the towel sculpture in the corner a lot harder to attack today. One of the ladies I worked with noticed I was less than focused.

"Jo, what's up with you today? You seem out of it." She wasn't looking at me, but rather the laundry filling the room.

"Oh, nothing. I'm getting to all that now." I pulled a single towel out of the pile and half of it came crashing all over the floor.

My co-worker laughed and bent down to help me. "Uh huh. Nothing," she said sarcastically.

"Okay, so you know how I've been talking to that guy who's quite a bit older than me?"

She grinned wide. "Yyeaahhh..." She loved hearing all the romance gossip. And in a hair salon, there was more than enough to go around.

"Well, I'm going over to his house tonight to watch movies and hang out. But I don't think anyone else will be there, and I'm super nervous."

"Ooohhhh. Because you think he's going to try to," she raised her eyebrows up and down and nudged me with her elbow, "Ya know..."

"Oh, gosh," I could feel my face reddening. "No. No, he's not like that. I'm nervous, because I'm afraid I'll say something awkward. And he'll see how much of a dork I am."

Stella stopped folding the towel she had in her hand. "What do you mean, 'He's not like that?'"

"Umm, I mean, we both disagree with sex outside of marriage. He knows I wear a purity ring, and he's mentioned before how he thinks it's really respectable that I have one. Plus, he hasn't even given me a full complement yet, so I'm not too concerned." I looked down at the slender silver ring with the word *Purity* carved in it. Many a guy from school had commented on it, but never in a supportive way. Virginity was looked at like something to hide and get rid of as soon as you could in high school. I hated that.

Stella looked down at it too. "You mean to tell me, he's okay with you not sleeping with him until you get married?!" Her shock made her tone get louder, and a few of the clients right outside the laundry room turned and looked our way.

"Yeah," I whispered, so she would take the hint to lower her voice as well.

She did not. "No way. No grown man is okay with that. He's just saying what you want to hear. Trust me, all men are like that. They can't help it." That wasn't the first time I'd heard that statement, and I was beginning to get tired of it.

"The man I'm going to marry will be more than just okay with it. He will cherish it. Respect it. Protect it. And if Seth doesn't do that, then he won't be the one I marry. But I think he is. I think he will. I've known him for at least five years now, and if he is just being what he thinks I want him to be, then he has been keeping up this charade for quite some time." I stopped trying to keep my voice down too.

"Listen, Jo," Stella put her hand on my shoulder to try and comfort me, "I know you have this idea in your head of how your husband will be. But your standards are too high. You'll never find someone that good. You need to be more realistic if you don't want to be alone your whole life." As soon as she was done with her sentence, her client's timer went off. Before I could even defend myself, she walked out of the room to go back to work.

It was just as well, because I knew that no matter what I told her, she wasn't going to see things my way. Most people wouldn't. Without factoring God into the equation, it was highly unlikely that waiting for my future husband the way I was, made sense. I knew my standards were high. But they were just the standards that the Bible lays out for a husband to be.

Even though nothing she said changed my mind in the slightest, it still bothered me. I couldn't quite put my finger on why. It shouldn't matter to me what she thinks. I had just been through that battle with William. Maybe it was because I knew there was a whole world out there with the same twisted view on relationships that they had, and I had no clue what to say to help them. There were not enough words to show my side of things.

I guess time will be proof, I thought to myself. I guess my marriage, whenever that comes, will be the evidence that God's way is the right way.

Just like that, God showed me there was more to be done here than simply fulfill a promise to me. In that moment, He showed me that this walk, this journey, could be used to do more than just make me happy. God could use this bringing together of two very unlikely people to show the world, or at least some of it, that His way is the best way. It changed the way I felt about Stella and William and all the other people who couldn't fathom a relationship based in purity.

I think many people don't understand purity in itself. Most of us have been told not to have sex before marriage. Or if you do, don't get caught. But we are rarely told why. I had the luxury of parents who not only understood the "why," but also the know how to instill this character trait in me. I could probably write a whole book solely on purity. There are so many other attributes that stem from purity.

Firstly, purity is a heart issue, not a flesh one. I've talked to girls before who have had sex in the past, and then come to know Christ. They felt like they could be redeemed enough to go to heaven. But they felt they could never be "pure" again. Purity and virginity aren't the same thing. Just as God wipes away all sin with the blood of Jesus, sexual sin is included. 2 Corinthians 5:17 (NIV) states, "Therefore, if anyone is in Christ, he is a new creation; the old has gone, the new has come!" This verse calls us new creations, meaning the sins of old aren't a part of us anymore.

With that being said, you can't just have sex outside of marriage and go on saying, "Oh, well, I'm forgiven. God will make me new every time." That's not how it works either. Romans 6:1–2 (MSG) says, "So what do we do? Keep on sinning so God can keep on forgiving? I should hope not! If we've left the country where sin is sovereign, how can we still live in our old house there?"

Seth is a prime example of my point. Before he got serious about his relationship with the Lord, he had sex with one other person he dated before me. At first, I was afraid this would bother me. I had saved myself for my future husband, and I was expecting a future husband who had done the same. But when he told me he was now choosing to remain abstinent until marriage, I saw a purity in Seth unlike I had ever seen, even in myself.

This is the reason why. According to Song of Solomon 8:4 (NIV), "Daughters of Jerusalem, I charge you: Do no arouse or awaken love until it so desires." This verse warns us not to awaken that desire in you for a sexual relationship because once awakened, it is far harder to resist. 1 Corinthians 7:2 (MSG) states, "It's good for a man to have a wife, and for a woman to have a husband. Sexual drives are strong, but marriage is strong enough to contain them and provide for a balanced and fulfilling sexual life in a world of sexual disorder."

For me, refraining from sex wasn't terribly hard, because I had never experienced it. Seth, on the other hand, had. He had tasted the temptation and still chose to endure the wait. For Seth to say "no sex until marriage" was much harder than it was for me for that very reason. And still, he did. No compromise and no remorse.

You might be wondering why it's important to wait until marriage for sex. It's astounding how many people don't know why. Amongst many reasons, these are the ones that helped me decide it would be worth the wait.

1. In Mark 10:8, the Bible, talking about two married people, says that they become one flesh. You tie yourself to that other person through sex. Whether you want to or not,

whether you mean to or not, whether you never see them again or not, you are tied together. Now, imagine how tangled up you'd be if you slept with multiple people. It creates spiritual knots in you that God never intended for you to have. Sex was originally intended for marriage only. Mark 10:9 (NIV) says, "Therefore what God has joined together, let man not separate." It says *what God put together.* God has a plan for you. He has someone He wants to link you up with—a planned person. And sex is intended to tie you to that person and that person alone.

2. Sex was designed to hold two people together. Because of this unique design, sex clouds the judgement in certain areas. When married, it helps to overlook the flaws in your spouse. But when dating, it clouds the judgement so you can't clearly see a person for all that they are. And maybe if you could see them clearly, it would stop you from marrying that particular person.

3. And this reason, I personally think, will reach you regardless of where your relationship with Christ stands. Think about going into a fancy store with perfumes and candles and all the smelly good items. There is always a "Try Me" sample in front of the product. This sample has no value, no worth. It's thrown away. The product, on the other hand, is valuable. It costs something. Now which one do you want to be? The one that holds value, or the one that is discarded after use. Just being a single whiff of the full package.

You see, I never wanted to be the sample. If a man wanted me, he was going to have to purchase the whole product. What's so glorious about this concept is that God did this for all of us. The Bible says that God paid a high price for you and me. We were bought with a price! We were not merely a sample. So don't treat yourself like one.

1 Corinthians 6:18–20 (MSG) states, "…these bodies that were made for God-given and God-modeled love, for 'becoming one' with another. Or didn't you realize that your body is a sacred place, the place of the Holy Spirit? Don't you see that you can't live however you please, squandering what God paid such a high price for? The physical part of you is not some piece of property belonging to the spiritual part of you. God owns the whole works. So let people see God in and through your body."

Don't just give yourself away. It belittles how infinitely cherished, costly, and treasured you are. And the person that God has designed to love you, will never want to take away your worth. They will only add to it.

Chapter Twenty-Three

The Talk

It had been seven months since Costa Rica. Seth and I spoke every day. We had moments of clarity where I thought surely he had heard God up on that mountain, too, and knew he was supposed to be with me. But neither of us had actually come out and said it. I knew Seth was mostly concerned about what my parents would think. And I also knew if I wanted anything to change, I was going to have to tell him they were all right with it.

Tonight was going to be a prime opportunity. A few of us friends were going over to Seth and Trevor's house for a movie night. If I somehow got a moment alone with Seth tonight, I was going to tell him. Just come out and say it. Sink or swim. And man, was I nervous. While I was trying to apply my mascara, my hands were shaking just enough to mess me up, and I had little black dots all over my eyelids to clean off. I probably took the majority of my eyeshadow off with it. But I didn't have time to redo it—everyone was supposed to meet at their house at six.

I hurried out the door with a swarm of thoughts buzzing in

my head. I was so dazed with all my thoughts that the drive to his house flew by. I knew God wanted me to tell Seth everything I had planned to say, but I was still so hesitant to say it.

I pulled into the driveway, and to my surprise I was the only car there, other than Trevor and Seth's trucks. Once again, our "group" hangout had dwindled down to Seth and me.

"Hey," I greeted Seth as he opened the door to let me in. "Where is everyone?"

"Oh, Trevor ended up having to work from home on some big project, so he isn't watching the movie. It's just you and me tonight. Is that all right with you?" he asked.

Of course it was all right with me, but now that "maybe if I have a free moment" just turned into all the time in the world. If I didn't tell him tonight, I had no excuse.

Seth went into the kitchen to make some popcorn, and I sat fidgeting on the sofa. I tried to act natural and not seem so rigid, but I don't think it was working, because Seth sat the bowl of popcorn down and said, "Are you sure this is okay with you? You seem tense."

Hopefully I was a better communicator than I was an actor.

"Yeah!" The word came out too loud. That wasn't terribly uncommon for me, but it still showcased my nerves. In attempt to redirect his attention, I asked, "What movie are we watching?" I walked over to the DVD collection under the entertainment console.

"You won't find it over there. It's actually on Netflix," he said, as he sat down on the couch in the same spot I was just in.

"Oh," I laughed nervously, "Right. Netflix for the win, I suppose."

I sat down next to him—not too close, but not the other end

of the couch either. He leaned forward to press play on the remote. When he leaned back onto the couch, he put his arm around me. He executed the move so effortlessly and smoothly, like it was business as usual for us.

That is, until he very quickly removed his arm and said, "Is this weird? I'm sorry, that was weird."

"No," I leaned forward and answered him quickly, "It's not weird at all. I love it." I smiled and leaned back onto the couch. Closer this time than before to reassure him that I was on board.

"Don't you think your parents will get mad?" he asked as he wrapped his arm back around my shoulders. Once again, that feeling of "home" swept over me like a wave. He was so familiar, even though we had never been here in this moment before. It was the best déjà vu I'd ever experienced.

"Actually, I've been wanting to talk to you about that. They are totally cool with us being..." I paused because I didn't know how to say what we were, "together."

"Oh." He smiled and looked down. That "together" word caught us both off guard. At least now it was out in the open. "How do you know?"

"Umm, they may have told me."

"Wait, so, they know I like you?"

He said it! He said he liked me! I'm fairly certain that most of the people in our lives knew we liked each other. I found it rather comical that he still thought no one knew.

"No." I answered. "They know I like you." I knew I was blushing, but I didn't try to hide it this time. He said it first, and I had nothing to fear anymore. It was such a relief to say that out loud. I realized that I had just said everything I needed to say in about two painless sentences.

"Oh, so … I guess, I guess that makes this a lot easier," he said and put his arm back around me. He started watching the movie like our whole world didn't just change. This was the moment I had been praying for, and it just so suddenly played out without any disclaimer or warning. It hadn't sunk in.

"Umm, I'm sorry, I wish I could be the kind of person who just sits here and enjoys the moment, but I have to know what you mean by that. What is 'this?'" My hands were fidgeting, and my face was getting hot. I was prepared to fight through the panic to get a clear understanding of where we stood after this conversation. So, I kept talking through the jitters, "Would I sound crazy if I told you I think you're the one I'm supposed to be with?"

I thought my heart was going to explode.

"No, it doesn't sound crazy at all. I think that too," he leaned in and answered. His eyes were locked into mine. I wanted to lean into him, too, but I couldn't move. I felt frozen. "You're sure your parents are cool with this?" He laid his head against the back of the couch and looked up at the ceiling.

"Yes, I'm positive. I've kind of told them everything," I admitted.

"That's so awesome. But there's a lot of other people that probably won't understand."

"Trust me, I know. Maybe we should still keep 'us' under wraps until I turn eighteen." It was only a few months away, we could keep a secret that long.

He grabbed my hand into his and look down at my fingers, analyzing them one by one. He didn't say anything for a while. "You sure you're okay with that? With all this? I don't want to make you uncomfortable."

"Hey," I tilted his face up to look me in the eyes, "I'm sure."

"You really are the greatest, you know that?" He squeezed my hand and grinned.

I fought all instinct to giggle like a middle school girl, but I think a little snicker snuck out.

"I'm really glad you think so."

"You know this means I'm committed to you. I wouldn't even consider this, if I didn't think you were the one. It's going to be difficult at first with everyone. But I know it's going to be worth it."

Worth it. He just used those two words I had encouraged myself with this whole time. The wait had been difficult, and that was instantly in this moment worth it. I knew whatever came next would be worth it too.

"Agreed. I'm glad we're on the same page." I didn't think my face could've smiled any wider. He said everything I'd been praying to hear.

We didn't watch any of the movie that night. I honestly couldn't even tell you what movie it was. We sat in that dimly-lit living room and let out every secret and silenced emotion we had felt since Costa Rica.

No stone was left unturned. It was as if a faucet had been turned on to its strongest pressure, and every drop of unknown was spilled out. I welcomed the airy emotion that replaced the tangled-up heavy one, right before I left his house that night.

He must have felt the same exhale of emotions, because as he was talking to me, the distance between us became smaller and smaller. Until somehow slowly then all at once, he was just inches away from my face. His breathe felt warm on my face.

"I want to take this slow." He barely whispered.

"Yeah, me too. I think we both are committed to doing this the right way." I smiled. His lips were so close to mine. My heart was pounding.

"Then why do I want to kiss you so bad?" He was no longer looking in my eyes but at my lips.

"It's just a little kiss. I don't think that would be so bad." All I had to do was close the paper-thin gap between us. But I was determined to let him chase me. I steadied myself.

"Yeah, well what will you parents think, if they knew I had kissed you?" I could tell everything in him was fighting back and forth to give into me.

"*I* think you should kiss me now."

"Do ya?" He said with a smirk, right before he leaned into me with a sweet gentle kiss. It was perfect. He was perfect. This was all so perfect.

I got in my car and texted Julia.

Seth and I just had 'the talk.'

It was all so surreal, I was almost numb from the suddenness of the change. It was the most beautiful numbing I'd ever experienced. "Thank you, God," I prayed out loud in my car. "You did what You said You'd do. Thank You."

And just like that, my story had a conclusion. Well, at least that chapter did. I had a "suddenly" moment in my life. Those "suddenly" moments are awesome. They are the moments where the promise you've prayed and believed for manifests. They are the big mile markers of your story. But if we aren't careful, we'll live our lives from suddenly to suddenly.

The Bible mentions the concept of seedtime and harvest—many times. This is where you plant a seed in your life. In my case, I planted a seed for my Mr. Man of God when I obeyed God and ended the relationship with Peter. I did this in expectation of a husband harvest. And yes, the planting itself was work. It was not an easy sowing. But the time in between the seed and the harvest, I believe, is the hardest season of farming.

The time season means the waiting season. Waiting is hard. There is a lot of unknown and uncomfortable variables in the waiting season. But this season is also the season of watering. This is the time God takes care of you and instills in you all the nutrients you need to grow and have a healthy harvest. The waiting is essential. The watering is mandatory. This is also the most intimate time with God, if you allow it to be.

The harvest is ultimately the goal, but God has so much to give in the waiting season. Don't live your life only looking for the suddenly and despising the watering. In fact, the majority of your life will be in watering seasons.

If you think about actual farming, there is one season of harvest, and the rest of the year is the spent on the sowing, watering, and waiting. And just like in real life, we don't dig up a plant every week to see if it's growing. Neither should we "dig up" the spiritual seeds we've sown by giving up on believing when things don't happen when, or how we expected them to.

Galatians 6:9 (NIV) says, "Let us not become weary in doing

good, for at the proper time we will reap a harvest if we do not give up."

We both knew there would be challenges with the stigma that accompanied our age-gapped relationship. And there were. It took some family members a minute or two to get used to the idea. They were concerned I would run off wild once I hit college. They were concerned that if we did break-up, the backlash would be detrimental; and I understood their concern. But this was different. This was right. This was God-ordained, and I had let go of caring what other people thought or said about us.

Letting go of those concerns was the best thing I could've done, because after the dust settled on the initial shock of our relationship, everything just worked out. His family was huge, with five other siblings; it was like family I never got to experience. I loved how close they were and how they had let me in on the whole Smith family experience. My parents loved Seth from day one. My dad and Seth had essentially become best friends. And with every passing month of a godly, healthy, and happy relationship, every spiteful word spoken to or against me was being proven wrong.

So many people said my standards were too high. That I would never find a man that could live up to my expectations. That "Mr. Man of God" was a fairytale and a long way off from the reality. That's why I was so proud to call Seth mine. Because he was the closest thing to perfect I'd ever found. He was justice sent straight from God. He was better than I could've dreamed. And every passing day he got better and better.

By this point, we were driving down an old country road, two years into the most blissful relationship I could fathom. The windows were down and the crisp afternoon breeze was dancing across my skin like a Broadway show. The air was heavy, hinting at rain. We were on our way to photoshoot Seth's sister had asked us to do. She was a photographer and wanted some couple shots to use for advertising.

"What are we going to do if it starts raining?" I asked with my hand out of the window feeling the air.

"I don't know, Seth, what are we going to do if it rains?" Erica asked Seth.

"It won't rain. We'll be fine," he answered, as a distant rumble of thunder growled in the background.

"Rain pictures might be cute, right?" I said lightly. "Although, my white dress might not have been the best idea."

Erica laughed. "Well, we can't let Seth's guitar get wet. We will take the pictures with his guitar first."

We pulled up to a beautiful entry way. It was blossoming trees as far as the eye could see lining a long stone road. Wherever the road lead to, I did not know. To the right was small wooden fence, and just beyond it was a pristine sparkling lake.

"This place is beautiful, Erica. How did you find it?" I asked.

She looked at Seth, and then back at me before she answered. "Oh, I've taken some other pictures here."

"Where does that road lead to?" I pointed down the long winding road.

"I'm really not sure. Are you ready? We should probably start before it rains." Thunder clapped again, closer and louder this time. "Seth, how about you have your guitar strapped around you, sit on the ground right next to her. Jordan, you look at Seth." Her camera started clicking a mile a minute.

We took pictures for about five minutes, and Seth said, "Oh, hang on. I want to get a couple pictures with my capo on the guitar."

I laughed. "I don't think anyone is going to even know what that is. I definitely don't think anyone will notice."

"Other musicians will know when they see the pictures. Gotta keep it authentic." Seth said as he ran back to the car to get the capo out of his guitar case. I thought it was odd when he returned without it.

"Ok, this time, Seth stand right behind her and Jordan, look at me and smile." Erica directed us on how to pose.

"What should I do with my hands?" I asked as I held them up at my face awkwardly.

She laughed and said, "How about you just turn and face Seth."

I turned around. Seth wasn't standing behind me like directed to. He was kneeling on one knee. With the guitar on the ground and a ring in his hand. "Hey, pretty girl, will you marry me?"

"... I found him whom my soul loves.
I held on to him and would not let him go ...."
—Song of Solomon 3:4 (AMP)

Epilogue

Living the Ever After

> *"Surely goodness and mercy*
> *shall follow me all the days of my life...."*
> —PSALM 23:6 (ESV)

I'm four years into marriage at this very moment writing this page. There has been goodness and mercy in every single day of it. We have a daughter with her own special calling and her own unique gifts. She's amazing. She has his eyes. Well, she has his everything. The only thing she got from me was attitude. And I'm just fine with that.

I hope she holds onto his everything. Because he really, truly is the closest thing to perfect I've ever seen in a human. I live with him day in and day out. I see all the hidden flaws he only lets out at home. And still, I think he's just as wonderful as that day up on a mountain in Costa Rica. Scratch that—more wonderful. He makes me want to be better.

He was worth all of it. He's worth more than all of it. If you don't remember anything else in this book, *please* remember this: **never be afraid of pain that produces something.**

Leaving Peter was painful. Waiting on God was painful. Being mocked and lied about was painful. The tear-stained pillows, the sleepless nights, the lonely holidays, the somber goodbyes—it was all painful. But all that pain produced something. Something of value.

If you always shy away from painful moments, you will miss meaningful growth. God can always bring purpose to your pain. If there is a decision standing between you and your Mr. Man of God, make it. Even if it hurts. Because the joy that comes after the tears is worth every drop.

I can only imagine what my life would look like if I had done things my own way. I probably would have married a perfectly decent man. He would be good but not great, comfortable but not motivating. I would most likely be dragging him along spiritually, eventually burning myself out. I'd miss out on the majority of my calling because I never had a helpmate, even though I would have a husband. I'd probably be fine but not thriving. And after years of trudging through mediocrity, I would probably end up divorced, never knowing that I had Seth Smith as an option right on the other side of obedience. And that's best-case scenario.

No matter where you're at in life at this precise moment, God wants to meet you here. This book was His invitation to you, asking you to join in on His plans, encouraging you that it'll be worth it in the end. I hope you accept. I hope you follow the Good Shepherd all the way to your Mr. Man of God. I hope you keep following Him after that. I hope you walk abundantly in your calling. I hope you thrive.

But above else, I hope you find that, regardless of who, what, when, and where your Mr. Man of God is, there is the Lover of your soul named Jesus. I hope you fall madly in love with Him.

"I have loved you with an everlasting love;
I have drawn you with unfailing kindness."
—JEREMIAH 31:3(NIV)

About the Author

JORDAN SMITH

JORDAN SMITH IS THE AUTHOR OF A Christian devotional blog, where she encourages others to focus on the goodness of God in the midst of life's messes. She travels around the world doing mission's work and preaching the Gospel. Wife, mother, and enthusiast of love, words, and worship, Jordan is an overthinker made useful by Jesus.

FACEBOOK: facebook.com/JordanWSmithBlog
INSTAGRAM: instagram.com/jwsmith_7816/
TWITTER: twitter.com/JordanWSmith_
WEBSITE: jordansmith.blog

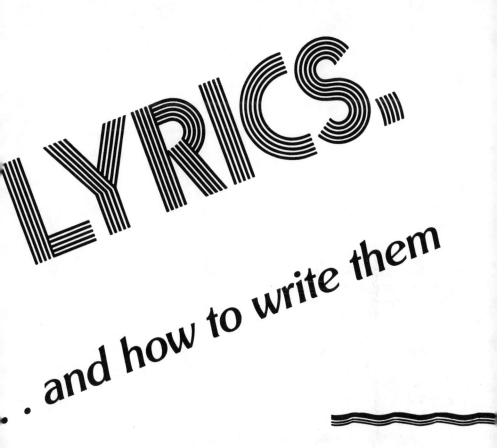

LYRICS...

...and how to write them

Jack Smalley

A FIRESIDE BOOK
Published by Simon & Schuster, Inc.
New York   London   Toronto   Sydney   Tokyo

Designed by Karolina Harris

Manufactured in the United States of America
10 9 8 7 6 5 4 3 2 1
Library of Congress Cataloging in Publication Data
Smalley, Jack.
Lyrics, lyrics, lyrics . . . and how to write them.

1. Music, Popular (Songs, etc.) —Writing and
publishing. I. Title.
MT67.S59   1987   784.5'0028   87-14940
ISBN 0-671-64068-2

● This book would not exist if it were not for the many talented students with whom I've had the pleasure of working through the years.

I am indebted to all of them for showing me what they wanted to know.

To Genève

Contents

Preface

Throughout all the years I've conducted a lyric-writing workshop, I have heard the same complaint: students grumble that their friends all love their songs, but they keep getting rejections from the professional arena. *And they don't know why.*

They don't understand the facts of life:

1. Friends will always like your songs.
2. Professionals are not your friends.

Friends *must* like your song, or the beer may not come out of the refrigerator. Or they may be accused of being disloyal. Professionals, on the other hand, have no loyalties except profit, so they judge a song on its potential as a money-making commodity. You will notice there is no mention of "artistic merit."

There is no formula for writing a successful lyric. If there were, you'd never get to see the professionals in the first place. They'd be churning out the hits themselves.

But there are tools. The successful lyricists, the craftsmen, understand the tools and know how to use them. They recognize the options. They understand what makes a lyric a strong contender in the professional world.

These tools I've categorized as techniques. By setting these techniques out and giving them names, they can be examined, analyzed, discussed, and clarified.

When you understand what you're doing, you'll do it successfully. You'll become a craftsman. You'll *know* when it's done right. And when it's right, you'll sell it!

Introduction

Before starting the actual work, we should clarify several points about a song so that we are on solid ground throughout this book. Let's start by defining terms.

The song itself is the **material.** It exists as a melody with a lyric.

Any performance of the song is a **production.** This production may be provided by a producer, a singer or an orchestra after the song has been accepted as material.

Consider, for example, a song written by Lennon-McCartney. Originally performed by the Beatles, the song may later have been covered by Ray Charles, then, possibly, by the Boston Pops. Each time, there's a different beat, a different singer, a different orchestral accompaniment and a different style.

The song as *material* remains the same. The production of the song may change.

Many of us now own synthesizers, drum machines and the facilities with which to make excellent demos in our homes. Let me remind you that a drum pattern that is programmed into a sequencer is not a song. It is simply a drum pattern. It may accompany a song. And it may in fact help you sell the song. But, again, a song is a melody with a lyric. If the song is sold, a new production of the material may be subsequently recorded.

With all this in mind, we can establish a premise: a song, as material, communicates.

The composer and lyricist have an idea in mind. They convey this message to an audience. If they are successful, the audience understands the message and reacts to it. This message will always be the same no matter what production values have been added.

On the performing side, the lyric becomes a **script** for the production.

Ultimately someone will get up on a stage and perform the material for an audience. Whether the stage is a publisher's office or a concert hall, the end results are the same: the lyricist has written words that a performer will interpret. It is the performer who will ultimately deliver the message to an audience.

And what is the message? What is the idea the lyricist presents to the audience? Obviously, it can be anything the lyricist wants to say. But let's consider an important point about our potential audience: most people are busy with their everyday jobs, the meeting of their obligations and the various stresses they experience as they go through the day. There is little romance there.

Many people, therefore, enjoy what are called *vicarious* experiences. They may watch plays, movies and television to see other facets of life. Vicariously, they may experience romance, danger or the excitement of travel.

People listen to songs to compare their feelings with others or to identify their own feelings. The performer, using the song material, tells about an experience, and the audience reacts by thinking, "I would like to have that experience." The audience lives out the experience with the performer.

We must make sure, therefore, that the message our script conveys is something an audience would like to hear. We must also make sure they understand the message. If we fail in either of these situations, we have an unsuccessful song.

As we realistically understand what a song is and what it does, we are better able to control its creation. We are not sitting out under the apple tree waiting for Erato, the Muse of Poetry, to whisper words in our ears.

We will have moments of inspiration, certainly, but we will better understand which part of the creative process is inspiration, and which part is the hard work of the craft.

The stronger the lyric, the better the song. Granted, an audience doesn't go down the street whistling the words, but when they think of a song, they are reminded of its message. And when the lyric and the melody combine to communicate with an audience, that is a hit song!

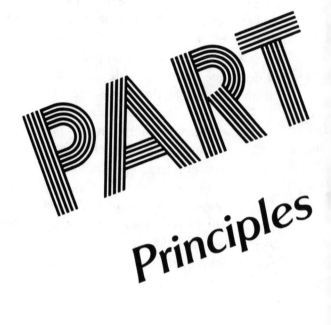

PART

Principles

ONE
of Lyric Shape

Form

Form can best be described as the way a song is laid out. It's what we've come to expect of a song's shape and is important in that it provides parameters for the composer and author as well as for the audience. Form tells us what goes where.

The idea of form undoubtedly started with primitive man. He looked at the universe and was awestruck. It was too big for him to handle. So he examined his own body: two arms, one on each side, two legs, two ears . . . a body in balance . . . form.

How was the first song created? Perhaps this is how it all began:

> Two cavemen, while lounging around the mouth of the cave one rainy afternoon, observed a flash of lightning destroy a tree. This amazed them. Neither of them could accomplish such an astounding feat. They also noticed the lightning came from "Up There." Whoever was "Up There" had some power.

The thing to do, they decided, was to send a message to this person, just to make sure they were all on good terms. The tribe was summoned, as it occurred to our cavemen that a great many voices were needed to be heard "Up There." A chant was started:

DON'T NAIL US WITH LIGHTNING!
DON'T NAIL US WITH LIGHTNING!
DON'T NAIL US WITH LIGHTNING!

As the night wore on, and the group became more emotional, the rise and fall of the chant became hypnotic. The various pitches assigned to the words became set. The first song was born.

The tribe's witch doctor, who had attained this important position because he was perceptive and understood these things, realized a little more information was needed so that the person "Up There" would better understand the message. He added:

WE DON'T WANT TO END UP LIKE THE TREE,
WE DON'T WANT TO BE AFRAID
WHEN WE GO OUT HUNTING,
WHEN WE GO OUT FISHING,
OR WHEN WE'RE JUST GOOFING AROUND.

To which, of course, the tribe responded:

DON'T NAIL US WITH LIGHTNING!
DON'T NAIL US WITH LIGHTNING!
DON'T NAIL US WITH LIGHTNING!

Well, it worked. The tribe didn't get nailed with lightning. And so they came to some very important conclusions:

1. Anything that fell in a cadence, such as the chant, prayer or mantra, should be respected. In particular, a repeated cadence, or chant, seemed to produce magic.
2. The section of the song sung by the witch doctor provided important information. (This became the first VERSE.)
3. The other section of the song, sung by the tribe, is the message. (This became the first CHORUS and the first HOOK.)

To this day the verse provides information about the message, and the chorus is the message. Throughout years of experimenting with form, these two sections have been shuffled about, appearing now here, now there. But no matter where they appear, their function is always the same: *the verse provides information and the chorus is the message.*

Both the verse and the chorus are complete statements within themselves, even though the two are interdependent for the full meaning of the lyric.

The one thing that obviously separates them is the fact that they each have a different metric shape. The melody for the verse will be different from the melody for the chorus.

As lyricists, we must understand form and how it works. This chapter examines the history and development of American song forms. By learning how the parts of songs have been fitted together throughout the years, we can better understand how lyric form works today.

• *Theatrical Form*

For many years the bulk of popular songs were written for the theater—from minstrel shows to Broadway. Although the theatrical form is much different from the forms used in today's music, the various sections—the verse, the chorus, the bridge—function in the same way as they do in more popular forms; they simply appear in different places.

The theatrical form is divided into two main sections, the VERSE and the REFRAIN. Within the refrain are the CHORUSES and sometimes a BRIDGE. As you examine these various sections, you'll discover what each section is and how it functions.

Verse

Since a musical play combines dialogue with song, a device is needed to provide a logical transition from one to the other. The verse provides this transition as it contains information needed to understand the message.

Look at this scene where the hero is about to sing a song to the ingénue—without transitional information:

SHE: Care for tea?
HE: Yes, thank you.
SHE: Sugar?
HE: (sings)

I LOVE YOU,

I LOVE YOU,

I LOVE YOU!

The audience can't be blamed if it laughs at this sudden leap from dialogue to song. The girl simply offers the lad a spot of tea, and suddenly he's down on his knees pouring his heart out. Some more information is needed:

SHE: Care for some tea?
HE: Yes, thank you.
SHE: Sugar?
HE: (sings)

NO SUGAR PLEASE,

TOUCH MY CUP WITH YOUR FINGERS,

I DON'T NEED SUGAR WHEN YOU POUR MY TEA

BECAUSE . . .

As the hero sings the verse, he tells the audience that he feels an intense desire for the girl and is taking advantage of the afternoon teatime to tell her of his consuming passion. After this transitional information, he can sing the chorus:

I LOVE YOU,

I LOVE YOU!

I LOVE YOU!

The musical and metric shape of the verse bears little or no resemblance to the chorus. It's as though they are two different songs. Sometimes, to make the transition smoother, a performer might "talk" the verse as the orchestra plays the melody. This helps the audience understand that the refrain starts when the performer begins to sing.

In 1902, Hughie Canon wrote a song that seemed to exemplify this form of verse and refrain. It was "Bill Bailey Won't You Please Come Home," and is considered a landmark in American popular music. Examine the verse to "Bill Bailey," and see what conclusions can be drawn:

ON ONE SUMMER'S DAY

SUN WAS SHININ' FINE

THE LADY LOVE OF OLD BILL BAILEY

WAS HANGIN' CLOTHES ON THE LINE

IN HER BACKYARD

AND WEEPIN' HARD

SHE MARRIED A B&O BRAKEMAN

THAT TOOK AND THROW'D HER DOWN

BELLERIN' LIKE A PRUNE-FED CALF

WITH A BIG GANG HANGIN' 'ROUND

AND TO THAT CROWD

SHE YELLED OUT LOUD

Quite a few things are happening in this verse:

1. **A setting.** A scene is described in words. The audience can now imagine a place where the story unfolds.
2. **Previous information.** The audience is told what happened just before this scene. This is the transitional information the audience needs so it can accept the premise of the story.

The verse, then, tells *what the song will be about.* Verses in today's songs still fulfill this classic function.

Refrain

The refrain is rarely used in today's form, so the word itself has fallen into disuse. In fact, there are even some disagreements about what the refrain actually is. Consider the refrain to be *everything after the verse,* and to include choruses and bridges.

The refrain contains the message. It may be, "Don't Nail Us With Lightning," or simply the "I Love You" that the hero sings to the young lady pouring tea. Whatever the message is, the refrain contains only the information needed to get this message across.

The audience rarely remembers all the words to the verse of a song, because they recognize it as merely transitional information. However, they will remember the refrain of a song if they recognize the message. Obviously, if the message is worth remembering, the song becomes successful.

Let's look at "Bill Bailey" 's refrain. This refrain contains four choruses, A, B, C, and D. There is no bridge. Notice that each chorus contains only the information needed to get the message across.

A	WON'T YOU COME HOME, BILL BAILEY
	WON'T YOU COME HOME
	SHE MOANS THE WHOLE DAY LONG
B	I'LL DO THE COOKIN', DARLIN'
	I'LL PAY THE RENT
	I KNOW I'VE DONE YOU WRONG
C	'MEMBER THAT RAINY EVENIN'
	I DROVE YOU OUT
	WITH NOTHIN' BUT A FINE-TOOTH COMB
D	I KNOW I'M TO BLAME
	NOW, AIN'T THAT A SHAME
	BILL BAILEY, WON'T YOU PLEASE COME HOME

The verse to "Bill Bailey" seems to be "outside" the actual song. This was the case in most theatrical forms. After the public knew the songs, they could remember the transitional information and the verses became less important.

Usually, after the song was a success, only the refrain was performed.

Even though this book is concerned primarily with the lyrics of a song, it is necessary at this point to make an important observation about the shape of the melody. Obviously this affects the shape of the lyric as well, and it's precisely this musical shape that made "Bill Bailey" such an important song in the development of form.

The chorus A presents a melody, a thematic statement. The chorus B presents a variation on this melody—new notes but in a similar metric shape. C starts the same as A, but varies slightly on the last line, and D is drastically different from the other three.

In outline form, the musical shape of "Bill Bailey" is defined as:

A: 1st musical theme
B: 2nd musical theme
C: 3rd musical theme
   (variation of 1st musical theme)
D: 4th musical theme

Lyrically, the story is presented in much the same form:

A: 1st theme: She wants Bill to come home.
B: 2nd theme: We find out what she's willing to do to clinch the deal.
C: Variation on 1st theme: The focus is back on Bill.
D: Summation: She's willing to cook, pay the rent and even accept all the blame. She repeats her desire for Bill to return.

The form defined by "Bill Bailey" lasted well into the

first decade of the century, reaching its peak in 1910 with a Shelton Brooks song called "Some Of These Days."

Other composers, in the meantime, experimented with the form, making changes they felt improved the breed. In his song "Waiting For the Robert E. Lee," Lewis Muir discovered he could repeat a chorus:

A: 1st musical theme
B: 2nd musical theme
A: 1st musical theme repeated
C: 3rd musical theme

A further variation was provided by Jerome Kern in a 1914 stage show called "The Girl from Utah." The song was "They Didn't Believe Me," and it established the following form:

A: 1st musical theme
B: 2nd musical theme
A: 1st musical theme repeated
A: 1st musical theme repeated

These musical devices worked very well as there was less and less *new* musical material for the audience to remember. If an audience could leave the theater humming the tunes, the composer had a hit.

Finally, in 1927, Kern wrote his masterpiece for a show called "Showboat." The song was "Ol' Man River," and it defined the following form:

A: 1st musical theme
A: 1st musical theme repeated
B: 2nd musical theme
A: 1st musical theme repeated

This form, with its immediate repetition of the A sections, gives the audience two good shots at the main theme before a 2nd theme is presented. This variation, or B section, coming as it does between the main theme sections, is known as the BRIDGE. And the main themes, or A sections, are known as CHORUSES.

Let's examine a complete song in this form to see the various sections at work.

"THE GIRL"

Verse

WHY PRETEND THAT I'M NOT ANNOYED

AT PARTIES WHERE EACH GIRL IS "BOY'D."

PEACHES IN CHAMPAGNE

OYSTERS ON THE SHELL

AN ENDLESS CAROUSEL.

A NOT SO MERRY-GO-ROUND THING,

A DIZZY RIDE, A ONE-TIME FLING

THAT MAKES THIS JESTER PUT AWAY HIS LAUGHS

INTO AN ALBUM OF FADED PHOTOGRAPHS

AND PICTURES SOMETHING NEW

THAT SOMEHOW LOOKS

AMAZINGLY

LIKE YOU.

Refrain

A(1)   IT SUDDENLY

OCCURRED TO ME

THAT THIS MIGHT BE THE CHANCE

FOR A DOWN-TO-EARTH ROMANCE

THIS BOY HAS FIN'LY MET

THE GIRL.

A(2)   IT SEEMS TO ME

THAT SHE COULD BE

THE ONE I'VE WAITED FOR

HOW COULD I IMAGINE MORE?

THIS BOY HAS FIN'LY MET

THE GIRL.

B   COULD IT BE THAT ONCE IN A LIFETIME

THAT GIVES ROMANCE A START?

COULD IT BE THAT HUSBAND-AND-WIFE TIME,

SHOULD I LET GO OF MY HEART?

SAY,

A(3)   MAYBE SHE

WILL CARE FOR ME

AND MAYBE WE WILL BE

JUST THE COUPLE WHO WILL SET

(*)THIS WORLD IN A WHIRL

BECAUSE I'VE FIN'LY MET

THE GIRL.

The Girl: An Analysis

Verse

As an introductory statement, the verse gives quite a bit of transitional information. The audience is introduced to a person who is bored with the round of meaningless social events. He has discovered a new possibility: someone to love—someone with whom he can share his life. This is what the song *will be about.*

Refrain

Chorus A (1)
The singer realizes he is smitten. This is what the song is about—the message.
Chorus A (2)
There is no new information, but a simple solidification of the message. It simply moves the story along.
Bridge B
Here is a new metric shape (to agree with a new melodic shape). A new point is also raised: the possibility that love could lead to marriage. The bridge is able to introduce new information, as long as it is the same message from a new point of view.
Chorus A (3)
A happy ending is proposed. Notice that the chorus only hints at this conclusion—songs never really end. If they did, there would be no reason to hear the song again and again.

Metrically there is a variation at the point of the asterisk (*). A new line has been added to strengthen the ending. Technically, this changes the shape, and the last chorus could be labeled C to indicate its difference from A.

Occasionally, a line or two is added to the ending. The last line may be repeated for emphasis, or a statement may be made that finalizes a lyric. These lines are tags—lines that have been "tagged" onto a song.

A-A-B-A

As songs, and singers, left the theatrical stage to appear in concert situations, the need for verses diminished. The audience knew that the performer was on stage to sing a song and therefore didn't need transitional information.

For this reason, performers frequently ignored the verse during a performance. Eventually, songs not destined to be performed in a theatrical or story setting were simply written without a verse.

The form A-A-B-A became the classic shape of American popular music for many years. There were variations, of course, but the majority of songs conformed to this shape until well into the 1960s.

Since American music is a popular export item, this form became a worldwide standard. Examine, for example, the song "Yesterday" by Lennon-McCartney. Note that this song carefully follows the A-A-B-A form, as does Stevie Wonder's "You Are the Sunshine of My Life."

In the chapter on contemporary forms, I'll show how this shape evolved. But for now, it is important to understand the function of each section of the lyric.

TABLE 1

Verse   Transitional information.
         A setting.
         Previous information necessary to
         understand the lyric statement.

Refrain CHORUS
             A (1): The message.
             A (2): The message extended.
         BRIDGE
             B: The message from a new point
         of view.
         CHORUS
             A (3): Conclusion of the message.
         TAG
             A restatement of the conclusion.
         An extension of last chorus [A (3)]

• *Summary*

In a sense, each section of a song lyric can be thought of as modular. Even though they depend on each other to make lyric sense, each section performs its own function:

The <u>verse</u>, no matter where it's placed, will always provide information.

The <u>chorus</u>, no matter where it's placed, will always be the message.

A <u>bridge</u>, no matter where it's placed, will always provide a different point of view.

You may want to examine the lyrics of some of the earlier authors, such as Lorenz Hart, Cole Porter, Johnny Mercer, Oscar Hammerstein, Irving Berlin, Jerome Kern or Harold Arlen, to see how they each handled the forms.

• *The Blues*

Concurrent with the development of the theatrical type of song was the development of the blues. As a song form, the blues is completely indigenous to the United States and traces its beginnings to the black work chants sung during the dark days of slavery.

The shape is simple: there are no verses or bridges. One shape is repeated as many times as necessary to complete a story.

The individual stanzas consist of two identical lines, then a third line in a different metric shape to conclude the stanza.

"EARLY MORNIN' BLUES"

GOT UP THIS MORNIN,' FEELIN' SO LOW DOWN
GOT UP THIS MORNIN,' FEELIN' SO LOW DOWN
MY BABY LEFT ME, AND RUN OFF TO ANOTHER TOWN.

SHE'S GOT A HEART LIKE A ROCK THROWN IN THE SEA
SHE'S GOT A HEART LIKE A ROCK THROWN IN THE SEA
SHE'S THE KIND OF WOMAN I SHOULD JUST LEAVE BE.

BUT, LAWDY, LAWDY, LAWDY, I LOVE THAT WOMAN SO
BUT, LAWDY, LAWDY, LAWDY, I LOVE THAT WOMAN SO
GONNA LOOK FOR MY WOMAN, BUT I DON'T KNOW
WHERE TO GO.

This shape, repeated without variation, is the entire form of the blues. There are no verse or chorus statements, but simply as many stanzas as are needed to complete the lyric statement.

Musically, each chorus of the blues is exactly twelve measures long. There is also a basic chord progression that defines the blues.

● *Contemporary Form*

Early Rock and Roll

In the mid-fifties and early sixties, a new form developed. Based again on black music, primarily the blues, this form came to be called rock and roll.

In the early development of the form, the sections— such as verses and choruses—fulfilled the same functions as in the theatrical form, but were shuffled around and appeared in new places.

The verse still contained transitional information, but once again became an integral part of the song. The story depended on this transitional information. Therefore, the verses were always performed.

The chorus was still the message, but was shortened to the point that it contained *only* the message. Frequently, in fact, the entire chorus was in a blues format and was simply the title of the song repeated over and over. This repetition made it easy for the audience to remember the message. Since the chorus was so short and sweet, it became known as the "hook." The success of this hook—and the message it contained—defined the success of the song.

To demonstrate this form, let's rewrite "Early Mornin' Blues" as an example of early rock and roll:

"EARLY MORNIN' BLUES"

Chorus

A EARLY MORNING BLUES, REALLY GOT ME DOWN,
EARLY MORNING BLUES, REALLY GOT ME DOWN,
HOW COME YOU LEFT ME, MOVED TO ANOTHER
TOWN?

Verse

B(1) DON'T YOU KNOW YOU WERE MY BABY,
THINGS WERE GOIN' RIGHT.
IF I DIDN'T SEE YOU, BABY,
I COULDN'T LAST THE NIGHT.

B(2) WE WERE DOIN' FINE,
FINE AS WINE.
NOW THE SUN'S COME IN MY WINDOW,
SEES YOU'RE GONE, AND IT WON'T SHINE.

The sections of the lyric in early rock and roll are defined in Table 2:

T A B L E 2

CHORUS
A: The message (hook).

VERSE
B: Transitional information needed to explain the reason for the message.

Motown

In the late sixties the form was redefined by a record/publishing company in Detroit. The new form caught on immediately and became known as the "Motown Sound."

In a basic sense, the new form simply reversed the earlier rock and roll shape. The verse was once again placed *before* the chorus so the transitional information could lead the listener to the hook. The chorus, or message/hook, was still short and sweet and easy to remember. See Table 3.

An important development, in terms of the new form, was the relative seriousness of the lyric. These were no longer simple little bubble-gum statements, but rather a delving into the innermost feelings of the singer. For the first time the words were more than a device to get the singer's mouth open so the melody could come out. The song lyrics were starting to say something important about life.

A version of our "Early Mornin' " lyric in the new Motown shape would work like this:

Verse

A(1)   I KNOW ALL ABOUT PAIN AND HEARTACHE

THEY'RE WITH ME NIGHT AND DAY

I TRY NOT TO LET YOU SEE HOW I FEEL

BUT BABY, THERE'S NO WAY

(Primary statement in which the performer is introduced and tells why the song is being sung: there are negative feelings and heartaches.)

Verse

A(2)   'CAUSE EV'RY TIME YOU WALK OUT THE DOOR

I ALWAYS TRY TO SAY NO;

OH, PLEASE,

DON'T GO!

(Primary statement developed with one new piece of information: the object of the performer's love wants to leave. This is the reason for the painful feelings.)

Chorus

B   EARLY MORNIN' GIRL,

DON'T SAY GOODBYE!

EARLY MORNIN' GIRL,

DON'T SAY GOODBYE!

NO, NO, NO, NO, NO,

DON'T SAY GOODBYE!

(This is the message, the reason for singing the song. The performer is in love with an "early morning girl" and can't stand the thought of her leaving.)

The chorus gives no new information. Any new insights will be given in subsequent verses. But the chorus is the hook.

TABLE 3

VERSE
A: Transitional information needed to explain the reason for the message.

CHORUS
B: The message (hook).

If the song is successful, the audience will remember *two lines* from the entire song:

EARLY MORNIN' GIRL,

DON'T SAY GOODBYE!

These two lines are the total message. The audience, when thinking of these two lines, will be reminded of the information given in the verses, even though they may not remember the lyrics word for word. But, if the hook is successful, they *will* remember the chorus. If the audience cannot get the hook out of their minds, the song is a hit!

In the earlier theatrical forms, a song could be performed without a verse. As I mentioned, the audience knew the performer was on stage to sing songs. The contemporary forms completely depend on the verses. The two lines that make up the chorus of "Early Morning Girl" make little sense without the information given to us in the verse.

Even though they may be shuffled around into various shapes and forms, the continuing function of the verse is to supply information, and of the chorus is to provide the message.

The Motown shape was immensely successful and is now the definitive shape of most of today's music. But the evolution of form is an ongoing thing. Always be on the lookout for form variations. Try your own hand. If you have a hit, you may be the instigator of a new form.

Again, for demonstration purposes, I'll paraphrase "The Girl," and put it in the Motown form to compare the A-A-B-A form with the A-A-B form:

"THE GIRL"

Verse

A (1)   I TASTED LOVE BEFORE

AND IT WAS GOOD;

AS FAR AS IT WENT

IT WAS GOOD TO ME.

BUT I KNEW THERE HAD TO BE MORE.

A (2)   'CAUSE IT WAS NEVER LIKE THIS,

AFTER OUR FIRST KISS

I KNEW WHAT I'D BEEN LOOKING FOR!

Chorus

B   YOU'RE THE GIRL,

YES, YOU'RE THE GIRL,

WO, WO, WO,

YOU'RE THE GIRL.

Referring back to the analysis of the theatrical form of "The Girl," this new version follows the same format:

A(1)

Primary statement in which the performer is introduced and states the reason for singing the song: the performer has been superficially in love before.

A(2)

Primary statement developed with a new piece of information: never before has the singer had this kind of emotional experience.

B

The message. The summation of the lyric in the strongest, most dramatic way. No wasted words, no new information. The audience will remember the statement. They will be hooked.

This constitutes one time through the song. In the older forms this would have been called the refrain. At this point, all subsequent verses simply reinforce the information necessary for understanding the message.

Verse

A (3)   I'VE HAD A LOOK AT LIFE

AND IT WAS GOOD;

AS FAR AS IT WENT

IT WAS GOOD TO ME.

I COULD KNOCK AND OPEN ANY DOOR.

A (4)   BUT NOW THAT I'VE FOUND YOU,

EV'RYTHING IS NEW,

AND I DON'T HAVE TO LOOK ANY MORE

Chorus

B   YOU'RE THE GIRL,

      YES, YOU'RE THE GIRL,

      WO, WO, WO,

      YOU'RE THE GIRL!

The Bridge

As its name implies, a bridge gets us from point to point. In the older, theatrical forms, the bridge was placed between choruses, and looked at the message from a new point of view. It *bridged* the choruses.

The bridge still serves the same function, in the sense of bridging parts of the lyric. But now it's more often at the end of the chorus.

The bridge can take a look at the message from a new point of view and shed new light on it. It can impart information that might not fit well in a verse and also serve as a momentary respite, a "breather," before launching into another verse.

Don't feel you must have a bridge in your lyric. It's a nice addition, and is becoming a reasonably standard addition to today's forms. But if you don't need it, don't feel you have to put one in.

TABLE 4

A: VERSE
Contains only the information needed to tell the audience what the song is about. We meet the performer, and find out why the performer is singing this particular song to us.

B: CHORUS
The message. Frequently the title of the song. Contains no new information, but sums up the information given us in the verse. Designed to hook the audience (they may not remember the verse word for word, but they must remember the chorus).

C: BRIDGE
Supplied when a direct return to a verse doesn't make sense, and further explanation is needed. Provides a smooth transition from chorus back to the next verse.

Summary of Contemporary Form

Some songs are still written in theatrical forms—or in combinations of both forms—but the form set forth in Table #4 is the most common of today's popular music.

• Summary

With the modular concept in mind, you've seen how verses, choruses and bridges have been moved around into many different configurations. Let me remind you there is no hard and fast rule about the placement of each section. The only thing to keep in mind is current taste. What does either the audience or the producers/publishers expect in the way of form? Lyricists competing in the marketplace must make careful decisions about whether to conform or to buck the prevailing forms.

You may want to take a look at some material from the fifties or sixties, particularly songs written or performed by Chuck Berry, the Everly Brothers, the early Beach Boys, Jan and Dean, and Bobby Darrin.

Then for comparison, look at later material such as Motown, or songs by Carole King, Billy Joel, Peter Gabriel, Paul Simon, Cynthia Weill and Barry Mann. Look also at later performers such as Lionel Ritchie, Madonna, Prince and Cyndi Lauper. It might be wise, also, to check out what's happening in country, rap, punk and techno-pop.

Meter

To meter is to supply in a measured or regulated amount.

In any metered situation, we measure something. A speedometer measures how fast a car is traveling, and gas and electric meters measure the amount of energy the home-owner uses.

Metering language is simply measuring it and supplying fixed amounts.

• *Measuring the Lyric*

The syllable is the basic unit part of a word. To measure a line, total the number of syllables used in each word. (That last sentence used a total of eighteen syllables: to mea-sure a line, to-tal the num-ber of syl-la-bles used in each word.)

Prose is not metered and therefore not supplied in measured amounts. When using prose, any sentence may be any length.

Poetry is metered. Each line of poetry contains a fixed number of syllables. Once that amount is decided upon, the poet measures each following line so that it conforms to the chosen meter.

The process of measuring a line is called *scansion*. The purpose of scanning the line is to find the accented syllables. When this is done, a *cadence* appears. A cadence is simply a repeated measured amount, the same number of syllables appearing over and over again. A drill sergeant, for instance, counts a cadence for his marching troops.

The ear responds to a cadence. It recognizes the fact that a cadence is being supplied, and the number of beats that make it up. This recognition is known as *rhythm*.

When scanning the line, simply look for accents or beats that meter the line. This can be tricky, however, because a word by itself seems to have an accent, yet when placed with a group of words the accents may shift.

In a group of words, the first word that contains only one syllable (such as the word "in" that begins this paragraph), is usually not accented. The accented word may not fall until the second or third word in a set of single-syllable words. The first five words in this paragraph would be accented as follows:

in a **GROUP** of **WORDS**

Words that contain more than one syllable usually contain an accent: SYL-la-ble, for instance. Or con-TAIN. If you're in doubt, recite the word or group of words out loud. The accents usually come quite naturally. If there is still some

TABLE 5

Monometer	1 metric foot
Monostich	1 foot per line
Dimeter	2 metric feet
Distich	2 feet per line
Trimeter	3 metric feet
Tristich	3 feet per line
Tetrameter	4 metric feet
Tetrastich	4 feet per line
Pentameter	5 metric feet
Pentastich	5 feet per line
Hexameter	6 metric feet
Hexastich	6 feet per line
Heptameter	7 metric feet
Heptastich	7 feet per line
Octometer	8 metric feet
Octastich	8 feet per line

lingering doubt about the accented part of a word, consult a dictionary. You'll see the word broken into syllables with the strongest syllable accented.

To measure a cadence of lyric, count the number of accents in a representative line. Subsequent lines that fall in similar positions can then be metered to contain the same number of accents as the model line. The first line of this paragraph would be measured thus:

To MEA-sure a CA-dence of LYR-ic, COUNT the NUM-ber of AC-cents in a REP-re-SEN-ta-tive LINE.

Each capitalized syllable represents an accented part of a word or group of words. In lyric poetry these accents are called beats. By counting the accents you can establish that the line has nine beats. For the rest of the lyric, each similarly placed line should contain the same number of beats as the model.

People tap their feet in time to the meter of music or lyric poetry. Since the foot comes down on a beat, the distances between accents, in poetry, are called feet. In the parlance of poetry, the measured line above contains nine feet.

The various measurements of feet per line are named in Table 5.

Although words and groups of words are not accented uniformly, there are certain recurring patterns. By identifying patterns, you'll find the groups of words that make one foot.

A combination, for instance, that is weak-weak-STRONG, as in the example "in a GROUP," is called an anapest. The next grouping, "of WORDS" or "weak-STRONG," is called an iamb. Each grouping represents one foot, even though each foot contains a different number of syllables. Table 6 may help the lyricist in recognizing the various groups that make up a foot of lyric.

T A B L E 6

NAME OF FOOT	SCANSION	EXAMPLE	EXAMPLE SCANNED	PRONOUNCE
Iamb	- /	Delight	de-LIGHT	ta-TUM
Trochee	/ -	Going	GO-ing	TUM-ta
Anapest	- - /	Appertain	Ap-per-TAIN	ta-ta-TUM
Dactyl	/ - -	Merrily	MER-ri-ly	TUM-ta-ta
Spondee	/ /	Headlong	HEAD-LONG	TUM-TUM
Amphi-brach	- / -	Believing	be-LIEV-ing	ta-TUM-ta
Pyrrhic	- -	With a	with a	ta-ta

Examples:

Hel-LO	iambic monostich
Hel-LO my FRIEND	iambic distich
hel-LO my LOVE-ly FRIEND	iambic tristich

HEY there	trochaic monostich
HEY my FRIEND	trochaic distich
HEY my LOVE-ly FRIEND	trochaic tristich

When working with music, whether composing music to an existing lyric, or setting a lyric to an existing song, pay attention to the flow. Music is scanned in exactly the same way as lyrics. When the foot comes down, that is a beat, whether musical or lyrical. Set the beats of lyric to the downbeats of melody, otherwise there won't be a proper marriage.

If there is a problem, change either the melody or the lyric. It's reasonably easy to change the meter of lyric by adding or subtracting a syllable:

SAY you LOVE me	trochaic distich
and SAY you LOVE me NOW	iambic tristich

● *Stanza*

The next measurement is the number of lines it takes to complete a statement. This is known as a stanza. A stanza may contain any number of lines of lyric, but the most common contain three or four lines.

"Bill Bailey" uses three lines per stanza, as does "Early Mornin' Blues." Each stanza contains a completed statement.

The theatrical version of "The Girl," on the other hand, uses stanzas of six lines to complete the statement. The verses of "Early Mornin' Girl" contain four-line stanzas and the chorus has six lines. The A-A-B version of "The Girl" starts with a five-line stanza (A 1), then has a three-line stanza (A 2), and the chorus has a four-line stanza.

The reason for pointing out all the examples is to show that there is no set rule as to the number of lines there must be per stanza.

The various names of measured stanzas are:

> **Couplet: 2-line stanza**
>
> **Tercet: 3-line stanza**
>
> **Quatrain: 4-line stanza**

If more lines are required, we refer to them as doubles. The six-line stanza in "The Girl" is a double tercet.

A special form of a five-line stanza is called a limerick. It usually begins like "There was a young lady from . . ."

In discussing the measurement of feet, I pointed out that each *similarly placed line* should contain the same number of beats. This means the first line of each stanza should contain the same foot measurement. The second should be similarly measured, and so on. For example, the following first lines are all iambic tristichs:

BILL BAILEY

A   won't YOU come HOME bill BAI-ley

B   i'll DO the COOK-in' DAR-lin'

C   'mem-BER that RAIN-y EVE-nin'

The first line of the last stanza (D) breaks the meter and establishes a different cadence. This is purposely done. It signals the start of a final statement. When a cadence is broken, the ear immediately recognizes the difference. Since a cadence can become hypnotic, break the trance by breaking the cadence. This becomes a signal that something new and different is about to happen.

D(1)   **i KNOW i'm to BLAME**

In stanzas A, B and C, each second line contains a different number of feet than the first line. This cadence, too, is broken in stanza D. The second line contains the same number of feet as the first:

D(2)   **now AIN'T that a SHAME**

Each tercet of blues contains another kind of meter. The first two lines, being identical, contain the same number of feet. The last line breaks the cadence and wraps up the statement.

For a comparative evaluation, let's place the first two stanzas of the theatrical version of "The Girl" side by side:

it SUD-den-LY	it SEEMS to ME
oc-CUR'd to ME	that SHE might BE
that THIS might BE	the ONE i've WAI-ted
the CHANCE	FOR
for a DOWN to	how could I i-MA-
EARTH ro-MANCE	gine MORE
this BOY has FI-n'ly	this BOY has FI-n'ly
MET	MET
the GIRL	the GIRL

The cadence is broken in the last stanza (as was pointed out earlier with the presence of the asterisk) by the addition of the extra line. This signals the summation and ending of the song.

Look at the scansion of "Early Mornin' Girl":

> **i know ALL about PAIN and HEART-ache,**
>
> **they're WITH me NIGHT and DAY.**
>
> **i try NOT to LET you SEE how i FEEL,**
>
> **but BA-by THERE'S no WAY.**

A second verse should contain exactly the same scansion, since the melody to the second verse will naturally be exactly the same as the melody to the first verse. The accents shown above fall on the strong beats of the melody.

If you are setting a lyric to an existing melody, it helps to sense the meter of the music in terms of weak/strong relationships. This way, the accents of the lyric will fall on downbeats of the melody.

Conversely, if you are writing a new lyric to which a melody will subsequently be set, being aware of the scansion helps you keep subsequent verses the same, so the melody will work for all verses.

• Summary

The ear responds immediately to any kind of metered or measured cadence. Once any cadence is established, the ear tends to expect a repetition of that cadence.

The lyricist uses a break in cadence to draw attention to a specific section of lyric. This can work against the lyricist, however, if he or she wants to maintain a flow. An audience may stop listening to a lyric as it puzzles out why a cadence is unexpectedly broken.

Scansion is the act of determining the strong and weak beats of a line of lyric. Scanning a model lyric determines the form and structure within the original parameters. This is a tremendous help when setting out subsequent stanzas. To maintain a flow it is necessary to scan all sections to make sure that all similar sections (all verses, for instance) are the same meter.

Most people are able to naturally sense the strong and weak parts of a word or line. However, like any other technique, this can be practiced.

I find myself unconsciously scanning lines in my head. I may recite a sentence I've just heard, or said, in a metric "sing-song" fashion, counting the feet as I go. Through analyzing other authors' lyrics, I notice that successful lyrics do not force the metric matching of individual lines. All the words used add to the meaning and are not included simply to fill out the scansion.

One thing you might want to check out, when analyzing other authors' work, is the number of feet in verses compared with the number of feet in choruses. See which has more—and see if you like what the other authors have done. You will draw some interesting conclusions that may affect your own work!

Rhymes

The technique of rhyming is easy to describe. It's simply the comparison of vowel sounds and the selection of those that are alike.

Consonants have no sound. They are simply ways in which the mouth or throat stops air from coming forth. Only vowels have an actual sound. Therefore, it's only vowels that rhyme.

Spelling has little to do with rhyming. "Ate" and "bait" rhyme. "Cow" and "blow" do not. The first example is called a correct rhyme, and the second, incorrect. The ear recognizes and anticipates correct rhymes.

If an incorrect rhyme is used, the ear recognizes this, and the rhythmic flow is interrupted. The listener may even stop listening to the song while he or she puzzles out the reason for the interruption. Obviously, since the lyricist prefers that the listeners keep listening, incorrect rhymes are poor choices.

• Placement of Rhymes

End Rhymes

The majority of rhymes fall at the end of lines, the last word of a line rhyming with the last word of another. Any lines may be selected to contain rhyming words. The most common fall into the following categories:

COUPLET: Two-line stanza with a rhyme on each line.

YOU WILL FIND THAT ALL OF THE TIME

WORDS AT THE END OF A COUPLET RHYME.

TERCET or TRIPLET: Three lines with a rhyme at the end of each.

THIS IS A LITTLE BIT HARDER TO WRITE

WE MAY HAVE TO SIT UP HALF OF THE NIGHT

FINDING THREE RHYMING WORDS TO RECITE.

QUATRAIN: Four lines, rhymes on every other line.

THE QUATRAIN IS A COMMON FORM

BECAUSE YOU CAN SAY MORE.

THE LINES THAT SEEM TO WANT TO RHYME

ARE SIMPLY TWO AND FOUR.

LIMERICK: Literally named after a town in England where the form was developed. Limericks are frequently used for "bawdy" poetry. For this reason, the form is usually reserved for comedic statements.

> THERE WAS A YOUNG POET FROM LIMERICK
> WHO NOTICED THAT RHYMING WAS QUITE A
> TRICK.
> HE'D SIT UP ALL NIGHT
> TO GET IT JUST RIGHT
> WHILE BURNING BOTH ENDS OF HIS CANDLE-
> WICK.

Internal Rhymes

When a rhyme falls anywhere *within* the lines, it's called an internal rhyme. It is a separate entity, having nothing to do with the end rhyme.

Authors of lyrics designed for the Broadway stage— Lorenz Hart, Cole Porter and Johnny Mercer, to name a few —were master craftsmen, and their lyrics frequently contained internal rhymes.

The problem with an internal rhyme is that it may set up an added cadence of sounds. If the internal rhyme is not made in succeeding stanzas, it may be noticed by the discerning ear.

I don't mean to say they should be avoided. It's just that an over-rhymed lyric can become obvious. The listener becomes too aware of the cleverness of the author, particularly if the message suffers.

> AN INTERNAL RHYME IS A MARVELOUS THING
> WHEN IT WORKS LIKE THIS IN A SONG.
> AN INFERNAL TIME MAY BE HAD BY ALL
> IF THE STATEMENT IT MAKES IS WRONG.

This is true, of course, of any rhyming situation. Never use a rhyme simply for the sake of the rhyme. The message is always more important than the rhyme.

Blank Verse

Many of us have been led to believe there must be a rhyme or there is no lyric. Don't overlook the power of a cadence. A rhythmic line that contains no rhyme is better than a poorly constructed line that contains internal and external rhymes without making sense.

Shakespeare rarely rhymed his lines. He kept to his cadences, and that was enough. There was, of course, the beauty of his language and marvelous imagery. In fact, any unrhymed five-foot iambic verse, like Shakespeare's, is called heroic blank verse.

There are many songs that contain no rhymes. The message, with its development, and the march of cadences are enough. It is better to sacrifice the rhyme when the meaning is clouded, or when a line is so hopelessly bent that it's no longer recognizable as English.

> **TO RHYME OR NOT TO RHYME**
>
> **THAT'S A FAIR QUESTION.**
>
> **WHETHER IT'S BETTER TO SPEAK OF LOVE**
>
> **AND KEEP THE LYRIC SINGING**
>
> **OR REDUCE A LINE TO A TWO-CENT RHYME**
>
> **IF OUR MESSAGE OUT THE WINDOW GOES WINGING.**

The last line of the above sonnet is hopelessly bent out of shape simply for the sake of the rhyme. The correct way to say the line would be, "If our message goes winging out the window."

> AH, TO RHYME OR NOT TO RHYME;
>
> TO SPEAK OF LOVE'S THE QUESTION.
>
> IT'S BETTER TO SPEAK THE SPEECH
>
> THAT CAPTURES A LOVER'S HEART
>
> THAN TO LAY A RHYME ON THE EARS
>
> THAT DAMAGES THE MIND.

Alliteration

We mentioned that only vowels are capable of end or internal rhymes. An alliteration is a form of rhyme in which the beginning sounds of words agree. In this case, the rhyming medium can be either vowels or consonants. This technique, coupled with strong cadences, can produce a rhyming effect:

> WHILE POLISHING POEMS, A POPULAR POET
>
> ELECTED AN ELEGANT STYLE:
>
> HE CAPTURED HIS CADENCES QUITE CAREFULLY
>
> REFUSING THE RICHNESS OF RHYME.

• Rhyme Scheme

The order in which the end rhymes of a lyric occur sets up another kind of cadence. The rhymes fall in measured places, which the ear recognizes and begins to anticipate. The measured placement of end rhymes is called a scheme.

A concise picture of .the rhyme scheme can be established by assigning numbers to the last word in each line. Every time a rhyme sound reappears, it is assigned the same number. The next rhyme is assigned the next number in sequence.

"Bill Bailey" contains rhymes only at the end of the final lines of each stanza, with the exception of the final stanza, where the metric form is changed. The rhyme scheme is as follows:

```
1
2
   3

4
5
   3

6
7
   8

9
9
   8
```

Remember, all similar numbers rhyme with each other. 3 with 3, 8 with 8, and 9 with 9.

The purpose for setting out such a scheme is to orga-
nize the material and see where the rhymes fall. This way the
lyricist can anticipate his needs.

• *Rhyming Dictionary*

The purpose of the rhyming dictionary is not simply to find
rhymes, but to check out *possible* rhymes. Suppose I wish to
rhyme "day." As stated earlier, only vowels can rhyme. The
long sound of "a" is the vowel sound. Working without a
rhyming dictionary, I'd have to try all the consonants I could
think of with the vowel sound "A."

> **bay**
> **bray**
> **bway**
> **chay**
> **(day)**
> **dray** . . .

. . . and so on until a word is suggested. This technique
is time-consuming to say the least. I can't possibly imagine
a word that ends with "chay." I might also overlook double-
syllable words such as away, birthday, bouquet or disobey.

A good rhyming dictionary presents every possible word
that rhymes with the given vowel sound. The lyricist can see
at a glance whether it lists a desirable word. By desirable, of
course, I mean a word that will work with or further the
message. Remember, a line that is bent out of shape or that
contains an outrageous rhyme will stop the listener in his
tracks.

There are several good rhyming dictionaries on the market. An excellent reference work is *The Modern Rhyming Dictionary* by Gene Lees, which has deleted many old and archaic rhymes and added new ones to keep up with contemporary usage.

In a pinch, a list of consonants comes in handy. Table 7 is a complete list of consonants and combinations of consonants. Couple these with vowels to find possible rhyming words.

• Working Procedure

Setting the Rhyme

Flow is one of the most important aspects of the lyric. Never use a word simply because it rhymes with another. Unless the rhyming word carries the statement further, or is in contextual agreement, it is no good and can be an "ear stopper." The rhyming dictionary helps avoid this pitfall. As soon as a rhyme scheme is established, a quick scan of a dictionary presents rhyming options. If no words are found that continue the meaning of the statement, changes must be made. The following procedures should illustrate this point.

A DAZZLING TOWN	1
NEW YORK, NEW YORK	2
I LOVE PORK	2

T A B L E 7

CONSONANT SOUNDS

B   BL   P   PL
    BR   PR
    BW   PW
    CH Q (KW)
C   DR   R   SH   SHR
D   FL   S   SK   SKR
F   FR   SL
            SM
    GL   SN   SPL
G   GR   SP   SPR
    GW
            SQ   STR
    HW   ST
H   SV
        SW   THR
J   TH
      T   TR
    KL   TW
K   KR   VL
        WR
      V
L   W
M   Y   ZH
N   Z   ZL

Easy vowels to sing: *ah, oh, oo*
Hard vowels to sing: *ee, i*

Easy consonants: m, n, l, r
Hard consonants: s, z, ch, sh

It's laughably obvious that the last line has no relationship to the statement. The lyricist may turn to the dictionary,
which yields the following rhymes:

> **cork**
>
> **fork**
>
> **orch.**
>
> **stork**
>
> **torque**
>
> **uncork**
>
> **weeding-fork**

There are three words that may be of possible use:

> **cork: reference to champagne**
>
> **fork: reference to food**
>
> **stork: reference to a nightclub**

The choices are extremely limited, and I know that these
are the *only* choices. That's the advantage of referring to the
rhyming dictionary. Since there are no other rhymes, I may
elect to remove "New York" from the rhyme scheme.

One possibility is to move the phrase and set "New
York" at the end of a *nonrhyming* line:

> **NEW YORK, NEW YORK,**   1
>
> **A DAZZLING TOWN**   2
>
> **_ _ _ _ _ _ _ _ _ _**   2

Now check the dictionary for words that rhyme with "town." It is a good idea to jot down any contextual words on a piece of scratch paper to refer to later.

Another possibility is to place "New York" in an internal position:

A DAZZLING TOWN	1
NEW YORK'S THE PLACE	2
_____	2

Now check the dictionary for words that rhyme with "place." The dictionary immediately presents the lyricist with many options that he or she would not have discovered otherwise. After all the options are exhausted, the lyricist can make the final selection of words for the rhyme scheme.

Utilizing the rhyming dictionary helps the lyricist to avoid poorly constructed or contrived lyrics to achieve a rhyme.

An immediate indication of a poorly constructed lyric is a line that is bent out of shape to ensure a rhyme solely to fit the scheme.

A quick rule of thumb is this: if you wouldn't naturally *say* the line as prose, don't say it as lyric.

Remember, this is the English language. If a line of lyric doesn't flow in terms of language, the audience will stop to puzzle the line out. But the song continues to be performed. When the audience tunes back in, the lyric has passed them by.

Let's work with a line that stops the flow:

TO FLY

COMING THROUGH THE CLOUDS, IT'S I.

The second line of the stanza is twisted to achieve a rhyme scheme. But it's not the normal pattern of speech. The second line would be spoken:

I'm coming through the clouds.

Something must be changed. A quick look at the rhyming dictionary yields the following possible rhymes for "cloud":

crowd

proud

I can set the first line as:

ABOVE THE CROWD

I'M COMING THROUGH A CLOUD

Unfortunately, the line doesn't make much sense. I've also lost the nice feeling of a two-word first line (the iambic monostich), which is short and to the point. Scanning the rhyming dictionary once again, there are the·following possibilities for "fly":

by

eye

high

sky

sky-high

try

Now there are several second-line possibilities:

TO FLY . . .

    AND WAVE TO THE BIRDS PASSING BY
    (too much Peter Pan)

    THE CORNER OF A CLOUD WILL CATCH MY EYE
    (nice alliteration)

    SPINNING THRU' THE SKY, FEELING HIGH
    (internal rhyme)

    I FEEL I OWN THE SKY
    (positive feeling)

    I KNOW I CAN DO IT IF I TRY

    (positive feeling, Peter Pan again)

The important point is that we haven't settled for a poor line. A little research yielded several better ones. Now there is a stockpile to choose from.

Setting the Form

The first stanza of a lyric becomes the working model. The number of lines per stanza is established; the number of feet per line is set; and a rhyme scheme is formed. This sets a pattern for similar stanzas. In the process of analyzing what we *have*, we are able to see what we *need*.

Follow the various steps we might take after that first moment of inspiration.

TO FLY	1
I KNOW I CAN DO IT IF I TRY	1
I'LL WAVE TO THE BIRDS PASSING BY	1

After the first congratulatory glow has worn off (I always feel that way when I actually get something on the page!), check to see how well the lyric flows. There is a jump between the second and third lines. For the moment, reset the stanza as follows:

TO FLY	1
I KNOW I CAN DO IT IF I TRY	1
(DUMMY)	?
AND WAVE TO THE BIRDS PASSING BY	1

The dummy line is used to get the sense of what an added line might do to the stanza. With the proper line, the lyric will flow better. Now experiment with a second stanza to get a sense of flow:

SO HIGH	1
I'D LIKE TO FEEL I OWN A PIECE OF SKY	1
(DUMMY)	?
(DUMMY)	1

One reason for starting the second stanza at this point is to see if it is possible to accomplish the iambic distich of the opening line and still make sense. (Both stanzas open well, so we're on a good track.) The second lines don't match metrically, but that can be adjusted later.

A good word with "flying" is "wings." To develop the first stanza, replace the dummy line:

TO FLY

I KNOW I CAN DO IT IF I TRY

GET MY WINGS

AND WAVE TO THE BIRDS PASSING BY.

At this point set a metric and rhyme scheme as a working model:

Scansion	Rhyme Scheme
iamb	1
iamb anapest iamb iamb	1
anapest	2
iamb anapest anapest	1

Now there is a pattern for adjusting the second line of the second stanza. The line was originally:

i'd LIKE to FEEL i OWN a PIECE of SKY

(iamb) (iamb) (iamb) (iamb) (iamb) = 5 feet

Having set out the scansion pattern, adjust the second line:

i FEEL like i OWN a PIECE of SKY

(iamb) (anapest) (iamb) (iamb) = 4 feet

The lines now match. The second one has been improved in the process, as it is more assertive and implies more strength. The second stanza now starts:

> **SO HIGH**
>
> **I FEEL LIKE I OWN A PIECE OF SKY**
>
> **(DUMMY)**
>
> **(DUMMY)**

Now try to complete the second stanza with a line from the stockpile:

> **SO HIGH**
>
> **I FEEL LIKE I OWN A PIECE OF SKY**
>
> **(DUMMY)**
>
> **AND A CORNER OF A CLOUD WILL CATCH MY EYE.**

The last line is not in metric agreement with its similar line in the first stanza, but for the moment, leave it alone.

At this point, consider a rhyme on number 2 of the rhyme scheme (wings). A glance at the rhyming dictionary produces the following words:

anything	**swing**
bring	**astonishing**
everything	**faltering**
king	**flittering**
sing	**hovering**
string	**spiraling**
thundering	

Since "wings" has a plural ending, none of the words are true rhymes. The most viable choice is "thundering," which seems to work well with clouds:

> SO HIGH
>
> I FEEL LIKE I OWN A PIECE OF SKY.
>
> THUNDERING,
>
> THAT CORNER OF A CLOUD WILL CATCH MY EYE.

The word "thundering," however, is uncomfortable, as it sounds as though the singer is doing the thundering. Since the dictionary yield is poor, it might be better not to make a rhyme with wings. (Notice the last line has been altered, too, to make contextual sense. Until we nail down the stanza, though, there is little reason to make an adjustment on that line.)

What might a person who is flying be apt to do? "Look down" is a possibility:

> LOOKING DOWN
>
> AND A CORNER OF A CLOUD WILL CATCH MY EYE.

This works. It gives a feeling of great height—the idea of looking down at a cloud. The two stanzas can now be set out for comparisons:

> TO FLY
>
> I KNOW I CAN DO IT IF I TRY
>
> GET MY WINGS
>
> AND WAVE TO THE BIRDS PASSING BY.

SO HIGH

I FEEL LIKE I OWN A PIECE OF SKY

LOOKING DOWN

AND A CORNER OF A CLOUD WILL CATCH MY EYE.

Now that the lyric flows well, adjust the last lines of each stanza to put them in metric agreement.

And <u>WAVE</u> to <u>EV'</u> ry <u>BIRD</u> that <u>PAS</u>-ses <u>BY</u>
(5 feet iambic)

A <u>COR</u>-ner <u>OF</u> a <u>CLOUD</u> will <u>CATCH</u> my <u>EYE</u>.
(5 feet iambic)

The stanza pattern is:

Scansion	Metric Feet	Rhyme Scheme
iamb	monostich	1
iamb anapest		1
iamb iamb	tetrastich	
anapest	monostich	2
iamb iamb		1
iamb iamb	tetrastich	

The two stanzas are in complete metric and rhyming agreement. The alliteration has been saved to punctuate the last stanza, which will undoubtedly lead to a chorus. Subsequent verses will be written to fit this pattern.

Any lyric deserves the time and effort to research good rhymes, and after the thought is determined, follow the pattern to establish a proper cadence. The cadence of the lyric is *very* important.

If you work in this manner, you'll discover how you can

be both free and creative. You can move back and forth within the material, jotting down lines, trying them out, not worrying too much about meter until you have to, and making sure you have good rhymes. Set your own procedures. Find your own methods of working. The whole point of this chapter is to show how a good procedure can help you write a successful lyric.

• *Summary*

Rhymes, like metric cadences, contribute to the flow of the lyric. If this flow is interrupted, either by a rhyming word that doesn't make sense, or lack of rhyme at an expected place, the audience may stop listening while it puzzles out this interruption. Meanwhile, of course, the song goes on. When the audience tunes back in, it may be too late for them to understand what has transpired during this lull, and they could lose interest in the song.

Being aware of a rhyme scheme helps to avoid these pitfalls. Plot the position of rhymes within a lyric and then shift the words around so that those that are consistent with the lyric message can be selected or properly placed.

A technique I've practiced, in order to make contextual rhymes (rhymes that make sense with and further the story), is to examine every option by making lists, or stockpiles, of potential rhymes for lines of lyric. I then study each word in my list to see whether its meaning is consistent with the message my lyric conveys. Those that are not consistent, I discard. The bonus is that new lines of lyric occur to me as I check my lists. These, too, are stockpiled.

Since any art, craft or technique should be practiced, you may want to try making up lists of rhyming words. One way to do this is to observe something around you. Then set out one line of lyric about this observation. Don't even ponder the line, just jot it down.

Now, make a list of every possible rhyme you can find for the last word in your line. Make a stockpile of words that develop your observation about the thing, person or activity. If there are no rhyming words that satisfy you, try rewording the line.

After you have a satisfactory list, arrange your words into a story sense. I'm always amazed to see how the bare bones of a message come through with the simple reciting of a list of words.

Of course, the last thing to do is try your hand at a quatrain or two, using your stockpile of words.

The important part of this procedure is to *not* get bogged down. I find that if I think of too many things at once —scansion, meter, rhymes or meaning—I freeze up. I am freer when each part of the process is done without the restrictions of the other parts. Finding rhymes without having to think about meter, for instance, seems to make the job easier.

Once any part of the process—scansion, meter, rhymes or meaning—is finished, you are free to really concentrate on the other parts. This way you can move words or lines about until the lyric feels natural.

PART

Principles o

TWO

Lyric Development

This section deals with the basic presentation and development of *ideas* for a successful lyric. The various chapters describing the methods and techniques within this section are interdependent: one chapter cannot exist without the others. But we'll look at each step along the way separately.

Remember: these are techniques. Ultimately you will write your lyrics without consciously thinking of these various techniques. But if you get a good handle on them now, and fully understand them, they will help you write clear, concise lyrics.

Think of yourself as your own editor. These techniques will help you to understand where and why the lyric went wrong, and how to correct it. But, better than this, as you write, and particularly when you think you've finished a lyric, you'll *know* when it's working.

The Message

• *Plot*

It has been said there are only seven basic plots. We commonly think of a plot as the twists and turns of a story. In fact, the dictionary refers to a plot as the plan of a story.

If, however, there are truly only seven basic plots, they are not just "boy meets girl." A plot must have deeper meanings so we can hang our messages on them.

Let's take a look at the seven basic plot headings:

Love
Hate
Loneliness
Happiness
Sadness
Jealousy
Revenge

It's apparent that the seven basic plots are not stories, per se, but are emotions or states of mind.

The plot of "Bill Bailey" is loneliness. The message, based on this plot, is "She is lonely." The plot of "Early Morning Girl" is pain. The message is, "It hurts me to say good-bye." And so we see that a plot is an emotion or state of mind on which the message is based.

By starting with an emotion, we can build a successful story by making definitive statements about the emotion and carrying these statements to a logical conclusion. We then place actors in a story situation to work out the emotions involved.

Emotions are universal. Everyone has emotions and can identify with—and respond to—a story that is based on an emotional appeal. Without an emotional base, our actors are shadows moving on an empty stage.

The emotional plot with the most universal appeal is love. Everyone would like to experience love. That's why so many song lyrics deal with this plot. There are subheadings under this plot—as with any plot—that deal with "unrequited love" or "puppy love." But the main idea, the plot, would be love.

All successful stories are based on one or more of these seven plots. Some of the headings do not make as successful a song as they do a story, play or movie. So, for our purposes, we can invent a few plot headings of our own.

There was a period during our recent history, for instance, most notably during an unpopular war, when "revolution" was an accepted plot heading. There have been, and will continue to be, many successful "religion" songs. During the high points of the civil rights movements of the sixties, there were successful "uprising " songs that found their way into standard repertoires.

The successful narration, whether story or song lyric, is based on an emotional plot heading for its message. The audience recognizes the emotion, through the message, and responds to it. The successful lyricist recognizes the message and develops it in a lyric statement.

• *Theme*

A theme is the extension of the plot or message into a moralistic kind of statement:

Revenge leads to Guilt
Love leads to Happiness

A theme is indigenous to the story form, whether a play, a book or a movie. The plot is developed into a theme, and the story acts out the development.

Song lyrics don't develop themes. A story, book, movie or play comes to an end. Once we've read it or seen it, the chances are we won't go back to see or read it again. A song doesn't finish. We never know whether Bill Bailey comes home. Therefore, we'll listen to the song again and again. Each time we experience the plot of loneliness and respond to that message. We naturally hope for the best, as she puts out such a convincing story.

The bridge in the theatrical version of "The Girl," adding a new point of view, implies the possibility of marriage. The audience, aware that the plot emotion is love, responds to this message and hopes all will turn out well.

The audience has a vicarious experience through the lyric. They experience the emotion as an ongoing, *now* situation. They know that in reality the song was sung last night, the night before and the night before that, and it will be sung tomorrow night and so on. But at the moment of listening to the song, the audience shares an emotional experience with the singer. A thematic development, such as love leads to marriage, need not take place, because we are actively involved in the love experience as it happens at the moment of performance.

The audience recognize an emotion. And when you paint it larger than life in a lyric, it will touch them. The emotion becomes an important comment. It becomes successful.

• *What Is the Plot?*

This is the first question we should ask ourselves when setting out a lyric. Once we know our plot, every single word in the message must be consistent with that plot. Anything that strays from the plot must be recognized and erased.

Imagine yourself as a photographer. When you hold your lyric "photograph" up to the audience for inspection, they must be able to understand it immediately. So you *focus* on the plot to the exclusion of everything else. And you *enlarge* the plot so it's easily seen.

One of the reasons for thinking in these terms is that in the performance of a song, there is a lot of competition for the listeners' attention. There is the melody, the beat and the charisma of the singer's performance. If a new plot is suddenly introduced, or there are too many subplots, the audience is asked to think of too many things at once. They'll tune out.

• *Ongoing Information*

For practical purposes I must admit that audiences don't lean back in their chairs and say to themselves, "Aha, this song is about loneliness." But the subliminal activity is there. The opening statements spell out the emotional plot in an enlarged way:

WON'T YOU COME HOME, BILL BAILEY . . .

. . . CHANCE FOR A DOWN-TO-EARTH ROMANCE . . .

MY WOMAN'S GOT A HEART LIKE A ROCK CAST IN

THE SEA . . .

I KNOW ALL ABOUT PAIN AND HEARTACHE . . .

TO FLY . . .

In each case, the opening line tells the audience what the song is about. They sense an emotion and are prepared to follow the message.

But remember that the audience is being fed the lyric one line at a time. There is also competition for the audience's attention—the melody, the physical presence of the performer, etc. Perhaps they're dancing to the beat. The mind categorizes experiences and sensations and decides whether it must keep track of them.

We walk into a room. A clock is ticking on the wall. We hear it. Someone then walks into the room and engages us in conversation. The clock is ticking, but we no longer hear it. The mind has categorized the ticking of the clock as on-going information and has filed it away while it responds to the conversation. If the clock suddenly starts barking like a dog, we'll immediately become aware of it and stop listening to the conversation!

Suppose I tell you it's midnight. You immediately assume it's dark. This becomes ongoing information. Then I tell you it's noon in Australia. This is a true fact, but it's conflicting information, because the sun is suddenly shining. We must think of both phenomena as happening at the same time. This is difficult. We don't know on which to concentrate. It's distracting to tell both stories at once, as we are faced with two conflicting pieces of ongoing information.

The thought processes are the same when listening to a song. We sense the plot emotion, categorize it as ongoing information and we file it away, like the ticking of the clock, so we can listen to the complete performance as an entertainment.

If we suddenly receive conflicting information, we become distracted and have to go back to the file cabinet and check out our information. While we do this, we're *not* listening to the song. And since there is no chance to go back— the performer goes on singing—we lose track of the story line, and ultimately lose interest in the song.

As long as every word in the lyric is consistent with the plot, the audience has no trouble accepting the message.

An audience, as a collective body, is not too willing to

think. They are there to be entertained. The entertainment may be a good cry over a sad song, but it's still entertainment. So when we set them up with an opening statement that indicates a certain emotion, they settle back to share the experience. They accept each succeeding line of the lyric as long as it stays on the subject. When they hear conflicting information, they don't know which piece of information to listen to and as a result, simply stop listening.

Unfortunately, the audience may be one person—the prospective buyer of your song. Publishers' and producers' eyes tend to glaze over when the message strays from the plot. And because it's such a subliminal thing, nobody is sure why the song is suddenly boring.

The point is that it's not always easy to tell *when* the song has strayed from the plot. Examine the lyric carefully, and learn to spot the message that strays from the original emotional plot.

For a guideline, rephrase the initial question. Rather than ask, "What is the plot?" ask: "Why is this song being sung?"

If you can reply, "Because I'm in love," or, "I'm in pain," or "I'm lonely," then you know why the song is being sung. You know your plot. You can adhere to the message.

• The Message In Focus

To help my classes recognize plot deviations, I've invented the song, "Fred From Chicago":

> HOLDING YOU CLOSE TO ME
>
> FEELING THE BREATH OF YOUR WORDS ON MY EAR
>
> THERE'S A KNOCK ON THE DOOR,
>
> MY OLD FRIEND, FRED, IS HERE.
>
>
> FRED FROM CHICAGO,
>
> FRED FROM CHICAGO,
>
> YEAH, YEAH, YEAH, IT'S FRED,
>
> FRED FROM CHICAGO.

The message in the first two lines of the verse implies a love plot—you and me, breathing hard, holding each other close.

This message is literally interrupted by the knock on the door! And the message in the chorus simply tells us that Fred comes from Chicago. There is no ongoing information about this! Fred has burst into the song . . . and ruined it.

You can imagine the audience rising en masse and demanding their money back. They were all set to experience a nice love song. Not only did old Fred interrupt *our* love-making, but the audience's as well.

The song doesn't focus on the plot and, therefore, sends two messages. The audience doesn't know which message to respond to. They end up responding to neither.

I made the problem very obvious in "Fred From Chicago," but you will be amazed at how often old Fred sneaks into lyrics. He's always lurking about, impatient to jump in and ruin a song.

Don't let him in. If you're holding someone close and his or her hot breath is burning your eardrums, you don't want anyone around—except the audience who is vicariously enjoying the experience with you.

Let's go back for a moment and look at the lyrics we've been using as examples. The lyric content of "Bill Bailey," for instance, never strays from "loneliness." There is only one thing on that girl's mind: she wants Bill back. That is the focus of the lyric. That is the message.

Suppose she decides, along about the third stanza, to "find me a new B. and O. brakeman," whose name, by the way, is Fred, and he runs the midnight train out of Chicago. The plot would be lost. At that point, the entire thrust of the *new* plot heading would focus on a different emotion or state of mind: Hope.

Imagine the young man who's been smitten by "The Girl," deciding in the bridge that he would rather remain a bachelor. That would give him weekends to go off fishing with his old friend Fred. That would give the audience a chance to demand, "Why did you bother singing the song? You're either in love—or you're not!"

There are no deviations from the plot in any of the song lyric examples we've examined so far. The audience does not have to consider any other circumstances.

Here's a motto. Write it in capital letters, and pin it to the wall above your desk:

ONE PLOT = ONE SONG

● *Summary*

The message sent to an audience through the song lyric can be boiled down to one or two words that indicate an emotion or state of mind.

At the beginning of this chapter, I listed the seven basic plots. Practically all works of fiction or prose send these messages to the audience.

Lyric writers utilize this idea as the departure point or underlying meaning of their lyrics. The trick is to recognize what the message is.

Lyricists may have to add words to the list of basic emotions to modify the message they want to send. They may, for instance, write a lyric about "hopeful love," or "foolish love," or about loneliness that can run the gamut from "hopeless" to "suicidal." They might have to invent new states of mind that adequately describe the message.

After they've recognized the message, though, they must stick to it. And the way to recognize the message is to ask the question, "Why is this song being sung?"

It's good practice to analyze other songs. Try to figure out what the messages are in other material.

Another way to practice—and to garner material for future song lyrics—is to observe life around you, and make up plot headings describing what you see.

For instance, look at the people around you in the checkout line at the market. Pay particular attention to what they're buying. That young man, who's bought a frozen dinner, is obviously lonely. Is he hopeful, hopeless or suicidal? Can you think of a song title to describe this plot heading?

Or that young couple buying bags and bags of chips, dips, and six packs of beer. What kind of a party is it going to be? Would you like to attend? Why?

Besides being great practice, this tunes you in to life around you. As a lyric writer, you must be aware of life's vicissitudes before you can send any viable messages about it.

• The Message: Working Procedure

Operative Words

A definition for "operative" is "functional." An operative word is a working word—a word that causes an immediate reaction in the listener's mind.

The operative word can be a verb, noun or adjective. It's a word or phrase that creates the necessary ambience for the continuity of the lyric.

When we set out the operative words of a lyric, we begin to recognize the plot. This provides a method of recognizing compatibility—a way of seeing whether the lyric is staying within the boundaries of the plot.

The operative words in "Fred From Chicago" are:

Holding . . . close
Feeling . . . breath
Knock . . . door

There is a sense of motion from "holding" to "feeling," which stops abruptly at "knock," the point at which the lyric goes astray. If, for instance, the lyric would move from "feeling" to "touching," then there would be a compatible flow. And old Fred would disappear.

Here are the operative words from "Early Mornin' Girl":

Pain
Heartache
With me
Try not
No way

Walk
No
Don't go

Notice how each word or phrase sets a thought in motion—a thought that moves the plot along.

Let's insert an incompatible word or phrase in the above list to observe the result:

Pain
Smile
Heartache
With me
New York
No way
Suzie
Walk
Run

Notice how each time an incompatible operative word is inserted, the plot turns in a new direction. In each case we literally have a new song:

(I'm in) PAIN
(But I'm) SMILING

The emotion is no longer pain but hope. The entire emphasis changes, and we must follow this plot to its logical conclusion.

HEARTACHE
(go) WITH ME
(to) NEW YORK

This had better be explained! There must be an extremely logical reason for suddenly appearing in New York. Not only has a setting been introduced (which will be covered in a following chapter), but it wouldn't surprise me if old Fred had moved out of Chicago!

NO WAY
SUZIE

A new character is introduced to the audience, who thought all along that we were singing to them as surrogate loved ones. Suzie is Fred in drag.

WALK
RUN

We frequently find words that have automatic couplings, such as walk and run. These are "clichés," phrases that create immediate reactions. In the proper usage they work great. The use of clichés is covered in a later chapter.

Lyric Development

Operative words are of the utmost importance. In the first place, they help to pinpoint the plot. As we go on, we'll see how they help us in every area of the message.

You may find, as I frequently do, that the plot doesn't come immediately to mind. I never sit down at my desk, determined to write a lyric about a Lost Puppy Love. Usually, I simply have an idea for a lyric, and set it out:

SITTING IN MY ROOM

STARING AT THE PATTERNS ON THE WALLS

SILENT TELEPHONE

WOND'RING WHY NOBODY EVER CALLS.

So far, I'm not doing any conscious examining. I've simply started some nice lines on the page. I like them, so I continue:

SO I'LL GO ON DOWN TO THE BAR

HAVE A LITTLE BEER WITH SOME FRIENDS . . .

. . . and I suddenly wonder where the inspiration went. For some reason, I'm unable to continue the lyric. I go out to the old apple tree and wait for that mysterious voice to whisper the next lines in my ear, but it remains silent.

The moment has come to do some serious work. I begin by setting out the operative words:

Sitting
Staring
Silent
Wondering

I begin to see a flow from word to word. The sense I have is of *loneliness*. There's a chance that this is the plot for my message.

The operative words in the next stanza are:

Go
Friends

These two words have nothing to do with loneliness. "Go," for instance, is the opposite of "sitting." "Friends" are not "silent." The flow has been interrupted.

As soon as I move out of the room and into a social situation, I am no longer lonely.

From an audience point of view, the move from the room to the bar constitutes new information. They have to stop and reconsider the whole lyric.

In real life, of course, the story might be consistent. I'm sitting in my room, I feel lonely, so I go out and down a few with my old friend Fred who just blew in from Chicago.

But not in a song lyric. Why is this song being sung? Because I'm lonely—right now, at this moment—and I want to share the experience with you, my audience.

As soon as I realize, by setting out my operative words, that I'm writing about loneliness, I can go on with the lyric. I go into that room. I put myself in the situation so I can feel the emotion I'm writing about.

I look at the walls. Stare out the window. What do I see? Can I describe it lyrically to heighten the imagery of loneliness? I start a new list:

A deserted street
A naked light bulb hanging from the ceiling
Dust in the corners
Upholstery torn
Television set

I've got to be careful, when adding to my list, that I remain consistent with loneliness. That television set might provide me with entertainment and relieve my loneliness—unless it wants quarters and I'm fresh out.

Setting up a list like this stimulates new ideas. I begin to actually live in that room. For instance, the idea of quarters for the television makes me think of the "Magic Finger Massage" one finds in hotel beds. Anything there?

As I get back to my lyric, I find that I use only one or two lines from my stockpile. But I'm in control of my plot. I'm able to communicate the sense of loneliness to my audience.

It might be tempting, as another direction, to wonder, "Why am I so lonely?" One logical reason could be the absence of a loved one. And so, after "wondering why no one calls," I might start:

WOND'RING WHERE YOU ARE
REMEMB'RING HOW YOU LOOK
THE WAY YOUR HAIR TOUCHES YOUR CHEEK

. . . and I'm in trouble again. No loneliness there. Once again I set out my operative words:

wondering
remembering
look
hair
touches
cheek

The first three words can work because they're compatible with loneliness. The flow stops at "touches," and I sense I'm into a new plot: Love.

The two plots, Loneliness and Love, could be compatible. Loneliness seems to be defined as and intertwined with "Love, absence of." The problem here is that I've changed my focus.

The solution to the problem is to keep focused on the subject at hand. Instead of going on with a lengthy description of the loved one, I get back in that room:

> SITTING IN MY ROOM
>
> STARING AT THE PATTERN ON THE WALL
>
> SILENT TELEPHONE
>
> WOND'RING WHY *YOU* NEVER CALL

The audience now has a piece of information that is compatible with the rest of the ongoing information. I can now speak of my loved one in the past tense, as I remain in my lonely room.

> WOND'RING WHERE YOU ARE
>
> REMEMB'RING HOW YOU LOOK
>
> THE WAY YOUR HAIR *TOUCHED* MY CHEEK
>
> WHEN I . . .

The focus has returned to *my* loneliness. The ongoing information is compatible. The audience will accept the lyric.

• *Summary of The Message*

WHY IS THE SONG BEING SUNG?
> Know your plot.
> Focus on the plot by using compatible operative words.
> Keep aware of ongoing information.

AVOID:
> Secondary plot.
> New information that conflicts with ongoing information.
> More than one message.

FORM:
> The VERSE tells what the song will be about.
> The CHORUS tells us what the song *is* about.

REMEMBER:
> ONE PLOT = ONE SONG

This last chapter about the message is one of the most important in this book. That's why I've set out a summation in outline form.

You might want to keep this outline handy when working on lyrics. More important, you might be able to *add* to the outline. I'm sure you'll discover more and more of your own techniques as you work.

What always amazes me about my own work habits is how quickly I forget my techniques when I'm in the throes of trying to solve a tricky lyric problem. That's when I look back at my own reminders of what to do.

Don't forget the lists! As you begin to understand your plot and the message you want to send, start jotting down any words you can think of suggested by the plot. This is similar to the psychologists' technique of free word association.

After culling out the inconsistent words, rearrange the words into a sequential order. This could be the bare bones of your lyric.

For the time being, work without the restrictions set by meter, scansion and rhyme. Come up with ideas.

Sometimes, if you don't have any ideas for a lyric (I don't know how many of you are able to sit down at your desk and immediately start writing!), try thinking of a single word. Then jot down the next word that the first word suggests. As you increase the list, start looking for messages or plot headings. You'll be astounded at how often this technique leads to a successful lyric.

Finally, try to have some plot headings tucked away from your observations at the market or from a social gathering. (My wife sometimes has to nudge me with the admonition, "You're staring at those people, again!")

The most important thing is to always *practice* being a lyric writer!

Story Points

The plot must happen to someone. The actors need a vehicle to act out their emotions. Who these actors are, how they behave, the actions they take and the reactions they have are the *story points.*

Within the framework of a song, there are several built-in factors. First, there is a singer, and there is the audience's acceptance that the story has happened, or better, *is* happening to this performer. The singer, then, becomes our actor. He or she is *actively* involved in the story.

Second, there is the *suspension of belief.* This term means an audience is willing to forego reality and pretend that something is happening that is not actually happening.

The singer, for instance, might seem to be singing to someone. The words to the song are, possibly, "I love you."

In a reality situation, the audience might be tempted to look around the room for the object of the performer's love. Who is this delightful creature?

When the audience suspends their belief, they pretend this love object is there. Frequently, in fact, the audience becomes the *surrogate* loved ones. They feel the singer is singing to them.

The next phenomenon with a song lyric is that the audience seems to be privy to *secret information*. In the theater, the audience receives secret information as an "aside." An actor removes himself from the ongoing action and literally tells the audience some important piece of information.

Remember the old melodramas where the mustachioed villain cries, "Aha, me proud beauty." In a loud stage whisper, and smoothing his mustache, he tells the audience the vile and despicable plans he has for the proud beauty and her handsome hero.

This is still present in today's wrestling matches. Notice how the "villain" delivers punishment to the "hero" in a way that the referee can't observe the awful deed. But everyone makes sure that the audience sees this dreadful piece of villainy. It's a way of making sure the audience knows which side to root for.

In a song lyric, much of the content is in the nature of an aside. The audience feels they are listening to the singer's actual thoughts. In reality, this is impossible. But when the audience suspends belief, they accept this possibility without hesitation. The singer, as an aside, recites an appraisal of a situation. The audience hears the thoughts and shares the reaction.

Why? Because the song works on an *emotional level*.

Let's look at this from another point of view. Suppose I were to tell a story. As I start—"Once upon a time there was a beautiful girl named Snow White . . . "—the audience gets caught up in the *story points*. "What happened next? Where did she go? What did she do?"

What the audience doesn't realize is that buried within this lovely story is a plot—Love—and a theme—Love Conquers Evil. At the end of the story, remember, the handsome prince comes and kisses Snow White, awakening her from a deathlike sleep. They presumably live Happily Ever After. When telling a story, the plot and theme are buried within the activity of the story. The entire package, or message, is delivered painlessly as the audience follows the twists and turns of the story points. They learn something about life and themselves as they digest the story into a blurry realization that, yes, Love does Conquer Evil.

Snow White, of course, is a tale—an actual story. It has a beginning, middle and end. Nearly everyone has read it, seen it as a Walt Disney movie and possibly told it as a bedtime story. Each time it is a finished experience because the story comes to a conclusion.

A song lyric, on the other hand, doesn't state the theme as broadly or obviously as a story. Nor does it come to a conclusion. The audience senses the song lyric as an experience happening to the performer *at the moment of performance.* How could anyone know how the story is going to turn out? Obviously, there is hope that there will be satisfactory conclusions to the lyric message. But, just in case, the audience is willing to listen to the song *as many times as the performer is willing to perform it.* Since the performance is usually recorded, there is ample opportunity to listen to it.

If I tell you a "real life" story, such as, "I'm in Love!," it is in bad taste to ask, "What happened next? Where did you go? What did you do?" You instead ask, "Who is she?" Or make congratulatory remarks like, "Gee, that's wonderful." You become involved with my emotion to the degree that you share my pleasure.

In a song lyric, *the plot is the message.*

The manner in which the lyric delivers this message to the audience is the *story points.* The difference is this: if I tell you a story, you become involved with *third persons.* You understand my message to the degree that you get involved with what happens to Snow White.

In a song lyric, you worry about what is happening to the *singer.* You become involved in how the singer feels. Why? Because on an emotional level, whatever is happening to the singer is happening to the audience.

• *Laundry List*

This device, the opposite of a story, is used in many lyrics. I mention it here to make a comparison with what constitutes a story.

There is motion, either actual or implied, in a story lyric. Something is happening, either to the singer or to the person the performer is singing about.

The laundry list, on the other hand, simply recounts, point by point, the pertinent facts about the message. There is no action, and nothing is "happening," other than the recounting of the list.

Laundry lists recount things or reasons or ideas, or whatever the lyricist wants to add. I could list the reasons I love you, for instance:

> **. . . you're the promised breath of springtime**
> **. . . you like New York in June**
> **. . . you're three times a lady**

There is no action, and nothing is happening other than the reeling off of the list.

• *Working Procedure*

Let's break this down to a procedure by once again changing our operative words. As we do this, we'll sense stories developing:

"EARLY MORNIN' GIRL"
1. **Pain**
   Heartache
   with *ME*

The operative word "me" starts a story. The performer is experiencing the emotion. We now have an actor onstage to work out the plot.

By changing the operative word, we can see how the story might change:

2. **Pain**
   Heartache
   with *YOU*

The roles of performer and audience have been exchanged. Nothing is happening to the performer, except to notice a problem the audience is having. The performer now proceeds to give the audience some "advice." This is a new message.

3. **Pain**
   Heartache
   with *HER*

A new actor is introduced. Everything now happens to a third person. This shift of emphasis dilutes the message by destroying the relationship between the performer and audience. The singer keeps pointing "offstage" while asking the audience to consider something that is happening "off there."

The song might have to describe this third person, which wastes time. There have to be reasons how and why the performer knows this person's problems. This is not to say that it can't be done, but it is a difficult lyric when the audience is constantly paying attention to inconsequential story points in order to understand the plot.

There is a very important distinction between plot and story point:

> **Plot** (emotion) is the basic premise of the lyric.
>
> **Story point** is the framework in which the actors act out the plot. In selecting the actors and grading the three possibilities, we can draw these conclusions:
>
> **First Person:** Strongest in terms of dramatic statement. The singer has opportunity to perform and is the active participant. The audience relates to the singer as being actively involved in the story.
>
> **Second Person:** Weaker. The audience is now the active participant, while the singer is relatively passive. The singer's position is compromised and he or she must tell the audience what to experience. The singer is no longer the actor, but the director.
>
> **Third Person:** Weakest. Neither the singer nor the audience are active participants. Attention

is shifted "offstage." Distracting story points may emerge, as the audience is asked to consider the singer's involvement (onstage) with another personality (offstage). The offstage personality is the *active* participant. (A solution to this problem is discussed in Section 3, Narrative Form.)

● *Summary*

"Telling the story" is the process of creating actors and actresses who send the messages to an audience.

These people may be active participants in a story or the observers of a situation or story.

It's important to decide which of these actors or actresses is singing the song: me, you, he, she, we or they. A love song, for instance, is probably strongest when sung by "me"—about "you" and "me." As an observer, though, I sing about he, she or them.

Even though the story requires from an audience a suspension of belief, it must still be believable.

There may be secret information the audience requires in order to understand the message.

Unlike a movie, book or television show, the audience is more involved in an emotion or a state of mind. It's difficult, in a song lyric, to get too involved in a convoluted story.

AND: the story never ends.

One of the most important experiments to perform on a song lyric is to change the pronouns. Don't lock into who the storyteller is until you've tried several different people.

A nice way to practice this is to take one of your lists of

words from previous chapters and decide who is the best person to flesh out the story. Or, you might try inventing a little story and telling it from everyone's point of view. You'll discover some new insights by trying this.

Finally, one of my favorite games is to write a quatrain that places my actor or actress in a story in which they can act out the message. The rule is: don't use the actual plot word. "He," for instance, must tell "her" how he feels about her without using the word "love"!

The Setting

The setting is where the story takes place. It can be concrete or abstract, but it's always there. Everything happens somewhere.

In the list of operative words I introduced "New York." This gave the lyric a *concrete* setting. I directed the audience's attention to a specific place.

In an *abstract* sense, the setting for "The Girl" is within the performer's mind. The singer asks himself questions, and the audience is in on this secret information.

Frequently a setting can be very subtle. Consider the title (and opening line) to Stevie Wonder's song "Isn't She Lovely?" An important setting has been made. There are three people involved:

1. The performer, who is asking the questions. Wisely, this device keeps the focus on the singer as the active participant. The questions arise from the singer.
2. The audience, who hears the questions. They are being asked to consider the points the singer makes and are, therefore, active.

3. "She." Nonactive and offstage. She is in a non-specific somewhere. The audience, by respond-ing to the singer's questions, "creates" this offstage person. Mr. Wonder has formed a tri-angular setting to act out the message.

The preponderance of settings are in the abstract. That is, within the performer's mind. This setting enables the per-former to be the active participant.

Let's examine what happens when a concrete setting is made. An example is my room in the previous chapter, where I acted out the story points of loneliness.

The stages in Elizabethan theaters were bare. Physical scenery changes were impossible. As a result, William Shakespeare was forced to set scenery through dialogue.

Likewise, in the days of dramatic radio, the scene was set with dialogue. Sound effects could be added, and fre-quently music helped define a mood. The point is that a few well-chosen words can set a scene. But don't set a scene unless it's absolutely important.

To illustrate this point, imagine a television program in which the camera shows a dark, shadowy basement. A few cobwebs here and there, light barely filtering in through dusty windows, our expectations are that something mysterious is lurking in the shadows.

Now the scene shifts to a sunny meadow. We see two lovers sharing a picnic lunch. We expect there to be a rela-tionship between the basement and the two lovers. Some-thing is going to come out of that room and GET THEM!

Now, suppose that for the remainder of the story we *never see the basement again.* Nothing crawls out of the mildew. We keep waiting, but NOTHING HAPPENS.

We were given a piece of information—which we

picked up as *ongoing* information—that went nowhere. The basement had nothing to do with the story. When this happens, we are disappointed. We wonder why they bothered to show us the basement in the first place.

In the same way, a sudden shift to a *new* setting without a reason can be distracting, particularly if it conflicts with previous information. There must be a reason for *any* setting. And then if we jump to a new setting, there must be a logical reason for the switch.

Examine your settings carefully. Be sure you know where you are—and why. An audience will accept anything as long as it seems logical. Once established, though, the setting must be maintained.

● *Imagery*

Imagery is made up of nouns—the thing or things we are asked to imagine. The use of imagery is important to a setting because it calls up certain responses that help set a specific scene. This helps to establish a setting when the proper "things" are placed in it.

The observable things in my lonely room were each an example of imagery. Time is expressed through imagery. Rather than say "yesterday" or "tomorrow," we can call upon images of Model T Fords or spaceships to the moon, or Victrolas and stereos to reveal when the story takes place.

Compatible imagery can enhance a concrete setting— the cobwebs in the basement, for instance, or a silent telephone in the lonely room.

It is important to remember, though, that your New York may not be "dazzling" like mine. Or my Bakersfield may not be the same as yours. Be sure to use universal images, so that everyone immediately understands the setting. Use good imagery to take the audience where you want them.

• Working Procedure

Let's set out a hypothetical lyric. We'll create some problems and find ways to resolve them.

> SITTING IN THE BACK OF THE BUS
>
> WATCHING TELEPHONE POLES GO BY
>
> THINKING ABOUT MY LADY
>
>
> SITTING IN A SMALL CAFÉ
>
> MUSIC PLAYING SOFT AND LOW
>
> HOLDING HANDS WITH MY LADY
>
>
> SHE'S EV'RY INCH A WOMAN
>
> LIVING EV'RY MINUTE FOR ME
>
> SHE'S MY LADY
>
> SHE'S MY LADY

Operative words give us clues to the problems:

Sitting: bus	**(concrete setting)**
Watching: poles	**(plot = lonely)**
Thinking: lady	**(offstage person)**
Sitting: cafe	**(new concrete setting)**
Music: soft, low	**(new plot: seduction)**
Holding: hands	**(onstage person)**
She's: woman	**(offstage person)**
She's: mine	**(new plot: successful love)**

In terms of scene settings, we've visited three places:

1. The bus.
   The audience joins us on the bus. We are alone —counting telephone poles instead of talking to someone. This is ongoing information.
2. The café.
   The audience must leave the bus and join us at the café. We are not alone: the loved one is there too. Conflicting information.
3. Offstage.
   The loved one has actually been in two different places: offstage in the 1st stanza of the verse, onstage in the 2nd, and back offstage in the chorus. The audience has no idea where this person really is, or where she might turn up next.

Let's ask the question: Why is the song being sung? Subheadings under this question are:

1. **What is the plot?**
2. **What are the story points?**
3. **What is the setting?**

1. The plot suggested in the first stanza is loneliness, in the second, romance, and in the third, successful love. I must select one. Let's select loneliness.
2. The story point in the first stanza is traveling. More important, the singer is traveling alone. That relates to loneliness. I'll keep it.
3. We can travel on a bus. So I decide to stay there for the moment. Aware of the other setting problems, I decide to set the loved one permanently offstage. I can now set a new first stanza:

SITTING ON THE BACK OF THE BUS

COUNTING EVERY TELEPHONE POLE

'TIL I SEE MY LADY.

1. Remains the same.
2. The word "counting" is added. It contributes to the plot.
3. The loved one is firmly placed offstage, and a story point is added—traveling to the loved one.

Faced with writing a second stanza, I again ask the question: why is the song being sung?

The plot is loneliness, but it occurs to me that there is an addition to this plot: the singer is going to see his lady, therefore the condition is temporary.

Temporary loneliness. I realize that when I'm alone, I do nothing but think about my lady. Therefore, *anywhere* I am, this condition will prevail. Now there is a valid reason for a scene shift. The setting is actually *anywhere I am*.

I now set a second stanza:

1. SITTING IN A SMALL CAFÉ

2. MUSIC PLAYING OUR SONG

3. MAKES ME THINK OF MY LADY.

1. The scene shift is drastic, but there is a common word that carries it across: sitting. This is operative ongoing information. I've left the bus, but I'm still sitting *somewhere.*
2. The music is no longer soft and low, but is instead *our song.* This is a common experience and is compatible because it contributes to the plot.
3. The loved one is still offstage.

The plot is still temporary loneliness. There is no indication that the affair is over. The audience remembers line 3 from the first stanza: TILL I SEE MY LADY.

The chorus must now reinforce this statement by presenting the message:

CAN'T WAIT TO SEE HER.

This is a satisfactory line. The plot is solidified, and remains the ongoing condition.

The lyric can now be reworked in terms of meter and rhyme scheme. However, since all points are consistent, I know I'm in business.

PLOT:	**temporary loneliness**
STORY POINTS:	**thinking about the loved one**
SETTING:	**wherever I am.**

Time is a setting that occasionally causes problems. Past, present and future settings must be maintained. Consider the following lyric:

> **1. TOUCHING YOUR FACE WITH MY FINGERS**
>
> **MEMORIZING THE LOOK ON YOUR FACE**
>
> **I CAN SEE THE PLACE ON YOUR LIPS**
>
> **WHERE I JUST PUT A KISS.**

> **2. CALLED YOU LAST NIGHT FROM FRESNO . . .**

Stanza 1 places the audience in the present with the loved one. Stanza 2 shifts to past tense without the loved one. The audience is asked to move from a soft, intimate setting to a distant place. At least, however, it isn't Fred calling from Chicago.

The lyricist must decide where the singer is. The strongest place is *in the present*. It's from this position that the singer can think back on the intimate setting. This is a flashback and is perfectly acceptable.

> **I WISH I WAS TOUCHING YOUR FINGERS**
>
> **MEMORIZED THE LOOK IN YOUR EYES**
>
> **AND THE PLACE ON YOUR LIPS**
>
> **WHERE I LEFT A KISS.**

> **SO I'M CALLING YOU FROM FRESNO**
>
> **TO TELL YOU . . .**

By reworking the lyric, I've indicated that something that happened in the past contributed to the singer's condition. Since the focus is on the present as a setting, the singer can tell the audience how he feels *now*.

A cautionary note: The setting is *not* Fresno, but the present time. Fresno is a story point. It is there to indicate that the singer is removed from the object of his or her love. Don't describe Fresno. It's tempting to go into a small town vs. big town story. But that would be a different song. Fresno is not the message.

Inherent in the idea of a setting is the overindulgence on the part of the lyricist—making a setting for its own sake. For example:

> **TREES**
>
> **LEAVES FALLING DOWN**
>
> **TURNING BROWN**
>
> **SUMMER'S GONE**

> **TREES**
>
> **EMPTY BRANCHES IN THE SKY**
>
> **WAVING GOOD-BYE**
>
> **SUMMER'S GONE**

This is a tone poem. A setting and a mood is established, but *no one is there.*

It's the proverbial tree that falls in the forest: with no one there, is there any noise? There are certainly vibrations. It takes a human ear to translate the vibrations into noise or sound. And it takes a human heart to feel an emotion.

The audience begins to wonder why they're in that forest. Provide them with an actor. This actor has a reason for being in the forest. The audience then can share that reason:

> **TREES**
>
> **LEAVES FALLING DOWN**
>
> **TURNING BROWN**
>
> *MY* **SUMMER'S GONE**

If this is not acceptable, the audience can make an assumption in the first several stanzas. But an actor should be included down the road.

> **TREES**
>
> **EMPTY BRANCHES IN THE SKY**
>
> **WAVING GOOD-BYE**
>
> **SUMMER'S GONE**

The audience, at this point, will assume the singer is in the forest. We prove it later in the chorus:

> **MY SUMMER'S GONE**
>
> **AND I'M . . .**

Be sure to know your setting. The easiest way is to ask, "Where is the singer?"

When performers are placed in the strongest vantage point, they are actively involved, and they deal with the emotional plot as a current message.

● *Summary*

The summation of this chapter is best presented as a series of questions used as a check list. When you know the answers, you present a compatible setting at all times.

- Do you know where the singer is?
- Does the audience?
- Is the setting abstract?
- Is the setting concrete?
- If the setting is concrete, is it truly a setting or a story point?
- Do all operative words maintain the setting?
- If there are third persons, do you know where they are?
- Does the audience?
- Can you use imagery to describe the setting?

Universality

When something is universal, potentially everyone in the world understands it. As we concluded in Section 1, emotions are universally understandable.

When describing an emotion, a point of view can frequently cause problems. The lyricist is inclined to get too personal by focusing on a story point that is not universal—causing the audience to lose the impact of the plot.

A good lyric idea frequently comes from a personal experience. I've been through something and consider myself an expert on the subject. So I sit down to communicate my feelings to the world:

> Last evening I went to a club and saw this ravishing creature across the room. As she danced, I noticed that she twisted her elbow in a most intriguing way when she dipped.
>
> On closer scrutiny, I discovered a cute little freckle on this marvelous elbow. As the lights flashed, this freckle seemed to spin through the room like a lightning bug—now visible, now disappearing.

Everything else in the room disappeared into a hazy mist. Only this freckle, bobbing and weaving as it twisted my heartstrings, pulled me into a web of love.

Obviously, a lyric is necessary. This is too important an experience to keep from the world. I know my plot: love. The setting: a night club. My message must be:

THE FRECKLE I LOVE

How many people will relate to this story? How many freckle freaks are there in the world? Yes, the plot (love) is universal, as is the setting. But the story point is so highly personalized that the plot is totally lost.

George Harrison may have had this same experience. But he simply said, "Something in the way she moves . . ."

Wisely, he recognized the story point: the *way* she moved, not *what* she moved. His story point was universally accepted.

Once you have an experience, get outside yourself and observe it. Find out what the basic ingredient of the experience is. In other words, make sure you have the universal story point.

Getting outside an experience is not always the easiest thing to do. Most people don't understand the technique. And yet they do it all the time.

How often, for instance, do you solve someone's problems by telling them, "What you should do is . . ." (How many times, by the way, do they take your marvelous advice?) When you give this advice, you are looking at their problem from the outside. You are not actively involved in the problem. You are being objective.

They, on the other hand, are inside the problem. It's affecting their lives to the degree they cannot solve the problem. It's overwhelming. They are subjective.

If you get outside your problems, you can deal with them in an objective way. When faced with a large bill, for instance, for which you have no money, do you go into the bedroom and cry? That's subjective. Or do you call your creditor and explain that you're having a little problem and you'll be a little late. If you do, that's being objective.

When you're *inside* the problem, you're being subjective. When *outside,* you're objective.

Being in love with a freckle was being inside the problem, therefore subjective. I could see nothing else. The freckle is nothing more than an object that triggered the experience of love. I can now exchange the object for something more universal. I'm outside the experience and can handle it objectively.

As humans, we are faced with touching experiences every day of our lives. As lyricists, we must have these experiences so we have something to write about. But when writing the lyric, we must remain objective at all times.

• Working Procedure

Let's suppose a reality situation: She has just told me she never wants to see me again. She even gives back the ring. The love affair is over.

The feeling hits me hard, but as a lyricist, I don't want to waste the experience. I immediately start a lyric.

IT'S HER FAULT THE AFFAIR IS OVER

I WAS WILLING TO PUT UP WITH A LOT

IT'S HER FAULT WE NEVER HAD ANY FUN

WE'D ALWAYS ARGUE ABOUT WHERE WE'D GO

SHE WANTED DINNER AT THE BEACH

I WANTED A HAMBURGER AT TOMMY'S

SHE LOVED A ROLLER COASTER RIDE

AND ROLLER COASTERS MADE ME SICK.

COME TO THINK OF IT,

I'M GLAD THE AFFAIR IS OVER!

I'm inside the experience. I'm hurt, angry and have decided to use the lyric to vent those feelings. I'm being subjective.

The first thing is to get outside the experience. As soon as I do, I realize that *I'm* the one experiencing the lost love. She is offstage. When I point my vindictive finger at Her, I distract the audience. They begin to wonder if everything is really her fault—could I really be that perfect? I want them to feel sorry for me, after all, not her.

After all this soul-searching, I find my universal plot: Lost Love. Now I look for a universal story point and setting. Striving to overcome my subjective feelings, I start an objective outline:

PLOT: **Lost Love**
STORY POINT: **Places we had such fun**
SETTING: **Present time, looking back**

I understand now that all the places we visited are no longer points for an argument about what we'd do that evening. They become story points that I can either change or use to heighten my plot.

I can stir up the audience's empathy by telling them that right now, as I stand before their very eyes, I'm an object of pity—one who has just lost the Love of his life. They will relate to *me,* onstage, not *her,* offstage.

Now I'm ready to start an objective lyric:

1. **I'LL NEVER SEE HER AGAIN**

2. **NEVER GO TO THOSE PLACES WE HAD SUCH FUN**

3. **I'LL HAVE DINNER AT THE BEACH AND THINK OF HER**

4. **AND A ROLLER COASTER RIDE WILL NEVER BE THE SAME**

1. The message is expressed. The audience is told what the song is about.
2. This is the line I discovered in my objective thinking. "All those places" is a nondefined story point setting. From that point on, I could go to a laundry list of "fun" places.
3. The audience accepts my settings as *possible* fun places because they are compatible with the plot. They know, however, they can provide their own fun places, if they wish, because the story points are universal "everywheres."

4. My laundry list is still compatible with Lost Love. Instead of making me sick, the roller coaster ride reminds me of how wonderful she was.

I'm ready, now, to rework the lyric into a rhyme scheme and formal meter. I have a chance at a successful lyric.

Let's experiment with another procedure in arriving at universal objectivity. My car has just been repossessed. I'm inside the experience, and it's quite traumatic.

First, the financial problem. Where will I get the money to either get the car back, or buy another? Very soon I realize how immobile I am without my wheels. I can't get to the shopping center. I can't see my friends. Worse, I can't take HER out. It occurs to me that I'm the victim of a malevolent universe. Something out there is determined to get me!

The experience is so important that it's obviously worth a lyric! If I stay subjective, though, I'll write about the importance of an automobile in my life.

Unfortunately, since the audience is always objective, this will come off as a humorous song. Even though they are vicariously sharing the experience with me, they are really *outside* the experience.

They will begin to wonder why I feel so sorry for myself. It was, after all, my fault that I didn't meet my car payment obligations. They will also see the objective solutions: get a bike, ride the bus or walk. If She means so much to me, I should crawl on my hands and knees, if necessary, to be with her.

The audience will see through my subjectivity, and, rather than regarding me with empathy, will see me as a fool.

To turn my subjective experience into a universally acceptable lyric, I must decide what I'm really writing about.

What emotion am I feeling? What is the plot? Why is this song being sung? Several headings and subheadings present themselves as possibilities:

1. PLOT: Love
   A: Determined love
      1. Story Point: no obstacle can keep me from her.
   B: Realization of love
      1. Story Point: everything that happens makes me think of her.
   C: Friendly love
      1. Story Point: when I can't see my friends, I miss them.
      2. Story Point: will my friends miss me?
2. PLOT: Loneliness
   A: Immobility
      1. Story Point: can't get to see her.
      2. Story Point: can't see my friends.
   B: Imprisoned
      1. Story Point: can't get out of . . .
         a. this place
         b. this mood
         c. this love
         d. this town
3. PLOT: Wanderlust
   A: Travel (desire to)
      1. Story Point: haven't seen:
         a. New York
         b. Europe
         c. Shangri-la
         d. etc.

B: Travel (fulfilled)
   1. Story Point: I've been to:
      a. New York
      b. Europe
      c. Shangri-la
      d. etc.

The outline could go on for several pages. The important thing to notice is the flow. Each idea leads to another. Starting with the subjective experience of losing my car, I may end up with a lyric titled, "I've Been Everywhere In The World!"

I've used a technique to move from the subjective to the objective. I have a wide variety of plots and story points from which to draw and can now forget the car and write an objective lyric that will communicate universally.

• Summary

Even though a song lyric is inspired by a personal experience or observation, it must be expressed in such a way as to be universally understood.

When a lyricist is involved in the story in a highly personal way, he or she is subjective—in a sense, the subject of the story. It is difficult at best to produce a universal message if you are too involved in an explicit, personal way.

The trick is to get out of the story—to stand off and imagine the same story as happening to somebody else. Ask yourself, "Am I still interested in the story?" If not, "How can I make it more interesting?"

Let the actor or actress be the object of the story. Then look at them and imagine the story happening in a universal way. Become objective. It's the singer's feelings that have been hurt.

One of the techniques I've employed, in order to get out of my own way, is to write a prose paragraph about the experience. Prose does not have the restrictions of scansion, meter and rhyme.

When I'm finished, I underline all the operative words and a bare-bones plot emerges. I get a sense of the underlying message I want to send.

Another technique is to draw up a list of operative words describing a feeling about an experience or observation. Again, a bare-bones plot might emerge.

But the most amazing adventures occur when I simply write out a sentence and start making story point exchanges. Sometimes even pronoun exchanges get me off and running:

> **I walked around the block today.**
> **She walked around the block tonight.**
> **They walked around the hill tonight.**
> **We drove around the hill last night, and . . .**

I urge you to experiment with these techniques for developing a lyric—particularly when you're staring at a line of lyric and wondering, "What comes next?" The techniques are all designed to help you stop wondering—and start writing!

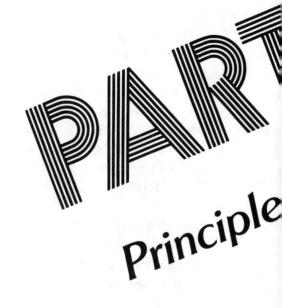

PART

Principle

THREE

f Lyric Style

This section of *Lyrics, Lyrics, Lyrics* deals with the various styles of lyric presentation. An understanding of these styles will help in selecting the best style for a particular lyric. This doesn't mean a lyric can always be pigeonholed into a certain style. Some lyrics work in a combination of styles, or in a categorical style invented by the lyricist.

The purpose of this section is to present you with some options. You may be working on a lyric that isn't coming together—because you're trying to put it in the wrong style. Being aware of the options—and experimenting with various styles—enables you to bring your lyric into the best possible focus.

Another reason for considering a stylistic approach to the lyric is to remain consistent. Once you understand that the lyric—or portions of the lyric—is in a specific style, it's much easier to keep the lyric in focus. If, for instance, you're working in a dramatic style, you can see how you must maintain tension for the singer.

After examining the styles presented, check out some current songs, and see if you can get an idea of their style. The purpose is to form some conclusions of your own, as I've only scratched the surface of possible styles. Just remember: consistency is the key word here. If a lyric drifts too much, you will surely lose your audience.

Dramatic Style

A drama, according to the dictionary, is a work for the theater. I'm taking advantage of the word to categorize a lyric style that is neither comedic nor a love song, although either of those styles could be "dramatic."

A formula for drama is:

TENSION MOVING TO RELEASE

Here is a thumbnail description of a three-act, dramatic play:

ACT I: **Get the hero up a tree.**

ACT II: **Throw rocks at him.**

ACT III: **Get the hero down from the tree.**

The first act introduces tension. In a dramatic story this story point is frequently some obstacle the hero must overcome. Act II increases the tension by adding a second story point. Finally, Act III accomplishes release—the hero overcomes the obstacle or solves the problem.

This principle of tension/release is inherent in all artistic works. In the story above, the hero is placed in a predicament from which he must logically extricate himself.

In music, this principle is accomplished by moving from a dissonant chord to a consonant chord. In a painting, we see jagged lines or clashing colors expressing tension, a rounded or flat line and harmonious colors expressing release.

To categorize a song lyric as dramatic, *the singer should be in a condition of tension.*

When a book, movie or play expresses tension/release, the story moves to a "completed" action. A dramatic song lyric, however, may never move to "release." Rather than tell a story, the lyric expresses an emotion through the story points.

Inherent in tension is *implied* release. Although it's not a hard and fast rule, this is the device to rely on in the song lyric. Let's look at some of our lyric examples to see how this works.

> **"Bill Bailey"**: The opening line, "Won't you come home," sets the tension. She's been left alone and is in trouble. Subsequent lines increase the tension. When she admits she's to blame, it is the implied release. The audience hopes that Bill will relent and return to her loving arms.
>
> **"The Girl"**: The tension here is a basic universal problem—the hero is considering whether the time has come to settle down with The Girl. The audience is sure he'll make the right decision.
>
> **"Early Mornin' Girl"**: The hero's pain and heartache is the tension situation. The second stanza increases the tension when the loved one threatens

to leave. The implied release is the anguished cry in the chorus, "Oh, Please, Don't Go!"

The strongest presentation of a lyric is in the first person, with the performer in a present-day situation. The performer tells the audience about the predicament he or she is in *at the moment*. Obviously, any release is in the *future*.

The release, whether implied or actual, must be consistent with the plot. In this context, it is apparent how the lyric about the lonely room violated this principle as soon as the performer was allowed to go out for a beer.

This was release but the wrong kind. In a lyric, our only release is the removal of the *cause* of our loneliness—for example, being reunited with the loved one.

If the lyric goes so far as to unite the two lovers during the performance of the song, the message is diluted. Suspension of belief places the performer in that lonely room at the moment of the performance. A lover walking through the door would solve the problem and finish the story. There'd be no point in ever singing that song again.

• *Analysis of Dramatic Style*

Studying, analyzing and categorizing the work of other authors is a must for any lyricist. These four great standards are superb examples of the dramatic style:

"You've Lost That Lovin' Feelin' "
"Bye Bye Love"
"Yesterday"
"Never Can Say Good-bye"

Each of these songs states the tension in such a way that the audience immediately understands there is a problem or obstacle.

The problem implies a universality of emotional plot and story point. The problem must be a universal problem, and it must be stated larger than life. Small problems are not interesting enough to sing about.

The following example is a lyric about the age-old problem of the end of love. The comparison of this lyric to the thumbnail description of a three-act play will show how analyzation works:

Verse 1: Tension stated. (Act I: get the hero up a tree.)

WAITIN' FOR THE MORNIN'

PAYIN' UP MY DUES

WON'T PICK UP THE PAPER

I CAN'T STAND NO MORE BAD NEWS

WHEN SHE CLOSED THE DOOR,

SHE TOOK TOMORROW WITH HER

HARD TO REALIZE

HOW MUCH IS OVER.

HERE'S THE SUNRISE,

DON'T WANT TO SEE IT COME!

Although a *specific* problem is not stated, it's apparent that the singer is in a state of terrific tension. This is an unhappy parting.

At this point, there is no clear story point. Has there been an argument? Is this a permanent parting? Or, what had been the nature of the relationship?

All of this is irrelevant, however, as the song deals with a universal situation. There has been a parting of two people, and the audience will usually insert their own reasons for this unhappy event. It's usually *assumed* they're lovers. What is interesting now is that the singer has been placed high in the branches of a dramatic tree.

Chorus: The message. The summation of tension and payoff to Act I:

> **AIN'T NO EASY WAY TO CRY.**
>
> **NEVER BEEN NO EASY WAY TO SMILE AND SAY,**
>
> **"I CAN MAKE IT ALONE."**
>
> **NEVER BEEN NO EASY WAY TO SAY GOOD-BYE.**
>
> **NEVER BEEN NO EASY WAY TO CRY.**

The message is not a story about a breakup, but rather an anguished statement about how the singer feels about the situation. This is true universality. Everybody knows there is no easy way to cry. The audience, agreeing with this message, feels empathy for the singer.

**Verse 2:** Tension reinforced. (Act II: the rocks are being thrown
at the singer):

> NO ONE LEFT TO TALK TO
>
> GOD HELP ME EASE THE PAIN
>
> I'M THROWN OUT IN THE WEEDS NOW
>
> LIKE AN OLD TIN CAN FILLIN' UP WITH RAIN.
>
>
> LEAVE ME SLEEPIN'
>
> AIN'T NO KISS TO WAKE ME
>
> NO USE KEEPIN'
>
> MY DREAMS ABOUT HER
>
> DAYLIGHT'S CREEPIN',
>
> DON'T WANT TO SEE IT COME!

This information adds to the doomlike immediacy of the
situation. There is an insinuation that the singer would welcome death as a release from the situation. The singer really
means business when he makes this strong a statement.

At this point, of course, the chorus is restated. _Yet, there
is no third act!_ Remember the earlier statement that a song,
as opposed to a story, _never ends._ The singer is doomed to
an eternity of uneasy ways to cry.

If, however, the audience establishes empathy for the
singer and recognizes the message as a universal emotional
statement, they will root for the singer. The implied release
lies in the hope that there will be a happy ending.

Narrative Style

The early Greek dramatists recognized the problem of relaying "secret" information to an audience. Rather than use the "aside," they invented the idea of a chorus—a group of people who were removed from the action and could clarify things for the audience. This device is still referred to as the "Greek chorus."

Over the centuries, this chorus was reduced in number, until a single person was used to comment or relay information. This person is known as the narrator.

The audience recognizes the narrator's role. The narrator is an observer and is detached from the action and so can suitably comment on it for the audience's clarification.

• The Observer

This is the primary form of the narrative style. The performer has witnessed an action and wants to tell the audience about it.

This "action" is usually offstage. The narrator may occasionally have been an active participant in the action, but at the point of performance, the singer is removed from the action and assumes the true narrator's role.

Song lyrics that fall in this category are:

"Bill Bailey, Won't You Please Come Home?" (Remember: "*she* cries," not "*I* cry")
"Eleanor Rigby" *
"American Pie"
"The Fool on the Hill"
"Abraham, Martin and John"
"Some Girls"

* Note that some titles in this section appear in several lists, as they are examples of combinations of styles. Many narrative lyrics fall into several categories.

● *The Storyteller*

Occasionally the narrative style is a little like telling a joke or bedtime story. No point of view is made. The audience is not asked to think of any deep meaning. There is simply an entertaining story to be told. Songs in this category are:

"Copacabana (At the Copa)"
"Frankie and Johnny"

• *The Preacher*

A problem arises in the narrative style when the lyricist states a definite point of view. This is the situation when the lyricist wants to make a social comment.

Most audiences don't like to be preached to and told how they should act or what they should do. For instance:

> **Long hair is dirty, and you should . . .**
> **Equal rights are important, and you should . . .**
> **War is wrong, and you'd better . . .**
> **The world is coming to an end, and you'd better . . .**

These may all be important statements; however, the audience is there to be entertained, and so the lyricist sugarcoats the message.

The trick is to turn it back on the performer. As an example, look at the old comedic device of the pie in the face. It's funny when the comedian is hit. If the audience is hit, it's not funny anymore.

The narrator makes the statement as though he or she has observed a situation, and tells the audience how he or she is going to react:

> **Long hair may be dirty, but I'm going to . . .**
> **Equal rights is important, and I will . . .**
> **War is wrong, and I'll never . . .**
> **The world is coming to an end, and I'd better . . .**

This frees the audience to decide for itself whether it agrees with the narrator. Nothing is pushed down its collective throat.

Here are some examples of narrative lyrics in this style:

> "Imagine"
> "Blowin' in the Wind"
> "I Believe"
> "Hair"

• The Confider

Included in the narrative style is the relating of a personal experience. The narrator tells the audience about something that happened to him or her. The problem here is maintaining universality. No one wants to hear about someone's daily activities, from brushing teeth to saying good night. Make sure the personal experience is something that interests an audience. There must be a good reason for telling the story.

Examine the following lyrics for examples:

> "Little Green Apples"
> "Isn't She Lovely?"
> "Mr. Bojangles"
> "Up, Up and Away"

• Analysis of Narrative Style

The narrative style makes copious use of the third person "he" or "she." The singer is simply an observer. There may be some philosophical conclusions; however, the usual practice is to simply make the observations and let the audience draw conclusions.

"David Daring" is a mythical young man the narrator has observed. David's lifestyle has made such an impression on the narrator that he feels the audience should get to know him.

That is the presentation of the lyric as a song. Actually, of course, David is simply a creation of the lyricist, who wants to describe a sort of "free soul" personality.

There is, of course, an underlying reason for the narrator to tell about David. There is a message.

Verse

DAVID DARING WALKED THE STREETS WITH EMPTY IN HIS POCKET,

HOLES IN HIS SOLES AND DREAMS FOR PRETEND;

AND SO ON A MONDAY, HE THOUGHT THAT HE'D PLAY.

HE HAD TEN SILVER NOTHINGS TO SPEND.

BUT WITH PRETEND TO SPEND,

THERE WERE SO MANY THINGS TO BUY;

SO HE SHOPPED 'TIL SOMETHING CAUGHT HIS EYE.

IT WAS A BALLOON,

THE BIGGEST BALLOON THAT YOU'VE EVER SEEN,

AS BIG AS THE MOON,

WITH POLKA DOTS LIKE APRICOTS AND GRASSY

GREEN BETWEEN,

SUDDENLY HE KNEW WHAT HE'D NEVER KNOWN.

HE MUST HAVE THAT BALLOON FOR HIS VERY OWN.

Chorus

DAVID DARING,

DAVID DARING,

WISE IN HIS EYES AND FAIR IN HIS HAIR.

WHEN YOU COUNT TO A HUNDRED, THE WORLD'S

NEW AGAIN.

DAVID DARING'S ALREADY THERE.

The verse is actually in three sections:

The first section establishes David's personality as a free-spirited dreamer. The style of the lyric also establishes a kind of mythic quality, to make the audience aware that he is not a real person. This realization is important so the audience will consent to go along with the story—to suspend, for a moment, their beliefs.

The second section describes what David is going to do, and how he's going to do it.

The third section establishes something else in David: a purpose. Without this purpose, this epic quest, the audience would lose interest in David as a hopeless case. The desire for the balloon gives the audience an investment in David: they hope he will be successful in accomplishing his desires.

The chorus, in this lyric, does little more than repeat David's name and affirm the mythic attributes that make him worth singing about.

DAVID DARING WALKED THE STORE WITH HOPE IN HIS EARDRUMS

SAYING AND PRAYING TEN NOTHINGS WOULD SUFFICE.

THE PROPRIETOR OF THE BIG BALLOON STORE

TOLD HIM TWENTY SILVER NOTHINGS WAS THE PRICE.

BUT WITH PRETEND TO SPEND

HE COULD BUY ANYTHING IN SIGHT,

SO WITH HIS BRAND-NEW BALLOON, PREPARED FOR FLIGHT

HE FLEW TO THE STARS.

HIS THERMOS WAS FILLED UP WITH EXTRA AIR.

THERE IS LIFE ON MARS.

HOROSCOPES AND TELESCOPES REPORTED DAVID
THERE!

SUDDENLY HE KNEW WHAT HE'D NEVER KNOWN:

HE COULD HAVE THE UNIVERSE FOR HIS VERY
OWN.

DAVID DARING,

DAVID DARING,

WISE IN HIS EYES AND FAIR IN HIS HAIR.

IF YOU COUNT TO A HUNDRED, THE WORLD'S NEW
AGAIN.

DAVID DARING'S ALREADY THERE.

The established form is followed by setting out three sections to the verse:

> The first verse has David satisfying the first of his quests: he buys the balloon. This act sets the stage for the next leg of the adventure.
> The second section gets David off the ground.
> The third section once again establishes in

David a quest. This is a much deeper realization in that the first was a desire for a balloon as the means to an end, but this realization involves the entire universe!

The message becomes much clearer here: the narrator has seen in David an example of how dreams can come true. Besides enjoying David's personality, this is the basic reason the narrator wants to tell the audience all about David Daring.

DAVID DARING WALKED THE SKIES,
UNDERSTANDING EV'RY MOMENT.
KNEW IT WAS TRUE THAT THE EARTH'S REALLY
SQUARE.
THE MAN IN THE MOON SAID, "WHAT A FINE
BALLOON,
BUT I THINK THAT IT'S SLOWLY LEAKING AIR."

DAVID DARING WALKED ON AIR AS HE TRIED TO
KEEP HIS HOPES UP.
SPRAWLING AND FALLING, HE LANDED IN A HEAP,
BUT LUCKILY FOR ALL, A HAYSTACK BROKE HIS
FALL,
AND HE'S UNDER IT NOW FAST ASLEEP.

DAVID DARING,

DAVID DARING,

WISE IN HIS EYES AND FAIR IN HIS HAIR

IF YOU COUNT TO A HUNDRED, THE WORLD'S NEW

AGAIN,

AND DAVID DARING'S ALREADY THERE.

The form is broken in this last part of the lyric. This is partly because the song is already long enough, but also to signal the end coming. The scansion indicates the first section of the verse is repeated, and the second and third sections are dispensed with.

The first verse in the wrap-up creates in David a kind of omnipotence. He understands everything. How the audience would enjoy this knowledge! However, there is also some disturbing news: the adventure is about to end. Did David, like Icarus, fly too high? This is left up to the audience.

The second verse lets David off the hook. He may have flown too high, but his landing is soft. This ending lets the audience decide for itself the implications of David's flight.

Icarus was destroyed. David was saved. This seems like an ending, though a moral is not pointed out. The song told David's story, but can dreams really come true? Again, it's up to the audience to draw conclusions.

The Valentine

In a pure form, the valentine is a clear statement of love. There is no tension/release as in the dramatic style. In most cases the valentine is expressed in the first person; there is little interest in a performer describing a love affair between two other people, as in the narrative style.

The message of this style is always pure unadulterated love. A subtitle such as unrequited love would place the lyric in the dramatic style, as the singer is in a state of tension.

The danger in the valentine style is banality. There are hundreds of songs with the title, "I Love You." (I might mention here that a song title cannot be copyrighted.) New ways of expressing love must be found for the lyric to be viable. A clever statement must be made, otherwise the audience will have heard it before.

• Code Words

It's interesting to note that each pair of lovers has their own little codes. They believe they have developed a private system for expressing their love without the public at large knowing what's going on.

The surprising thing is how universal these codes are. For instance, there are the three words in the phrase "I Love You." Therefore, "Knock Three Times, I'll Meet You In The Hallway" has immediate universality. Surprised lovers turned to each other and said, "That's us." It became their song. In an abstract code situation, many pairs of lovers are well aware they act coy and demure in public, but become tigers when alone. "Behind Closed Doors" became their anthem.

The codes must have a certain recognition factor—a bit of the cliché—yet smack of a private signal. These songs cause lovers, young and old, to squeeze hands when they hear the words that salute their private reminders of love.

• Laundry List

The laundry list, as a lyric device, works best in a love song. In this form, the lyric presents a list of the loved one's best features. From "All the Things You Are" to "Three Times a Lady," these attributes are the reason the performer is smitten.

Universality, as usual, is the key. The lyrics must use descriptions or analogies that apply to all loved ones. "I Love the Freckle On Your Elbow" may be the beginning of a laundry list, but it is hardly universal.

A list may answer the posed question, "How do I love you?"—as in "let me count the ways."—or "Why do I love you?"

Lists such as these may also be springboards for ideas. It's possible to start one place and end in another. Using the last technique, "Why do I love you?," the lyricist may respond with, "(because) You Light Up My Life."

The John Denver standard, "Annie's Song," provides a marvelous example of the use of a laundry list in a love song. The verse is a series of analogies. The loved one is "like a . . .

> . . . night in a forest,
> . . . mountain in springtime,
> . . . etc."

The chorus recites the eternal, timeless list that is demanded of all lovers, in a heartfelt plea for permission to drown, die, and so on for the sake of love.

If the lover is willing to go that far, the audience knows that he or she means business. Great lovers throughout history, whether real or fiction, have died for love. Audiences now seem to expect this kind of total commitment as proof of the depth of the lover's feelings.

Looking for fresh devices, I asked my workshop students to compile a list of actions, rather than analogies, that are implied expressions of love. These actions might include:

> Knowing the proper wine.
> Remembering anniversaries (counting from the first *minute,* by the way!)
> Squeezing toothpaste tubes from the bottom.
> Taking out the garbage!

● *Names*

At first glance, this device seems to lack universality. Identifying a loved one by name seems to exclude everyone else. In actuality, the name becomes a story point. The message is still love.

The audience recognizes this and accepts the fact that the performer just happens to be in love with "Laura," "Michelle" or "Sweet Caroline."

There's a good chance the audience vicariously identifies with the named loved ones. And the possibility exists that if Sweet Caroline is in love, there might be a chance for the rest of us. The psychological factors are beyond the realm of this work, except for one pertinent fact—there have been few songs in this style utilizing boy's names. (Can you think of anything other than "Chuck E.'s in Love?")

● *Narrative Valentine*

When the lyricist provides the performer with an experience that either leads to a love affair or solidifies the affair itself, the song is a narrative valentine. A *story* is being told rather than an outright expression of love. The technique has universality, as everyone has their own "special" circumstances relating to their love affairs.

Examine, for instance, the lyrics to "Tie A Yellow Ribbon," and note how slight, dramatic overtones are included. Every story should have an implication of tension.

In the narrative valentine, the emphasis is on the *release* side of the story, on the idea of a love affair. It's as though the audience picks up the thread of the story just a few lines before " . . . and they lived happily ever after."

Symbols

A symbol is a device that represents a thing, action or emotion. Without symbols, people would be unable to communicate. Words themselves are symbols for things or actions. Even the letters making up the words on this page are symbols for various sounds.

A symbol, then, is not the thing itself, but the device that sums up in the listener's mind all the information he or she has about the thing. The symbol is closely associated with the thing and represents all its attributes or qualities.

The lion is a symbol for courage. A lamb, on the other hand, represents the attributes of meekness or the qualities of playfulness. Counting on the lamb's entire family is a symbolic action that puts us to sleep.

Symbols make a complicated statement in one or two words. In a song lyric, where brevity is necessary and time is of the essence, this is an absolute blessing. A good symbol can be thought of as a picture, and we know that a picture is worth a thousand words.

● *Personification*

In this kind of symbolism, the author creates a person or creature who *is* all the attributes of an emotion or quality. When the abstract emotion or quality is presented to the audience as a "real" person, there is an immediate recognition. Villains personify Evil, just as the Hero represents absolute Good. And is there anything purer than the Hero's Lady Love?

The list includes Mothers, Dads, Husbands, Wives, Lovers, Santa Claus, Easter Bunnies, the Boss, Uncle Sam, Smokey the Bear, David Daring and anyone else who represents a condition or quality.

The important piece of advice is not to tamper with symbols that have become stereotypes. Mom represents unconditional love, and her apple pie is everything good about America.

Wives usually represent Fidelity. Husbands, unfortunately, seem to represent the opposite quality—they play around a lot, particularly in country music.

Lovers, of course, are the objects of affection, therefore, perfect. How could anyone love an imperfect person?

Personification is an excellent tool for the lyricist. The important part of the technique is to recognize that the technique is being used. In other words, don't describe a person just for the sake of inventing a personality. Endow this person with all the needed characteristics. Let the audience recognize in this person the epitome of what you want to represent.

Consider, for example, this list of titles:

> **"Eleanor Rigby"**
> **"Sweet Georgia Brown"**
> **"The Fool On the Hill"**

"Sophisticated Lady"
Princess Leia
"Billie Jean"
You

Eleanor Rigby is the absolute embodiment of loneliness. And no one in the world is sweeter than Georgia Brown, Lennon/McCartney's person on the hill is the ultimate fool, and Duke Ellington's Lady is the ultimate sophisticate. There's no song about Princess Leia, but isn't she a great Princess? And poor Billie Jean, who is not his lover, but just a girl who is trying to get something going. The ubiquitous "you" exists in many songs, such as "I Just Called to Say I Love You."

On the negative side, it's usually dangerous to personify evil in a straightforward manner. Negative personalities are best described with comedic overtones. Just as we like to whistle in the dark, the audience feels more comfortable when they can laugh at:

"Bad, Bad Leroy Brown"
"Lucretia McEvil"
"Thriller"

Notice that proper names become the symbolic personification of a segment of society:

"Bill Bailey"
"Mr. Bojangles"
"Sweet Caroline"

Bill Bailey is every man who's deserted every woman. Sweet Caroline is the surrogate teen, and Mr. Bojangles draws our sympathy as the archetype senior citizen cast off by society.

In the same vein, don't forget:

> **"Ol' Man River"**
> **"Lady Madonna"**
> **"Honey"**
> **"Lover"**
> **"Husbands, Wives and Lovers"**
> **"Levon"**
> **"Rhinestone Cowboy"**

Since the dawn of storytelling, symbolic people have been the voices of certain emotions, characteristics or qualities. They are part of our mythological heritage. Let them speak their parts. Let them be bigger than life. Then they can do their jobs.

• *Emblems*

Most people commonly think of an emblem as a badge or object. The cross, for example, is the emblem of Christianity. A flag is the emblem of a country. On a mundane level, a certain seashell represents a brand of gasoline.

An emblem, then, is a *material object* that represents a thing or quality.

The heart, for instance, represents the attributes and qualities of love. It's startling to realize how many parts of the body are used as emblems. This list might be termed the "organ recital":

"Heart and Soul"
"My Heart Sings For You"
"Zing Went the Strings of my Heart"
"Body and Soul"
"I Only Have Eyes for You"
"The Eyes of Texas"
"Don't It Make My Brown Eyes Blue"
"The Windmills of Your Mind"
"Always On My Mind"
"Can You Read My Mind"
"He's Got the Whole World in His Hands"

Another type of emblem is the use of a location as representing certain qualities. Again, these must be universal stereotypes; the places must be recognized as having the attributes the lyricist desires.

Home is a strong favorite:

"The Green, Green Grass of Home"
"A House is Not a Home"

Various city names conjure up unique visions:

"New York, New York"
"Chicago"
"My Kind of Town"
"I Left My Heart in San Francisco" (two emblems in that one!)
"A Foggy Day" (in London town)
"Chatanooga Choo Choo"
"April in Paris"

Street names or parts of a city have a built-in characteristic:

> **"On Broadway"**
> **"Pigalle"**
> **"MacArthur Park"**

States create a state of mind:

> **"California Dreamin' "**
> **"California Girls"**
> **"Moonlight in Vermont"**
> **"A Little Bit North of South Carolina"**

Or countries:

> **"Spanish Eyes"**
> **"Brazil"**
> **"Canadian Sunset"**
> **"Born in the U.S.A."**

Abstract localities represent certain qualities:

> **"Over the Rainbow"**
> **"Heartbreak Hotel"**
> **"Hotel California"**
> **"Bridge Over Troubled Water"**

How about taking in the Whole Thing:

> **"Windows of the World"**
> **"You and Me Against the World"**
> **"Love the World Away"**

And then, on to the Cosmos:

"Star Dust"
"Fly Me To The Moon"
"Stairway to Heaven"

Closer to home is the song, "Take me Home, Country Roads," which uses real places like West Virginia, Blue Ridge Mountains and the Shenandoah River. But in the lyric context, they are every bit as symbolic as heaven.

We all have a picture in our mind of the ideal country road. And when it winds over the meadow and through the woods to Home, where a Mountain Mama, the Ultimate Earth Mother, wraps us in Unconditional Love as we press our cheeks to her Ample Bosom—well, that's worth singing about.

Notice that many of the objects represent emotions, whereas the locations are frequently indicators of a state of mind. People act one way on Broadway, another way on a Country Road.

Selecting, or creating, a good emblem can nail down a complicated quality in a word or two. Look for them or invent them. They can work for a song.

• *Tokens*

This third kind of symbolism is the use of an act or abstract image to represent a fact, feeling or event. People wear black, for instance, as a token of mourning, and shake hands as a token of friendship. Tokens are those nebulous images that represent feelings, characteristics or qualities.

Colors, for instance, affect everyone:

"Song Sung Blue"
"Mood Indigo"
"Look for the Silver Lining"
"Evergreen"

Certain days of the week represent a state of mind:

"Rainy Days and Mondays"
"Thank God, It's Friday"
"Saturday Night is the Loneliest Night of the Week"
"Sunday Morning Coming Down"

Or parts of days:

"Lazy Afternoon"
"Midnight Sun"

Or the months:

"June in January"
"April Showers"

Seasons:

"Spring is Here"
"A Summer Place"
"Autumn Serenade"
"Winter Wonderland"

Don't overlook the weather:

"You Are the Sunshine of My Life"
"Rainy Days and Mondays"
"In the Cool, Cool, Cool of the Evening"

As with emblems, the token represents a state of mind more than anything else. But that's logical: experiences on a lazy afternoon are much different from a winter wonderland. The lyricist describes how the singer is feeling by placing him or her in a certain locale. The audience recognizes this symbolism immediately.

• *Analysis of Symbols*

Symbols have a double meaning. First is the thing itself, what it actually is. The second is its symbolic representation: the emotion, feeling, characteristic or quality it expresses.

When Romeo says, "Juliet is the sun," the audience thinks of the thing itself—the sun—but then, since Juliet is obviously *not* the sun, they think of what the sun represents: warmth, love, light, life.

All the examples quoted above are song titles. There are many more examples within bodies of lyrics I cannot quote without running afoul of copyright laws. The point is, besides being good subjects for song titles, symbols can be most useful as words or phrases within the body of a song lyric.

Notice that many symbols are borderline banalities.

Hearts, for instance, have had a pretty good run. And blue is a very familiar color to singers and audiences. They're still good symbols, though, and in the right place can express a world of meaning.

Be inventive. Don't always rely on the old favorites. I was impressed with a student's use of the word "Victrola" to symbolize an old-fashioned setting. Quite a bit different from "stereo."

I once had an assignment to write a lyric about certain nostalgic things. So I started a list of symbols:

LACE CURTAINS WAVING AT THE (OPEN) WINDOW

KATYDIDS CRYING IN THE TREES

LEMON OIL GLEAMING ON THE FURNITURE

(which led me to:)

DUST COVERS OFF THE PARLOR SOFA

DOILIES PINNED IN PLACE

BACK-PORCH SWING

(which led me to:)

KIDS SWINGING ON A TIRE TIED TO A BRANCH

(This part of the list hints at some rhymes and the beginning of a form:)

LAYING ON SOME BAR-B-Q

THE LAWN WAS TRIMMED

(which led me to:)

THE GRASS WAS CUT IN THE MORNING

SO THERE'D BE NOTHING LEFT TO DO

(More symbols: the words in parentheses may be changed for future rhymes)

FOLDING CHAIRS LEANING IN THE SHADE OF A (TREE)

WHILE THE LADIES FAN THEMSELVES AND GOSSIP (TALK)

(or for an easier rhyme:)

WHILE THE LADIES FAN THEMSELVES AND CATCH UP ON THE NEWS

KIDS PLAYING TAG IN THEIR SUNDAY BEST

(which led me to:)

KIDS IN THEIR SUNDAY BEST

WAITING FOR THE GROWN-UPS TO SETTLE DOWN AND GOSSIP

SO THEY CAN START UP A GAME OF TAG

The final lyric used quite a few items from my stockpile. Each symbol I thought of was a springboard to the next symbol. Later on I wrestled with form, rhymes, scansion and meter.

The following lyric contains many rather strange and obscure symbols. It's the story of a person who's realized his own mortality, and, in a cry of anguish, wants to sing about it.

Verse

IN THE BEGINNING
THERE WAS ABSURD
A TRIP THROUGH THE TULIPS
A BOAT RIDE THROUGH THE TUNNEL OF LOVE

AND IN THE MIDDLE
THERE IS PLASTIC MAN
ALIVE AND LIVING IN PASADENA
A FREAK OUT IN THE SIDE SHOW

AND IN THE END
THERE IS THE PHOENIX
RISING FROM THE FIRE OF HIS FUNERAL
SPREADING MIDNIGHT WINGS OVER THE EMPTY
DESERT
LOOKING FOR TOMORROW
LOOKING FOR TOMORROW
LOOKING FOR TOMORROW

Chorus

HEY, MISTER BONES
WHAT KIND OF A TRICK HAVE YOU PLAYED?
MY COLLAR NEEDS TURNING,
THE CURTAIN'S BEGINNING TO FADE.

Bridge

> YESTERDAY'S A PIECE OF CHEWING GUM
> STUCK TO THE SHOE OF MY SOUL
> AND THE THINGS I WAS GOING TO DO ON A
> SOMEDAY
> ARE STILL JUST A NEBULOUS GOAL.

Chorus

> HEY, MISTER BONES
> GOT ANY MORE TRICKS UP YOUR SLEEVE?
> THE EVENING'S ALL OVER
> AND FOLKS ARE BEGINNING TO LEAVE.

> HEY, MISTER BONES
> I'VE GOT A LAST-MINUTE MESSAGE FROM THE
> FRONT
> THE TEAM'S WAY BEHIND.
> WE'VE GOT TO PUNT!

> HEY, MISTER BONES
> WHY DO YOU TREAT ME THIS WAY?
> THAT CIRCLE YOU'VE DRAWN IN THE DUST
> IS JUST THE BEGINNING OF THE END.
> END OF THE BEGINNING.
> END OF THE BEGINNING.

The lyric is in an odd shape. There is one long verse, then a series of choruses broken by a bridge. Symbology, in this kind of lyric, is necessary, as it's a little uncomfortable for an audience to be faced with "Hey, Mister Death."

The interesting thing about this lyric is all of the symbols, personifications and analogies are about the end of things. The last three lines, though, are the implied hope of immortality.

Let me repeat once more: a symbol is like a picture. One good symbol may be worth a thousand words of lyric.

The Sound of Sound

The pure state of this style is either totally meaningless sounds or a series of words that convey no concrete meaning.

The old be-bop phrase "oo-bop-she-bam" is a perfect example of meaningless sounds set to a rhythmic pattern. Scat singing, as performed by Ella Fitzgerald and Mel Tormé, where the performer improvises a rhythmic melody over the original song, uses this device.

A total lyric of meaningless sounds, however, is too highly specialized to be considered a marketable item. Individual performers usually improvise their own set of sounds.

The second device, strings of words that have no real meaning, can be considered as having value. Examples of this technique are the songs "Whip It" and "Shake Your Bootie."

Again, though, this is such a highly specialized device that it is difficult to sell on the open market. The performers who use this device are usually quite able to create their own material.

If you feel you have something really catchy, though, don't put it in a drawer. The following list of songs demonstrates the market value of this device:

"Mairzy Doats"
"Bibbidi-Bobbidi-Boo"
"Hut Sut Song"
"Ragg Mopp"
"Da-Doo-Ron-Ron"
"Boogie-Oogie-Oogie"

• *Control of Sound*

Within the body of a lyric, the lyricist can take advantage of the idea of sound for the sake of sound. Sounds become interjections of extreme emotion.

Just as a startled or surprised person might react with a meaningless syllable—"Wow!" or "Aah!"—the performer may feel the need to inject some reactive sounds into the performance.

The lyricist can control this by actually including the sounds as integral parts of the lyric. The sounds then become necessary and important.

The impact of a lyric depends on the choice of actual sounds. An examination of various effects helps to provide some ideas on this.

First, compare a consonant and a vowel. Experiment by saying the letter "T" without adding a vowel sound. Your tongue should stay behind your upper teeth, holding back your air supply. Only when a vowel is added, such as "oo," do you drop your tongue and release the air with the sound "tu"!

This experiment demonstrates the fact that a consonant literally has no sound of its own. It's a vocal stopping point. The various ways the mouth forms these stopping points lends a defined value to the consonants. The following consonants are soft, as there is little energy used in their formation:

D	S
J	SH
H	TH
L	V
M	W
N	Z
R	

In contrast, the rest of the consonants become explosives, as more energy is used to form them:

B	K
CH	P
F	Q
G (hard)	T
	X

Writers take advantage of this difference. For some reason a succession of hard sounds is catchy. A big hit from World War I was "K-K-K-Katy." Jack Benny, that marvelous comedian, got lots of laughs from "Cucamonga."

For the sake of lyric writing, we can classify the softer

consonants as passive, whereas the explosives become active.

If the performer must keep his mouth closed, he produces a humming sound. This is passive or introspective. The performer seems to be thinking things over. "Michelle, ma belle" is predominantly soft. There is an introspective, romantic feeling about the words.

An explosive sound, on the other hand, demands attention. "Walk Right Back"—all hard endings—becomes a command.

"At the Copa" takes advantage of the comedic, catchy "k" sounds, as does "Crocodile Rock."

The use of explosives as a hook is a workable technique. The proper sound can jerk an audience into a position of attention. "Stop In the Name of Love," "Help" and "I Just Want to Stop" are all prime examples of this method.

It might be wise, at this point, to comment on the difficulty of producing certain sounds. The vowel, "e," for instance, requires a constriction of the throat. Run the gamut of the vowels in a high voice. Notice how some are easy, some difficult. Try to avoid the more difficult sounds on higher musical pitches. Don't forget, performers want to sound good. If they have difficulty producing a sound, their performances may falter.

Various sounds in combination can produce a faltering effect. The more difficult ones can become tongue twisters. "Rubber baby buggy bumper" looks okay on paper, but try to get through it. I've found it very helpful to recite my lyrics in a loud voice. This experiment helps to pinpoint the more difficult sounds. I then do my best to rewrite them.

PART

The Lyric a

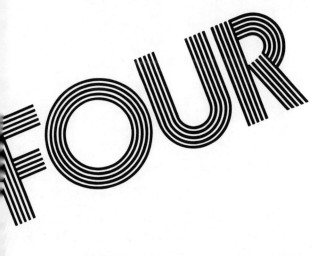

FOUR

Script

Up to this point I've presented the ingredients that must be considered when setting out a lyric. The next step is putting these ingredients together to form a cohesive form or statement.

By considering the lyric as a *script,* some conclusions can be drawn. First, there are people saying words. The words they say contribute to a story line. The way they say these words gives us insight into who these people are.

The author must have some definite ideas about these things before he sits down to write his story. Otherwise, he will get himself into impossible situations from which there's no way out.

Imagine, for instance, you are writing a murder mystery. And that you start page one with no idea who the murderer is. You can immediately see the problems: first, the placement of clues; second, the interplay of characters; and third, the logical ending.

In the mystery form, the author literally starts at the end of the book and writes backward. And, by extension, every literary form is really done this way. The authors must know the ending before they start with the beginning.

With all this in mind, let's examine the methods for doing this.

The Synopsis

A good story can be told in one or two sentences. This is called a synopsis—the bare skeleton of the story without any flesh.

An audience goes to a movie or a play and becomes so involved with fleshing out the story that it fails to see the synopsis. (Proof: the friend who tells about last night's movie, recreating every intricate twist and nuance of the story, and usually, near the end when nothing is making sense, says, "Oh, I forgot to tell you about the ...")

Let's break down some old movies to see what a synopsis looks like:

Casablanca
An American soldier of fortune helps the woman he loves escape from the Nazis. She is accompanied by her husband, a member of the French Resistance.

Wizard of Oz
A young Kansas girl seeks the Wizard of Oz to find the secret of happiness. She is accompanied by a

Scarecrow, a Tin Man and a Cowardly Lion, who seek, in turn, Wisdom, Love and Courage.

Midnight Express
A young man gets caught smuggling hashish out of Turkey and is imprisoned. He finally escapes.

These are the synopses. They look quite simple when set out this way. But look at all the hints there are for story points, settings, tension/release and, above all, emotional universality.

Most important, the synopsis gives the writer a clear idea of what he or she is communicating to the audience. The synopsis, in stark simplicity, tells exactly what's going on.

As I've said over and over, a song lyric should ideally present only one idea. When the author has a firm grasp on the idea, he or she can make sure each word in the lyric contributes to its expression.

Let's break some songs down into synopses:

"Bill Bailey"
A lady has thrown her lover out. Repenting, she wants him back.

"The Girl"
A young man has fallen in love and is contemplating marriage.

"Early Mornin' Girl"
You're leaving me. I can't handle it.

"Eleanor Rigby"
A lonely woman is waiting to die.

"Bridge Over Troubled Waters"
If you've got a problem, I'll help.

"Beat It"
Fighting solves no problems.

Again, the synopsis is a very succinct statement explaining what the song is about. Once the synopsis is set out, the lyricist knows what he or she is writing about.

REMINDER: Story synopses have endings, lyric synopses do not, because their endings are implied.

Not only is the synopsis a method of control, making sure the lyric stays with the message, but it is a device for finding new lyric ideas.

For instance, most lyricists see small life dramas around them all the time. They find themselves in flights of fancy, constructing stories about situations they are either in or observing:

The Hitchhiker
You hold up three fingers explaining you're going only three blocks. He indicates in the same way that he's only going one block. Speeding away, you "discuss" this with him.

The Conversation
You know they're talking about you by the way they whisper and cast furtive glances your way. You know exactly what they're saying.

The Too Rare Steak
You've been brought a steak that has been walked past the broiler on its way out of the kitchen. You rehearse your upcoming conversation with the waiter.

These are the little dramas of life to which you've added a story. Utilize the same process when creating a lyric. In fact, it's a good test to explain any lyric in synopsis form. If it can't be done, the lyric may be too complex, or may have strayed too far from the synopsis guidelines.

Check out a lyric synopsis for possibilities:

> "Bill Bailey"
> SYNOPSIS: A lady has thrown out her lover and, repenting, wants him back.
> PLOT: Love (lost).
> STORY POINTS: She'll do anything to get him back.
> SETTING: Unimportant.
> UNIVERSALITY: Good potential.

Now take a synopsis from a life situation and try the same thing.

> Too Rare Steak
> SYNOPSIS: My steak is raw, and I want the waiter to take it back.
> PLOT: Disappointment.
> STORY POINT: I want satisfaction.
> SETTING: A restaurant.
> UNIVERSALITY: Good plot and story point; very poor synopsis.

"The Too Rare Steak" has about as much potential for a song lyric as "The Freckle On Her Elbow." But the analysis yields some good ideas. The operative word "satisfaction" catches my eye. There already have been a couple of good songs that deal with this story point. But can I find a new way to say it?

Accepting the synopsis as having possibilities, I use a previous technique: change some words:

"My ____ is too ____, and I want ____ to ____."

I can find dozens of operative words to fill in the blank spots in the analysis:

My life is too dull, and I want it to change.

My nights are too short, and I want them to be longer.

My love is too far away, and I want her to come back.

Any of the above synopses could work as successful lyrics. Once I have a basic synopsis idea, I may have to reconstruct it for universality. But there is a method of control. I know what I'm talking about, and now the words will flow.

Casting the Lyric

The intelligent author of a play, movie or television episode puts a lot of thought into the creation of the characters. This is done in order for the characters to act "characteristically." In other words, the characters do everything that type of character would do, and nothing that type of character would not do.

Each actor then bases his mannerisms, speech patterns, etc., on the correct presentation of the character. When the author draws the character well, the actor knows what to do.

Therefore, the author must know the characters extremely well. Hypothetical family trees may be constructed. A part of the country—or world—from which the character comes may be chosen. The character's tastes and predilections will be ascertained. Much of this creative "research" will never be told to the audience except as the true presentation of this character.

Lyricists may have to go to such extreme lengths to know the characters in their song lyrics. They must know who their performers are. Look at this from a businesslike point of view. The reasons are clear.

Performing groups are, for the most part, self-contained. They write their own material. The style of the material is instrumental in creating the group's image. Few groups (there are exceptions) consider material from outside sources.

Single artists are more apt to consider material from outside sources. The single artist is the best avenue for the freelance songwriter. So it's important to know for whom the song is intended. That's why it's so important to know your characters.

• Casting the Song

The process of casting the song works in several ways. A lyricist may first write a lyric, then decide who could best perform it. Or he or she may write a lyric for a certain performer.

Each performer has a distinct personality, point of view and manner of presentation.

With this in mind, there is now a valid approach toward characterization. The performer who will perform the material can be considered the central character. The lyricist takes advantage of the performer's built-in personality and establishes a point of view based on that performer's persona.

A sample list of single artists should make this point clear:

Michael Jackson	Eddie Rabbit
Cyndi Lauper	Debbie Boone
Dolly Parton	Pat Benatar
Linda Ronstadt	Olivia Newton-John
George Benson	Rod Stewart
Tom Jones	Barbra Streisand
Melissa Manchester	Donna Summer
Prince	Barry Manilow
Teddy Pendergrass	Barbara Mandrell
Chaka Khan	Billy Joel
John Denver	Eydie Gormé
Anne Murray	Dionne Warwick
Frank Sinatra	Joe Williams
Stephen Bishop	Kenny Loggins
Ray Charles	Ray Parker, Jr.
Steve Lawrence	Pat Boone

Each of these performer's personalities is distinct. Chaka Khan, for instance, would not sing a song written for Anne Murray. Nor would Teddy Pendergrass consider a song written for Barry Manilow.

All of these artists have well-established personalities and always behave within them. Performers must be able to present material in a believable manner. If the material doesn't fit the character, the performance will not work.

This doesn't mean that a song is meant for one performer alone. Think of it more as typecasting. The various performers become generic—there is the Dolly Parton type, the Ray Charles type, and so on.

It's a good idea to draw up a list of performer types. Listen to various artists to become aware of the type of material they perform, and how the material is presented. A good typecast list provides a group of performers to whom you can submit the same material. If Dolly Parton turns it down, go to the next performer on her type list.

• *Characterization of the Lyric*

Let's examine some necessary points in terms of setting material with the right character.

First, consider the performer as the central character—the star. This means the audience will accept the performer as the actor who is involved in working out the story points.

Second, the character must be sympathetic. This doesn't mean the audience feels sorry for the performer—although that might happen. A sympathetic character elicits a positive response from an audience. They *believe* the character.

When the character is believable, the audience goes through the problems with the character and hopes for the best solutions. If the character is not believable, the audience loses interest and literally doesn't care what happens to him or her. This is disastrous.

Next, consider the story as an ongoing happening. No one is interested in yesterday's news. Even though, in reality, the song has been performed last night and the night before, the audience must get the feeling the performer is actively involved in the story as of right now.

Finally, present the story in terms of the character. This strengthens the believability. Consider the synopsis, and determine whether the character would actually be involved in such and such a story.

At the risk of belaboring the point, let's experimentally cast some performers in some movie synopses. This provides further insight into the process of typecasting in terms of sympathetic characters.

Wizard of Oz
Frank Sinatra, from Hollywood, seeks Mahatma Gandhi to find the secret of happiness. He is accompanied by Charlie's Angels who seek, in turn, Wisdom, Love and Courage.

Casablanca
Prince, an American soldier of fortune, helps Dolly Parton, his old lover, escape from the Nazis. She is accompanied by her husband, Elvis Costello, a member of the French Resistance.

Midnight Express
Pat Boone gets caught smuggling hashish out of Turkey. He is imprisoned and finally escapes.

This is not meant as a commentary on the inability of these people to perform in the roles mentioned, but only to show how the *established* personalities of these performers make them better for some characters than others.

Performers who sing songs in front of an audience tend to stay with material that fits their established image. This is not entirely healthy, as any performer should grow. But there's an adage in the entertainment business: if it isn't broken, don't fix it.

Therefore, it's a wise idea to align the characters with the synopsis. Otherwise, you run the danger of facing rejection after rejection.

Orchestration

The word, orchestration, seems to imply something musical. This is actually not the case. The connotation of the word is: to combine for maximum effect. Consider the orchestration of various synopses and characters.

Wizard of Oz
A young girl has been displaced by a cyclone, and her three friends are looking for abstract strengths of character, such as intelligence, courage and heart. Only a Wizard could get her back home and supply her friends with their missing ingredients.

If Dorothy was simply on the wrong street, and her friends needed relief from a headache, stiff neck and dandruff, any passerby could have directed them to the nearest drugstore.

Romeo and Juliet
Two young lovers, children of seriously feuding families, realize their parents will never agree to a

union between them. Depressed, they commit suicide.

If the two families were neighbors in present-day Burbank, California, and were not on speaking terms because the one family played heavy-metal music until all hours, the two young lovers would not have a really serious problem. Las Vegas is but a few hours from beautiful downtown Burbank.

Star Wars

A young man, with the help of his friends, rescues the beautiful princess from the evil, robotlike Commander of the bad guys.

If Darth Vader were not the ultimate personification of evil, even to the point of being entirely dressed in black, the rescue would have made little sense. It would have been like saving the Prom Queen from the school bully. A pleasant story, but not as seriously engrossing.

Examine synopses of material, and look at various ingredients. Implied with a plot is a problem: tension. The lyricist must orchestrate this problem with the correct character, the correct story and, if necessary, the correct setting.

In most of the previous synopses, strong characters are pitted against seemingly insurmountable problems. This is what is meant by "bigger than life." Uninteresting characters beset by small problems don't make headlines.

Examine lyrics. Note how operative words are used to emphasize the importance of the plot or character. When properly orchestrated, the problem threatens to consume the character, unless he or she overcomes it. And since in most cases the song hopes to imply a happy ending, the character must be endowed with sufficient strength to overcome the problem.

Note how the hero in "Early Morning Girl" is not afraid to admit that pain and heartache are with him night and day. As with most people, he tries not to let his feelings show. But he is ultimately strong enough, when faced with the separation, to tell his Love, "Don't Say Good-bye."

Given this orchestration—strong character vs. heavy emotional problems—the audience tends to root for the hero. Everything is believable. Everything works.

There's the heroine who is so upset over the loss of Bill Bailey she moans the whole day long! Not just a few minutes after breakfast. She'll do anything from cooking to paying the rent to assure his return. She's strong enough to shoulder the blame. She is sympathetically larger than life. Her character has been properly orchestrated to surmount the problem. The audience believes in her and hopes all will turn out well.

Don't be afraid to let your characters have strong feelings. As I mentioned, most of us don't want to expose our vulnerability. But it's precisely that exposition of feelings that an audience responds to in a song lyric.

• Working Procedure

Let's go back to an experimental lyric that shows different kinds of orchestration. Following the process through provides insights into the effects of various strengths and weaknesses. Start with a synopsis:

A character finds himself alone in a room.

The synopsis immediately shows there is no story. Even if the song explains to the audience that the character is lonely, it's a dull story.

I've already decided, however, that loneliness is the problem. So I'll orchestrate this problem for maximum effect:

> A character finds himself alone in a room. Looking out the window, he realizes the world has been destroyed. He jumps out the window.

Now the problem has been incredibly magnified. The character is the only one left in the entire world: maximum loneliness! Unfortunately, he lacks the strength of character to cope with the problem. The audience may not care that he does himself in. So, I'll give him strength to surmount the problem:

> A character finds himself alone in a room. As he looks out the window, he realizes the world has been destroyed. He realizes he's been given an incredible opportunity to start a new world!

The character's amazingly positive nature endows him with astounding strength of character. He is sympathetic, in that the audience hopes he will find someone of the opposite sex so that he will no longer be lonely. His search for this person may be the story.

Now let's experiment in another direction:

> A character finds himself alone in a room. As he looks out the window, he realizes there are no people walking along the sidewalk. He jumps out the window.

Now the problem is minimal—the solution too strong. No one would believe this story.

> A character finds himself alone in a room. As he looks out the window he realizes the world has been destroyed. "Good riddance," he mutters, as he goes back to bed.

In this synopsis, the problem has no effect on the character. The audience feels tricked: why bring up the story in the first place if nothing is going to happen?

Obviously, none of these synopses make good song lyrics. The point to all this is the importance of a well-balanced story. A song lyric, as well as a story, must be well-balanced for maximum effect, otherwise it is not believable and the audience will not care.

Now I'll try a song lyric synopsis:

> A character finds himself alone in a room. His lover has left him, totally destroying his world. Feeling alone in the shambles, he is determined to get her back.

This synopsis sounds viable. The problem is strong: the symbolic destruction of the world. The audience recognizes that when someone *feels* totally alone, they *are* totally alone. The character is sympathetic as he shows determination. The audience will root for him!

Breaking the lyric down to synopsis form provides an opportunity to check orchestration. When the situation is well-balanced, the audience will react to the message. They will remember the song because it has an effect on them. They experience something with the hero or heroine, because they care about them.

The synopsis also helps to develop the idea and to decide what feelings the operative words must express. After this is done, it's time to cast the song:

Male or Female?

I've been using the generic pronoun "he." The best choice is an either/or situation—that is, a lyric that could be performed by either a male or female vocalist, as this gives access to a broader market. Since the story concerns a lonely person (whose message is simply "loneliness"), it's possible to pull this off, as both sexes are certainly capable of loneliness.

Age?

This song is obviously not for the bubble-gum market. But if the character is too old, it might be hinting at an illicit affair—which may not be a bad idea! At any rate, mature is a good description for the character. This may even help to narrow down the male/female decision, if necessary.

Image?

Must be an emotional heavyweight, used to doing heavy material, capable of feeling the intense loneliness the song will project.

All this creative research helps in deciding who the character will be. When the final decision is made, I'll tailor the lyric for that particular generic type.

So far I've approached everything from a businesslike point of view. I have a character type in mind and should be able to give the performer a suitable script. My chances for success are excellent.

PART

Some Fina

FIVE

Considerations

These last few points are overall considerations that were not covered in other sections of this book. Therefore, I've reserved a special section for them.

• *Production Style*

Look once again at the movie synopses. Each story is produced in a particular style:

> *Wizard of Oz*
> **Style: Fantasy**
> *Midnight Express*
> **Style: Brutality**
> *Casablanca*
> **Style: Narrative reality**

These styles have a definite effect on the overall production. In terms of today's musical styles, consider the following list:

> **Rock and roll**
> **Pop**
> **Punk**
> **Country**
> **Jazz**
> **Broadway**
> **Blues**
> **Fusion**
> **Rockabilly**
>
> **Combinations:**
> **Pop/Rock**
> **Country Crossover**
> etc.

These various styles have a definite effect on the overall production. The lyricist should be acquainted with the feelings of these styles, and the artists who are noted for performing them.

The tempo can also be described:

Slow (Ballad)
Moderate
Bright

These are not precise tempi, but simply descriptive feelings. When used in conjunction with style descriptions, such as "slow pop," "ballad," "moderate country," etc., they provide a reasonably clear picture of the feeling of the material for production purposes.

Not only do styles indicate a production quality, but they are also indicators of the types of messages conveyed, and the selection of operative words to convey these messages.

It is useful to think of the performers who operate in particular styles in order to help define these nebulous qualities: Willie Nelson, a country singer (in spite of his remarkable performace of songs of the forties); Steve Lawrence, jazz/Broadway; Pat Benatar, rock and roll; John Denver, country crossover; etc.

By studying the material these generic performers select, a realistic picture of the various stylistic considerations develops.

• *Verbiage*

Think of a garden overgrown with weeds. The flowers get choked out. In a lyric, the line that's overgrown with words chokes out ideas.

It's easy to put too many words on paper. There are frequently many, many times when all lyricists just feel as though they might possibly have so many bright and witty things to say that there is just maybe not even enough room on a very, very large piece of paper to possibly contain all the really marvelous things they just might have to say!

There are fifty-six words in that last sentence! An example of excessive verbiage. When the exhausted reader finally finishes the line, he or she may not have any idea what was said.

There are both passive and active words. Passive words just lie there, whereas an active word springs to action and furthers the story line.

The neophyte lyricist will frequently use passive words to fill the metric count on a line. This deadens the lyric. A partial list of passive words may help the lyricist when editing for verbiage:

> **just**
> **possible**
> **might**
> **maybe**

These words are "hedgers." Cop-outs. "I just might go" has a passive quality. "I'm going" is active.

Pronouns can be eliminated. When hearing a lyric, the audience has a tendency to fill in the gaps. The context of the line usually indicates what pronouns are missing:

(You're)	"Three Times a Lady"
(She's)	"My Girl"
(I'm)	"Hopelessly Devoted To You"
(It's)	"Easy From Now On"
(I)	"Never Can Say Goodbye (to you)"

If a line is boiled down to its purest essence, the basic idea of the statement is immediately heard and understood.

Exchanging one word for a group of words works. Switching a line around works. Not enough room to say "it" —that's never a good excuse. That doesn't work.

Rule of thumb: **LESS IS MORE!**

● Clichés/Banalities

Clichés, by definition, are trite phrases or expressions. They may have value in the lyric because they elicit an immediate response from the audience. The proper use of a good cliché can boil a long message down to a very few words.

In a song lyric, there is relatively little time to get the message across. The lyricist does not have the luxury of a long span of time as in a novel or motion picture. Advertisers recognize this and use clever clichés to get their advertising message across in a limited amount of space or time. Check billboards, TV commercials and magazine ads for examples of the catch phrases that get their message across quickly.

The danger in clichés is banality. When a phrase is overused, it loses its value as a good lyric.

A clever cliché overcomes banality:

> "You're the Top"
> "I've Got You Under My Skin"
> "Jeepers Creepers"
> "Behind Closed Doors"
> "You Light Up My Life"
> "You Are the Sunshine of My Life"
> "Always On My Mind"

These are all "I Love You" songs stated in a refreshing way.

Current slang is a good source of cliché material. However, longevity is a problem. Will tomorrow's audience understand yesterday's cliché?

> Fine as Wine
> Twist and Shout
> Groovy
> The End
> Sock It to Me
> Get Down
> Grody to the Max

There's a fine line between the flagrant cliché and the lyrical line:

> "Blowin' In The Wind"
> "Country Roads"
> "He Ain't Heavy, He's My Brother"
> "Even the Nights Are Better"

It's a good idea to jot down current speech patterns. They become potential lyrics. When you can get a message across with a clever, and I mean clever, cliché, by all means use it.

• *Controversy*

A controversial idea is one that doesn't fit the accepted mold. When an idea is controversial, people will take sides, either for or against.

As a lyricist, you may have a problem presenting controversial material, as some producers and publishers don't like going out on a controversial limb. They don't like people taking sides. They want to sell to *everyone.*

But if you can place a controversial lyric, it may get people talking. And when everyone is talking, fame is the result.

Examine the following list of "controversial" people. Remember, they were controversial when they started out:

>Elvis Presley (Elvis the Pelvis)
>Beatles (Long Hair)
>Donna Summer ("Erotic" record)
>Randy Newman (Short People)

Not to mention:

David Bowie	Cyndi Lauper
Mick Jagger	Prince
Joan Baez	Madonna
Bob Dylan	Alice Cooper

These are all talented people. In some cases, the controversy may have been a finely calculated piece of promotion. In others, they truly were revolutionaries. Whatever the case, they were certainly talked about. But they also had the talent to back up their statements.

The point is this: if you are controversial, you may, at first, have difficulty in selling your material. It's a question of proper casting and visionary producers and publishers. But if you can get it going, your career may be established.

PART

Lyrics, Lyrics,

SIX

yrics: A Summary

You may want to use this summary as a step-by-step working procedure covering all sections of the book. Or you may want to keep it handy as a checklist when working on a lyric or in the important process of editing a lyric. By all means, add your own ideas about your personal work procedures.

1. Lay out one stanza.

For the first step, assume you have an idea for a lyric. Vague, perhaps, but nevertheless an idea. Avoid sharpening pencils, or tidying up desk tops, and jump right in!

Don't worry about meter or rhyme. Don't even worry about the shape of the stanza. Even if every line is a dummy line, *get something on paper!*

2. Set the plot.

You may have started with a title statement. Usually, this is your message. In later steps, you'll have opportunities to reexamine this message.

But suppose you're not sure of your message. This frequently happens. Sometimes, even with a title in mind, you may not be clear on what the message is. Start by examining the stanza you just set out. Even though this may be a dummy, there is a feel to the lyric. Ask yourself:

"Why is this song being sung?"

Jot the message on a piece of paper, and tack it to the wall in front of you. Look at it frequently. Make sure every word in the lyric pertains to the message.

3. List operative words or phrases pertaining to the message.

Examine as many options as possible. You may end up discarding much of this list, but there are sure to be many usable gems.

Working freely this way, you're not committed to meter or rhyme. You can set out whatever occurs to you. The practical consequence of this procedure, besides stockpiling a list of words and phrases, is the subliminal reinforcement of the message. You'll begin to understand what you want to say. For this reason, during this process, you may even find yourself changing the plot. Ideas beget ideas—let them flow!

4. Write the synopsis.

This could be Step 3, but I've placed it here since there may have been quite a bit of mind changing. You'll know when it's time for this step. And don't forget, up to the moment of performing the song, you can still make changes!

At this point you will begin to see your characters—who they are and what they do. Put them in a story.

5. Check for universality.

It's time to move from the subjective to the objective. Having committed to a synopsis, check whether the story (and message) will appeal to the world at large.

6. Set the form.

By now you probably have a nice pile of work sheets on the desk, but each step has helped you decide what you want to say.

Now set your message in the strongest form: dramatic, valentine, etc.

7. Cast the song.

Since most of our ingredients are on the table, it's time to decide who the performer is. Having a clear idea of whom, generically, the song is for will help in selecting language styles, etc.

In your mind, you should be able to see and hear this performer actually performing the material. Maintain a mood and a style—all necessary ingredients for a smash lyric.

8. Establish the model.

Go back now to your first dummy stanza. You should have collected enough material to make some good editorial decisions.

Rewrite the stanza, using all the collected ideas you have. Now's the time to pay attention to meter and rhyme. (Remember, by the way, not to rhyme just for the sake of rhyming. Make sure each rhymed word has something to do with the story point and message.)

Check the meter. Recite the stanza out loud to feel the flow.

Edit the stanza. Cut out all verbiage. Make sure each word counts. Look for passive words that lie there doing nothing.

9. Set the scheme.

Analyze the model; underline strong beats; and number the rhymes. When this is done, you'll know the shape of subsequent verses and you'll have established a control.

10. Complete the first working model.

Check out your list of operative words and phrases. Use them to start the next stanza.

Dive into your rhyming dictionary for rhymes that further the story. If none of the words have rhymes, get out the thesaurus. It's material-gathering time again. You have to fill in the blank spots in the scheme.

You may discover that while looking up a word in a reference book, other words and phrases will pop into your head. You may not use the actual words you find in a dictionary or thesaurus, but they inspire you to new ideas.

A line out of sequence may occur to you as you work. Using your scheme, see where it belongs. You may find yourself working backward and forward.

As lines develop, fill them in. Recite them. If they don't work, change them. Listen to yourself as you recite the lyric. Do you know what you're saying? Would an audience?

11. How's the hook?

Is it truly the summation of the message? Is it clear? Is it clever? Keep this in mind:

> The hook may be the ONLY LINE the audience will remember—or forget!

12. Edit the lyric.

Make sure each word works with the message. Make sure all statements have been made in the strongest terms possible. Don't be satisfied with cheap lines.

Check for "except for's." The lyric is strong . . . except for this line. If you hurry over a line when reading the lyric to someone else, it is usually an "except for."

Check for hidden meanings. The "heavy" line that makes the audience "think." Remember: a song communicates. If it doesn't, it is a failure. The "heavy" meaning may be a cop-out; you couldn't think of anything better.

If you have an opportunity to try your lyric on some friends, watch their body language. Remember, friends will say they love your song—if they don't, the beer stays in the refrigerator. So be on the lookout for glazing eyes, twitching muscles, trips to the bathroom and other signs of a lack of attention. Any of these signs are tip-offs to problems—from weak lines to unclear messages. Don't be afraid of these signs—look for them. Better to discover your problems before taking the lyric out into the "real" world.

13. Finally:

SELL THE SONG